Wisdom Revealed

Wisdom Revealed

The Message of Biblical Wisdom Literature
—Then And Now

Robert P. Vande Kappelle

WIPF & STOCK · Eugene, Oregon

WISDOM REVEALED
The Message of Biblical Wisdom Literature—Then and Now

Copyright © 2014 Robert P. Vande Kappelle. All rights reserved. Except for brief quotations in critical publications or reviews, no part of this book may be reproduced in any manner without prior written permission from the publisher. Write: Permissions, Wipf and Stock Publishers, 199 W. 8th Ave., Suite 3, Eugene, OR 97401.

Unless otherwise noted, Bible quotations are from the *New Revised Standard Version of the Bible*, copyright © 1989 by the Division of Christian Education of the National Council of the Churches of Christ in the United States of America. Used by permission.

Wipf & Stock
An Imprint of Wipf and Stock Publishers
199 W. 8th Ave., Suite 3
Eugene, OR 97401

www.wipfandstock.com

ISBN 13: 978-1-4982-1748-4

Manufactured in the U.S.A.

I dedicate this book
to students past and present
who have enrolled in my course "Acquiring Wisdom"
and who have taught me that wisdom, like fine food,
is better shared than partaken alone.

Draw near to me, you who are uneducated,
and lodge in the house of instruction . . .
Acquire wisdom for yourselves without money.
Put your neck under her yoke,
and let your souls receive instruction;
it is to be found close by. See with your own eyes . . .

—SIRACH 51:23, 25–27

Wisdom is radiant and unfading,
and she is easily discerned by those who love her,
and is found by those who seek her.
She hastens to make herself known to those who desire her.

—WISDOM OF SOLOMON 6:12–13

The Lord created me at the beginning of his work,
the first of his acts of long ago . . .
When he marked out the foundations of the earth,
then I was beside him, like a master worker,
and I was daily his delight, rejoicing before him always,
rejoicing in his inhabited world and delighting in the human race . . .
Happy is the one who listens to me,
watching daily at my gates, waiting beside my doors.
For whoever finds me finds life and obtains favor from the Lord.

—PROVERBS 8:25, 29–31, 34–35

Contents

Preface | ix
Acknowledgments | xiii

Introduction | 1

Part I – Beginnings: Conventional Wisdom

CHAPTER 1: The Book of Proverbs: A Quest for Practical Knowledge | 25

    Essay 1: The Personification of Wisdom—Lady Wisdom and Lady Folly | 137

Part II – Unconventional Wisdom

CHAPTER 2: The Book of Ecclesiastes: A Quest for Meaning | 47

    Essay 2: Qoheleth's Enduring Message | 68

CHAPTER 3: The Book of Job: A Quest for God's Presence | 73

    Essay 3: The Mystery of Suffering | 97

CHAPTER 4: The Song of Songs (The Song of Solomon) | 103

    Essay 4: The Pursuit of Love | 111

Part III – Wisdom in a Hellenistic World: Quests for Identity

CHAPTER 5: The Book of Sirach (Ecclesiasticus) | 117

    Essay 5: Scripture as Canonical and Deuterocanonical | 130

CHAPTER 6: The Book of Daniel | 135

        Essay 6: Judaism and Hellenism | 147

CHAPTER 7: The Book of Wisdom (Wisdom of Solomon) | 151

        Essay 7: Hope for the Afterlife | 164

Part IV – Liturgical Wisdom

CHAPTER 8: Wisdom Psalms | 171

        Essay 8: Wisdom and Torah | 179

Part V – New Testament Wisdom

CHAPTER 9: The Wisdom of Jesus | 185

        Essay 9: The Letter of James | 193

CHAPTER 10: Jesus as Wisdom of God: Matthew's Wisdom Christology | 198

        Essay 10: Christological Hymns and the Jewish Wisdom Tradition | 208

Appendix: Chronological Timeline | 217

Bibliography | 219
Subject/Name Index | 221

Preface

FROM THE EARLIEST DAYS, humans have sought to understand the nature of reality, going beyond their first and often mistaken impressions to a more profound level of truth. They have learned to discern life's patterns and to respond to life's vicissitudes by acting wisely, doing what brought everyone happiness and success. The Bible is a record of that journey. It represents the inspired attempt to become wise at the deepest level.

Through stirring teachings, the sages of the biblical wisdom tradition offer time-honored advice about some of life's most difficult questions, including the problem of pain, the suffering of the innocent, the nature of evil, the justice of God, and dealing with death. They also address such themes as friendship, virtue and vice, marriage and spousal choice, decision making, life priorities, child rearing, illness, and death. The insights offered in the biblical tradition and the efforts of the biblical sages to integrate faith, reason, revelation, and human wisdom rival those of the renowned philosophical schools of ancient Greece.

Our study of biblical wisdom literature includes an examination of Proverbs, Ecclesiastes, Job, Song of Solomon, Daniel, and selections from the book of Psalms. In addition, we will study two extraordinary wisdom writings viewed as scripture by Roman Catholics and Eastern Orthodox, namely the book of Sirach (also known as Ecclesiasticus) and the Wisdom of Solomon, the latter written only a couple of decades before the birth of Jesus Christ. We will conclude with a study of New Testament Christology, examining Jesus as sage and as Divine Wisdom.

While this set of books of the Bible has provided perspective, guidance, and consolation to generations of believers, I believe these books can also be of great significance for unbelievers who are still searching, precisely because of the focus on some of the great human problems, including suffering, educating our young, governing wisely, avoiding temptation and vice, growing in virtue, choosing better vocations, selecting friends, and choosing marriage partners.

In one sense wisdom authors are highly conservative, for they revere tradition, yet in another sense they are highly innovative and progressive, for they also revere their own experience and value their own insights. In the biblical tradition, the understanding, the knowledge, the good sense, and the insight that constitute "wisdom" ultimately come from God, but are accessible in three primary forms: wisdom taught by God, wisdom taught by nature, and wisdom that arises from reflection on human experience. In these writings, wisdom is the rare attainment of intelligence, sound judgment, ethical conduct, humility, and the distinctive piety identified in the motto of the book of Proverbs: "The fear of the Lord is the beginning of wisdom" (Prov. 9:10).

Distinctive Features

My goal in writing this book is to produce a commentary on the biblical wisdom literature that addresses the interests and needs of biblical students, providing guidelines for understanding the message of these ancient works and their application to twenty-first century readers. *Wisdom Revealed* is not an exegetical commentary, for it does not offer verse-by-verse analysis of the text. Neither is it a textual study, in which a scholar makes a case for a preferred reading. Instead it offers perspective on specific topics that arise as one follows the narrative, always with an eye on the big picture, namely, guidance for daily living.

This study divides wisdom literature into ten units, each book discussed as a whole, providing biblical, literary, theological, historical, and textual comments where appropriate. My goal is to proceed from text to understanding and from understanding to application. To that end, each chapter includes the following features:

1. overview of the book;
2. assigned reading from the book;
3. central theme of the book;
4. outline of the book;
5. analysis of the book;

6. an essay related to the book, and
7. questions to ponder.

Learning Objectives

Upon completion of *Wisdom Revealed*, readers will be able to:
1. Demonstrate an understanding of the biblical wisdom literature and its message in the original setting;
2. Demonstrate an understanding of the varied approaches to wisdom utilized by Israel's sages;
3. Utilize a variety of modern interpretive approaches to this literature;
4. Explain how the wisdom material relates to the remainder of the Bible;
5. Understand, appreciate, and carry out acceptable and effective biblical exegesis (reading "out of the text" its intended meaning instead of imposing on the text one's own biases and presuppositions);
6. Apply practically the teachings of the biblical wisdom literature to contemporary issues and concerns as well as to daily life.

Explanatory Comments

The methodology adopted for the topics and books under examination in *Wisdom Revealed* is based on a threefold analytical approach: contextual analysis, textual analysis, and thematic analysis. The following explanations clarify what these mean:

- *Contextual Analysis* – these segments provide background and/or introductory information on a particular book or unit, including author, audience, cultural, historical, and theological context;
- *Literary (Structural and Textual) Analysis* – these segments examine the structure (outline) of the book and supply exegetical commentary, including literary observations, theological insights, textual problems, flow of the argument, and connections between the section and the remainder of the book or unit;
- *Thematic Analysis* – this analysis of key themes from the book or unit provides an understanding of both ancient and contemporary

relevance of those themes and their importance to the book, the author, and the original audience.

Acknowledgments

THIS BOOK REPRESENTS THE final volume in the trilogy: "Adventures in Scripture." Writing *Wisdom Revealed*, like *Hope Revealed* (my commentary on the book of Revelation) and *Truth Revealed* (my commentary on the Gospel of John), has renewed my love for scripture, challenged previous conclusions and interpretations, and convinced me that the ancient biblical wisdom literature, properly understood, speaks as profoundly to the present as to the past.

My analysis relies on monographs written by Richard J. Clifford, James L. Crenshaw, Robert Gordis, Joseph W. Koterski, Peter Kreeft, Roland E. Murphy, Kathleen M. O'Connor, and Ben Witherington III. I acknowledge particular indebtedness to James L. Crenshaw's *Old Testament Wisdom: An Introduction*, Kathleen M. O'Connor's *The Wisdom Literature*, and Ben Witherington's *Jesus the Sage*.[1]

This commentary could not have been written without the editorial assistance of Mary Ann Johnson and the ongoing encouragement and support of my wife Susan. I am particularly grateful for the friendship and support of Dan Stinson, David Novitsky, and Walt Weaver, colleagues at Washington & Jefferson College. Each has read my manuscript and responded sagaciously. I dedicate this book to students past and present who have enrolled in my course "Acquiring Wisdom."

---

1. Their works are listed in the bibliography.

Introduction

No matter how gifted the author, inventor, or creator, every supreme achievement of the human spirit, whether in art, music, literature, religion, or science, necessarily builds upon the work of predecessors. It is they who have laid the foundation of the tradition and worked out the techniques utilized by their successors. Pioneers find their reward in breathtaking glimpses of new and unsuspected vistas, but they almost never attain the highest level of achievement. That experience is reserved for later practitioners.

When we encounter a great work that seems to have no forerunner, like the Hebrew Torah or the Homeric epics, we would do well to heed the words of Qoheleth: "What has been is what will be, and what has been done is what will be done; there is nothing new under the sun. Is there a thing of which it is said, 'See, this is new'? It has already been, in the ages before us" (Eccl. 1:9–10). The biblical wisdom literature is no exception to this rule. In spite of its universal significance, it is the product of a specific time and culture. In spite of its antiquity, it is the end result of a long process of development. It can therefore be fully understood only against the background from which it arose. This will entail a study of the period between about 960 BC and AD 100, examining the role of sages in early Judaism and some of the earliest forms, themes, and trends in biblical wisdom literature as they appear in Proverbs, Ecclesiastes, and Job, followed by a discussion of crucial material in books such as Sirach, the Wisdom of Solomon, and in the New Testament.

The Emergence of Wisdom: The Cultural and Historical Background

In ancient Israel there were three principal intellectual and spiritual currents, referred to by the Hebrew prophets Jeremiah and Ezekiel, who foretold the downfall of the Jewish state in 587 BC and who lived to see their prophecies come true. Jeremiah quotes his opponents as saying, "Come, let us make plots against Jeremiah—for instruction shall not perish from the priest, nor counsel from the wise, nor the word from the prophet" (Jer. 18:18). Ezekiel declares that in the day of disaster people "shall keep seeking a vision from the prophet; instruction shall perish from the priest, and counsel from the elders" (Ezek. 7:26). These revealing statements recognize three learned professions in ancient Israel: priests, who taught Torah; prophets, who delivered messages from the Lord; and sages, who dispensed advice based on observations of nature and human experience. These specialists left an imperishable record of their respective functions and goals in the three sections of the Hebrew Bible: Torah (the Law), Nebiim (the Prophets), and Ketubim (the Writings).

The Septuagint, the Greek version of the Hebrew scriptures, expanded the Writings to include a fourth category: Wisdom Literature, adding to that literature the books of Sirach and the Wisdom of Solomon. A tripartite division of scripture appears in Sirach: "How different the one who devotes himself to the study of the law of the Most High! He seeks out the wisdom of all the ancients and is concerned with prophecies" (38:34b–39:1). What is unusual about this division is that "wisdom" is placed second, after "law" but before "prophecy." The passage continues by extolling the activity of the scribe: "he preserves the sayings of the famous and penetrates the subtleties of parables; he seeks out the hidden meanings of proverbs and is at home with the obscurities of parables" (34:2–3).

Whatever the origin and early stages of the Torah, it may be regarded as certain that its final compilation took place during the Babylonian Exile (587–539 BC), which followed the conquest of Jerusalem and the destruction of the Temple, the center of public worship. The Babylonian Exile, therefore, threatened the extinction of the people and their faith. The sudden and surprising collapse of the Babylonian empire and the rise of the Persian empire (539–336 BC) gave the Jewish people a new lease on life. Cyrus II, the enlightened Persian ruler (550–530), permitted those Jews who so desired to return to their homeland and reconstitute their community life under cultural and religious autonomy. A century later, Ezra (a priest and a scribe) inspired the struggling Jewish settlement in Jerusalem to accept the Torah as its constitution. The Torah now proved an indispensable instrument for uniting and governing the Jewish community. Though a priest, Ezra instituted a major reform that stripped the priests of their religious and intellectual leadership, leaving them only in charge of the conduct of the Temple ritual. Instead of a hereditary priesthood, which all too often exhibited the marks of decadence and moral corruption, the spiritual leadership of the people became vested in scholars. Being recruited from all classes, they represented a nonhereditary, democratic element. The creative impulse in Judaism was henceforth centered in the synagogue, in which all Jews were equal and which became at once a house of prayer, study, and communal assembly.

The importance of this revolution, unparalleled in ancient religion, can scarcely be exaggerated. Ezra's successors, the scribes and the rabbis, not only preserved the Torah but gave it new life. By their painstaking study and interpretation of the biblical text they endowed the Jewish tradition with some of its most noteworthy characteristics—its capacity for growth and its fusion of realistic understanding and idealistic aspiration. Their activity made the Bible relevant to the needs of later generations confronted by new problems and perils. They contributed not only to the survival of the Jewish people but also to the background from which Christianity arose, for they formulated many of the basic teachings shared by Christianity and Rabbinic Judaism.

The period of the Restoration (also known as the Second Temple period), which followed the return from exile, was challenging and difficult for the tiny, modest, and insecure Jewish community, surrounded as it was by a welter of foreign peoples—Samaritans, Edomites, Moabites, Ammonites, Philistines, and later, Greeks. The small Jewish settlement was a tributary of the great Persian, Ptolemaic, Seleucid, and Roman empires, which arose in succession and for five centuries held sway over the Jewish community in this part of the world. The Maccabean War (167–142 BC) was followed by a period of independence (142–63), which proved to be only a brief interlude, ending with the surrender of the Hasmonean state to the Roman general Pompey in 63 BC.

The masses, burdened by poverty and fleeced by taxation, nevertheless held fast to their trust in the righteousness of God. They could no longer believe, however, that the reign of God would take place in history through normal human processes. Only a supernatural cataclysm could rout the forces of evil and usher in the era of peace. Hebrew prophecy was driven underground, emerging in radically altered form as apocalyptic. This new literature described the ultimate conflict between the forces of light and darkness and foretold the final triumph of good over evil, a triumph that must surely be imminent. Apocalyptic literature, with its promise of the advent of God's supernatural messenger, a messiah or anointed king, was initially frowned upon by the official custodians of normative Judaism. They were aware of the dangers of such mystical and extravagant hopes and of the despair likely to arise in the wake of unfulfilled expectations. Ultimately, however, the doctrine of a supernatural messiah became the faith of Pharisaic Judaism and of fringe groups such as the Essenes, a semi-monastic order of Jews revered for its piety, and of other messianic sects whose hopes for a supernatural deliverance grew stronger as the tyranny of Roman rule became increasingly intolerable. Among them were the Christians, who began as a Jewish sect but who differed in their recognition of Jesus of Nazareth as the heaven-sent Redeemer.

Thus, on two levels classic Jewish hopes lived on after the Babylonian Exile. On the surface were the written words of the great prophets preserved in the Bible. And on a deeper level was the submerged drive of the prophetic faith, finding new expression in esoteric circles as "apocalypse," a revelation of hidden mysteries. During the Second Temple period, both the Law and the Prophets had become scripture, a sacred core of authoritative books to which the entire people looked for guidance.

As we know, the Law, which was the province of the priest and later of the scribe, and the Prophecy, which was the experience of the prophet and later of the apocalyptist, did not exhaust the range of spiritual activity in early Judaism. A third strand was supplied by Wisdom (*hokmah*), which was cultivated by the sage or the elder. Wisdom was essentially an intellectual discipline, concerned with the education of upper-class youth. It is highly probable that the sage was a professional teacher whose function was to inculcate in his pupils all the elements of morality aimed at achieving worldly success.

It is clear that Hebrew wisdom was not an isolated creation in Israel. On the contrary, it was part of a vast intellectual activity that had been cultivated for centuries in the Fertile Crescent, especially in Egypt and Babylonia. Situated at the cultural crossroads of the ancient world, the Israelites were influenced from an early time by Eastern wisdom writings. These writings, which circulated far beyond the land of their origin, dated back to the Egyptian Pyramid Age (about 2600–2175 BC) and to the Sumerian era in Mesopotamia. But wisdom had a timeless quality, transcending time and culture. Though ancient sages reflected on problems of society as they knew them, these were human problems found in varying forms in every society. Thus the wisdom movement was fundamentally international.

According to the historian Charles A. Beard, one of the lessons of history can be summarized by the proverb, "The bee fertilizes the flower it robs."[1] This is particularly true of the Jews during the Exile and the Restoration. Although the experience seemed bitter to many at the time, the people came to realize that God was working for good. While the surrounding culture was regarded as a threat to Israel's faith, the Exile also awakened a new world-consciousness, enlarging Israel's faith to an extent never before seen, not even in the cosmopolitan age of Solomon. The exiles realized that they must look beyond their own community to the whole civilized world, if they would behold the glory and majesty of God's purpose in history. The time was ripe for a deeper understanding of the conviction that Israel was called to be God's agent in bringing blessings to all the nations of the earth.

This new understanding of Israel's special place in world history was magnificently expressed by an unknown prophetic writer in the latter part of the book of Isaiah, beginning with chapter 40. This anonymous poet, called Second Isaiah or Deutero-Isaiah, has been acclaimed as one of the greatest writers and poets of the Hebrew scriptures, a visionary with a distinctly universalistic vision.

The view that world-shaking events may have a double and seemingly contradictory effect on people's lives also characterized a small but highly literate and influential group of Palestinian Jews living in Judah under Persian rule during the fourth and fifth centuries BC. These sages flourished during this "Golden Age of Wisdom," a peaceful era of two hundred years aided by a common lingua franca (Aramaic) across the Persian empire, a new sense of Jewish identity, and a new internationalism. During this period the books of Job and Ecclesiastes were written and the wisdom material found in the book of Proverbs was collected and finalized.

The wisdom of the biblical sages, unlike the regulations of the priests or the oracles of the prophets, usually made no claim to being divine

---

1. Cited in Anderson, *Old Testament*, 425.

revelation. It was, of course, self-evident that God was the source of Hebrew wisdom, as of every creative aspect of human nature. Thus, when Isaiah described the ideal Davidic king who would govern in justice and wisdom, he envisions the spirit of the Lord resting upon him, "the spirit of wisdom and understanding, the spirit of counsel and might, the spirit of knowledge and the fear of the Lord" (Isa. 11:2). Some of wisdom's most fervent advocates went further. By endowing wisdom with a cosmic role, they sought to win for wisdom a status almost equal to that of Torah and Prophecy. In their most lavish praise of wisdom, the Hebrew sages attributed her with great antiquity, declaring her to have been established "at the first, before the beginning of the earth" (Prov. 8:23). In Job's magnificent "Hymn to Wisdom" (Job 28), wisdom is endowed with cosmic significance and is virtually personified (28:20–28). Sirach (Ecclesiasticus), written in the first half of the second century BC, also personifies wisdom: "I came forth from the mouth of the Most High, and covered the earth like a mist. I dwelt in the highest heavens, and my throne was in a pillar of cloud" (Sir. 24:3–4).

In Palestinian Judaism, where the study and interpretation of the Torah ultimately produced the Mishnah, wisdom was equated with the Mosaic Law. In the Diaspora, outside of Palestine, where Greek ideas were more influential, wisdom received a more philosophic interpretation. In the Wisdom of Solomon, the spirit of the Lord and wisdom are explicitly identified and are taken to encompass both the creation of the natural world and its moral government: "For wisdom is more mobile than any motion; because of her pureness she pervades and penetrates all things. For she is a breath of the power of God, and a pure emanation of the glory of the Almighty; therefore nothing defiled gains entrance into her. For she is a reflection of eternal light, a spotless mirror of the working of God, and an image of his goodness . . . ; in every generation she passes into holy souls and makes them friends of God" (Wis. 7:24–27). In some circles the earlier personifications of wisdom were taken literally and served as the point of departure for a complex development. In the case of Philo, the celebrated Alexandrian Jew of the first-century AD, wisdom assumed the doctrine of the Logos or the Divine Word, which became the instrument by which God creates and governs the universe. It is only a further step to conceive of the Divine Word as the intermediary between God and the world, even as a distinct "person" or "aspect" of the divine nature (cf. the Logos Hymn in John 1:1–5).

Ultimately, however, biblical wisdom's claim to authority rested on its pragmatic truth. The Hebrew sages insisted that the application of wisdom "worked," meaning that when coupled with human reason and careful observation, it brought human beings success and happiness. Its origin might be in heaven, but its justification was to be sought in society and nature: "keep sound wisdom and prudence, and they will be life for your soul and adornment for your neck. Then you will walk on your way securely and your foot will not stumble. If you sit down, you will not be afraid; when you lie down, your sleep will be sweet. Do not be afraid of sudden panic, or of the storm that strikes the wicked; for the Lord will be your confidence and will keep your foot from being caught" (Prov. 3:19–26).

The magnificent description in the Wisdom of Solomon (7:22b—8:1) hints at the complexity of the biblical concept of wisdom. The Bible, being an anthology of books and containing a rich array of natural, moral, and theological perspectives, nowhere defines wisdom. Rather, wisdom appears in many guises, including as (1) a "tree of life" (Prov. 3:18), (2) the "fear of the Lord" (Job 28:28), (3) instruction for moral formation, (4) human experience, (5) the mysteries of creation, (6) Law or Torah, (7) a mysterious divine call, and even as (8) a spouse.[2] Despite her inestimable value, the embracing of wisdom (Prov. 3:18; 4:8) is precarious, because there is more hope for a fool than for those who are conceited (26:12). Ben Sira said it best: "The first man did not know wisdom fully, nor will the last one fathom her" (Sir. 24:28).

Solomon: The Exemplar of Israelite Wisdom

The origin of Israel's wisdom movement is unknown. A vigorous Canaanite wisdom movement might have been assimilated by Israel in the premonarchic period, as suggested by various affinities between the book of Proverbs and the Ugaritic Ras Shamra literature. Balaam, the Babylonian diviner (Num. 22–24), was related to Israel's early wisdom movement. From the earliest period of Israel's oral tradition come the proverb (1 Sam. 24:13), the riddle (see Judg. 14:14), and the fable (Judg. 9:8–15), ancient types of Near Eastern wisdom. By the time of the early monarchy, sages were well-known and respected leaders in Israelite society. We are told that the counsel of Ahithophel, one of David's court advisers, was

---

2. Murphy, *Tree of Life*, ii.

"as if one consulted the oracle [word] of God" (2 Sam. 16:23). During Absalom's rebellion a wise Israelite woman used dramatic skill as well as literary inventiveness to present an imaginary case to King David (2 Sam. 14:1–24); later, during the same crisis, another wise woman negotiated with Joab (2 Sam. 20:14–22). The remark that the woman went to the people "with her wise plan" indicates that she was a recognized leader with professional standing, perhaps like the "wisest ladies" found in the Canaanite court in the "Song of Deborah" (Jud. 5:29).

The Bible regards Solomon as the source and symbol of its wisdom. Just as the Pentateuch was ascribed to Moses and the Psalms to David, so Israelites attributed much of their wisdom literature to Solomon, including the books of Proverbs and Ecclesiastes as well as the Song of Songs. Outside the Hebrew Bible, a vast literature was also attributed to Solomon, including the book of Wisdom. Though this tradition is not to be taken literally—this literature was written over a period of nine hundred years—these claims reflect the established historical fact that Solomon's reign was marked by wide international contact and internal prosperity, which contributed to the flowering of culture in general and to the intensive cultivation of wisdom in particular.

In biblical times, religious texts were often attributed to a famous person from the past. Such practice, called pseudepigraphic because authorship was falsely attributed, was commonly accepted in the ancient world, when "old" was considered superior to "new." In the biblical tradition, the attributed author was usually either a famous person from the remote past (such as Enoch, Moses, David, Solomon, and Ezra) or the actual author's own teacher (after his or her death). A pseudepigraphic work, then, was composed *as if* it were written by a person from the past, while the actual author remained anonymous.

The reasons for such practice are well known. For example, if an ancient or biblical author claimed her teaching was "new" or "original," few people would pay attention. But if she wrote in the name of a recognized authority, or if she transmitted what her teacher said (who may have learned from previous authorities), then people would be interested. In addition, writing in the name of a famous personage or authoritative teacher such as Isaiah, Daniel, or a disciple of Jesus stressed continuity with tradition, enabling the "actual" author to adapt or apply that tradition to new historical circumstances. Pseudepigraphy characterized the wisdom literature of antiquity, including the Jewish wisdom tradition.

Solomon's cosmopolitan interests admirably qualified him to be the patron of wisdom. When the Queen of Sheba visited from far-off Arabia, Solomon displayed his wisdom by propounding and solving riddles (1 Kgs. 10:1–10). During his reign Israel broke out of the confines of the former Tribal Confederacy, with its limiting religious institutions and perspectives, and enlarged its horizons of faith beyond the boundaries of the Mosaic covenant heritage. Solomon was extremely hospitable to the cultural influences of the Fertile Crescent, in particular fostering close relations with Phoenicia and Egypt. Close parallels between the *Instruction of Amenemope* (c. 1100 BC) and Proverbs 22:17—23:11 indicate that this section of Proverbs depended heavily on its Egyptian source. Parallels in form and content have also been found between Proverbs and the most important Canaanite wisdom text, the work of *Ahiqar*, which was so widely known in the ancient world that it became part of many literatures and was transmitted in about a dozen languages. Written perhaps as early as the seventh century BC, the text combines a narrative of the fall and subsequent restoration of the courtier Ahiqar with a collection of about a hundred aphorisms, riddles, fables, and instructions. The sayings, which may have originated in the Aramaic kingdoms of Syria, apparently circulated independently of the narrative.

Solomon appears on the pages of scripture as the wisest man who ever lived (1 Kgs. 3:12; 4:29–31). We are told that Solomon had a dream in which God appeared to him, granting him one wish. Because Solomon requested wisdom, God gave him riches and honor as well. Renowned for his literary brilliance, he is said to have composed three thousand proverbs and one thousand and five songs (1 Kgs. 4:32). His proverbs became the basis for the claim that he authored the book of Proverbs. Solomon might have composed or collected some of the proverbs, particularly those found in the oldest section of the book of Proverbs (Prov. 10–29), but we cannot be sure. According to later tradition, some of his "sweetest" songs made up the Song of Songs, though there is little evidence that Solomon composed these sensual love lyrics. Nevertheless, their association with Solomon and their popularity at wedding festivities established them firmly in Israelite life. Eventually the songs were accepted as sacred scripture on the ground that they presented an allegory of the covenant love between God and Israel.

During the patristic and early medieval periods, writing at a time when Christianity was becoming accepted in the Greco-Roman world not only religiously but as a philosophical tradition, Christians envisioned the three canonical books associated with Solomon as representing three stages of spiritual progression, parallel to the graded disciplines in the schools of philosophy known as ethics, physics, and logic: (1) *Proverbs* (ethics), meant for beginners, teaches how to live virtuously in the world; (2) *Ecclesiastes* (physics), meant for "*proficientes*" (middlers)—"sophomores" and "juniors" advancing in their studies—teaches to treat mundane things as vain and transitory; and (3) *Song of Solomon* (logic), meant for "initiates," teaches the love of God to advanced students.

The Sources of Wisdom Literature

The theories of scholars on the origins of the wisdom movement can be reduced to two sources: (1) the clan or tribe, within which moral guidance would have been transmitted in the home; and (2) the court schools, in which more technical instruction was available. The home must have served as a focal point for the training of youth, as suggested by numerous references to father and mother and the phraseology frequent in Proverbs: "my son/my child." Of course, the term "son/child" can be understood metaphorically to indicate a teacher-pupil relationship. The teachings would have been transmitted orally at first, forming the legacy about life and living that parents communicate to children. The everyday topics of the maxims in the book of Proverbs point to the oral sayings of common folk in society, which may have been collected by scribes. Eventually, however, evidence points to the role of the school, probably originally attached to the royal court (although there would have been no court schools in the postexilic period), as the direct source of the majority of the biblical wisdom tradition.

Wisdom has a long association with royalty and the court, as can be inferred from the role of Solomon, the mention of "the officials of King Hezekiah" (Prov. 25:1), and the many "king" sayings in Proverbs. One may infer from the reign of Solomon that court schools would have been necessary for the training of scribes and other royal officials. An analogy may be drawn between Israel and the courtiers of Mesopotamia and Egypt, where schools certainly existed. In Egypt a class of sages instructed children of the pharaohs and other potential bureaucrats. Eventually there developed a system of private education for which instructors began composing texts on correct speech, proper etiquette, and skills in interpersonal relationships. In Mesopotamia this class was associated with temple schools as well as with the royal court. As we learn from the book of Daniel, Babylonian scribes and sages were required to attain skills in interpreting omens and dreams (Dan. 2:2–6).

During the period of the Restoration following the Babylonian Exile, Jewish sages proliferated in Judah. Other than the mention of the officials of King Hezekiah in Proverbs 25:1, which suggests that a distinctive class of sages already existed in Jerusalem in the eighth century BC (800–700), additional evidence appears in the expression "the sayings of the wise" in Proverbs 24:23. The "words of the wise" in 1:6 and 22:17 also suggests a professional class. While the author of the book of Job is unknown, Job's three friends are portrayed as wise men steeped in conventional wisdom lore, as their speeches in Job make clear. According to Ecclesiastes, Qoheleth (the Teacher) was a sage who "taught the people knowledge, weighing and studying and arranging many proverbs" (12:9).

In Israel there were probably three separate settings for wisdom teaching: the clan, the court of the king, and the school. In the clan the father and the mother were the sages. In the royal court, the kings were associated with sages who advised them (see 2 Sam. 16:23; 17:14). Later wisdom writings give evidence of a house of learning, that is, a school in which sages instructed the young. As noted above, it is likely that Ecclesiastes emerged from school instruction. Qoheleth was probably a scribe or teacher who lived in Jerusalem. We learn from the book of Sirach that Ben Sira operated a school of sorts: "Draw near to me, you who are uneducated, and lodge in the house of instruction" (Sir. 51:23).

Sirach 38:24—39:11 contrast the wisdom of sages and scribes with the activities of persons engaged in other pursuits, such as farmers and artisans, witnessing to a distinct occupational consciousness of sages as a social class. While other occupations are admired, they are not honored as are the scholars, whose activities include (1) studying sacred literature; (2) preserving the sayings of famous people; (3) investigating the intricacies of parables, proverbs, and riddles; (4) advising rulers; (5) traveling widely and observing other cultures; (6) maintaining religious piety; and (7) leaving a legacy: "Many will praise his understanding; it will never be blotted out. His memory will not disappear, and his name will live through all generations" (39:9). The reference to "those who are wise" in Daniel 12:3 (dated generally to the Maccabean era and therefore to the mid-second-century BC) points to a group of trained scholars who serve as exemplars in society, praised and viewed in tandem with "those who lead many to righteousness."

The Literary Forms of Wisdom Literature

If we are correct in assuming that the wise constituted a distinct class within Israel, we may also assume that these sages used a characteristic mode of discourse. The introduction to the book of Proverbs (1:6) mentions four kinds of sapiential teaching that students must understand: the *proverb* (a basic similitude or likeness in which a given phenomenon is set alongside another as illuminating it significantly); the *parable* (a saying or narrative conveying a stinging message hidden within a clever formulation); the *"wise saying"* (a general category or collection of sapiential instruction); and the *riddle* (an enigmatic saying leading to reflection on the meaning of life and its inequities). By extension, all of the above use admonitions and warnings as powerful expressions of cultural truth.

A broader examination of the Hebrew wisdom literature reveals additional literary forms, which, taken together, constitute ten categories. The wisdom saying we call (1) *proverb* (*mashal*) is expressed in a short pithy form, characterized by the usual Hebraic feature of parallelism. While proverbs need not include a pedagogic intent, usually the saying is clearly didactic, describing a particular act or attitude as wise or foolish. Over time, the notion of instruction became central, placing a premium on its memorability. Having an eye for literary expression, the sages favored contrast, simile, alliteration, hyperbole, numerical sayings, and other memorable devices. Numerical sayings may be related to (2) the *riddle*, as in "what item is common to the things enumerated?" While no pure riddles have survived within biblical wisdom literature, there can be little doubt that ancient sages coined enigmas and that the solving of riddles belonged to the essential tasks of the wise. Several (3) *allegorical texts* stand out as worthy links with riddles, such as the clever description of old age in Ecclesiastes 12:1–8 and the exquisite advice about marital fidelity in Proverbs 5:15–23, in which a wife is likened to a cistern from which one drinks life-giving water. Cipher language functions on two levels at the same time and is particularly apt in allegorical contexts.

The category of (4) *hymn* was utilized by the sages to fashion their own kind of song, whether about Lady Wisdom (Proverbs 8) or about the wonders of nature and the inaccessibility of wisdom (Job 28). Perhaps the supreme rhetorical achievement of the sages was the (5) *dialogue or disputation*. Its peculiar characteristics include a mythological introduction and conclusion, the dialogue proper, and a divine resolution. The book of Job is a marvelous example (Job 4–26), for it utilizes these formal features to address the problem of undeserved suffering. The sages developed a special type of (6) *autobiographical narrative*, allowing them to communicate lessons from personal experience. Wisdom's deep roots in experience provide many lessons based on observation and reflection.

Another important literary form that the sages adapted to their own purposes is the (7) *didactic narrative*. An example of this "story-sermon" appears in Proverbs 7:6–23, where a seductress leads a young man to his ruin. The (8) *wisdom poem*, a poem containing numerous sayings or admonitions, is exemplified particularly in Proverbs 1–9, in the speeches in Job, and also throughout Sirach and the Wisdom of Solomon. This device shows a tendency toward alphabetizing (Proverbs 2:1–22 has twenty-two lines corresponding to the number of letters of the Hebrew alphabet), a practice related to the acrostic pattern in which each unit begins with the next successive letter of the Hebrew alphabet (see Prov. 30:1–31 and Ps. 34). The book of Job, characterized by the disputation speech that marks the dialogue between Job and the three friends, also contains a (9) *lament* (Job 3), a dirge regarding Job's birth. Although Ecclesiastes uses various genres, the most characteristic form may be termed a (10) *soliloquy*. In passages such as 2:12–17 and 2:18–26, Qoheleth proposes as points for reflection the value of wisdom and the value of toil. While the passage develops randomly, there is frequent reference to the author's personal observations and insights.[3] The book of Job contains a lengthy example (chapters 29–31), wherein the protagonist concludes his defense.

The Themes of Wisdom Literature

Within the biblical wisdom tradition, certain themes take on increasing significance: the fear of the Lord, God's self-manifestation through personified wisdom, the problem of innocent suffering, the meaning of life, the justification of God's ways, the limits of human knowledge, and the inevitability of death. Given the range of this literature, we may conclude that Israel's sages struggled with life's fundamental questions. Their way of addressing these, and the solutions they reached, point to a remarkable group of people.

The period of the Restoration, which followed the Babylonian Exile, has been described as "an age of small things" for the returning Jewish exiles. Living under Persian rule, there had been little prospect of Jewish

---

3. Crenshaw, *Old Testament Wisdom*, 37–39, and Murphy, *Tree of Life*, 7–13.

national greatness and power either then or in the foreseeable future. Exilic prophets such as Ezekiel and Deutero-Isaiah were vindicated by events, but their grand visions were not fully realized. The return from the Babylonian Exile was a triumphant fulfillment of the prophetic faith that God would not abandon the people and that they would be restored to their own land. That much had taken place, but little more. There was neither stimulus nor need for the grand prophetic vision. The unyielding insistence of the prophets upon righteousness as the basic premise of national well-being had become an accepted element of Jewish thought, but it was no longer particularly novel or especially relevant to the problems of the hour. It was then, in the early centuries of the Second Temple period, that wisdom reached its golden age, largely because of a basic shift in the primary concern of religious faith and thought.

While the Torah and the prophets agreed in placing the nation at the center, the individual gradually came to the fore. Personal happiness and success, together with individual fears and hopes, had been recognized in the Torah and by the prophets, but after the Exile the problem of individual suffering became central to thought. Increasingly, too, the prophets, whose basic concern was the ideal future of the nation, became concerned with the happiness of the individual. "It was the decline of faith in the fortunes of the nation, coupled with the growth of interest in the individual and with individual destiny, that stimulated the development of wisdom. Wisdom was not concerned with the group, but with the individual, with the realistic present rather than with a longed-for future."[4]

Wisdom's practical goals for temporal success appealed primarily to those groups in society that benefitted from the status quo—government officials, rich merchants, great landowners, even high-priestly families. The goal of upper-class education was the training of youth for successful careers. These needs were admirably met by the wisdom teachers who arose, primarily in Jerusalem, the capital city.

The upper-class orientation reflected in the book of Job emerges in the treatment of the book's basic theme—the problem of suffering. While fuller consideration is given to this issue later, here it suffices to note that wisdom writers could not ignore the inequities of the present order. At the same time, as representatives of affluent social groups, they did not find the status quo intolerable. The lower classes, oppressed by poverty

---

4. Gordis, *God and Man*, 40.

and marginalized at the hands of domestic and foreign masters, were deeply afflicted by the prosperity of the wicked and the suffering of the righteous. Holding resolutely to their faith in God, they were nevertheless unable to see divine justice operating in the world. Their solution to this problem was the espousal of the doctrine of the afterlife, a future world where the inequalities of the present order would be rectified. Thus the idea of life after death became an integral feature of Pharisaic Judaism and of Christianity.

The teachers of wisdom, on the other hand, felt no need to adopt these views. The sages of the conventional wisdom schools continued to maintain the old view of collective retribution here and now, where the sins or virtues of the fathers determine the destinies of the children (Prov. 13:22; 14:26; 20:7; Sir. 44:10–11). The idea of a future life is not mentioned in Proverbs, probably because the material is comparatively early. However, by the first century BC, the doctrine of an afterlife could no longer be ignored. In fact, it is clearly affirmed by the author of the Wisdom of Solomon: "But the righteous live forever, and their reward is with the Lord; the Most High takes care of them" (Wis. 5:15). The unconventional authors of Job and Ecclesiastes are too sensitive to overlook the undeserved suffering and prosperity in the world, yet neither accepts the solution of life after death, although both are familiar with it (Eccl. 3:19–21; 9:10). The author of Job lacks the tough-mindedness of Qoheleth. He cannot pretend to be indifferent to the hope for an afterlife. He wishes he could accept it as true, but he sorrowfully comes to the conclusion that the renewal of life after death is not given to mortals (14:7–19).

Wisdom literature, thus, falls into two classes. The first consists of (a) practical advice to the young on how to attain a successful and good life. This *conventional approach* is illustrated in the maxims found in the book of Proverbs as well as in the longer essays of Sirach. The second consists of (b) reflective probing into the depth of human perplexity about the meaning of life, often skeptically. This *unconventional approach* is illustrated by the biblical books of Ecclesiastes and Job. Though the sages of this reflective perspective had been trained to apply observation and reasoning to the practical problems of life, they were intrigued more by fundamental issues such as the purpose of life, life after death, the basis of morality, and the problem of evil. When they weighed the religious and moral ideas of their time by these standards, they found much that they felt compelled to reject as either untrue or unproved. Hence the speculative wisdom books are basically skeptical, at variance with the approach of the practical school. In seeking to penetrate the abiding issues of suffering and death, these rare wisdom teachers were unwilling to rely on tradition and conventional ideas. When they insisted on applying experience and reason to the ultimate questions of life, "they courted tragedy—but achieved greatness."[5] Both types of wisdom literature, however, isolated the human problem from the particulars of history, and in this respect they stand in contrast to most biblical literature.

Because a certain amount of wisdom literature is found in the Bible, with it comes the tension that exists between two ways of viewing humanity—as individuals or as groups within a particular historical context, or simply as human beings. In the biblical wisdom books, the communal themes that dominate the Torah and the prophetic writings—Israel's election, the eschatological "Day of the Lord," covenant and Torah, priesthood and Temple, prophecy and messianic hope—are hardly dealt with.[6] Although much of the wisdom literature was produced in the postexilic period, when the Jewish people were deeply conscious of being a worshiping community, references to acts of worship are strikingly few in the books of Proverbs, Job, and Ecclesiastes. Yahweh, the personal name of God, is not used in Ecclesiastes or, with few exceptions (notably chapters 38–42), in the book of Job. Even when the name is used, as in Proverbs, nothing is made of the special relationship between God and Israel. In this literature God is not identified as the one who brought Israel out of Egypt or who acted repeatedly in the people's history. Indeed, there are no explicit references to Israelite history or to outstanding Israelite personalities, with the exception of Solomon. In avoiding local or national divine names, progressive sages were seeking to express their concept of God in the broadest and most universal terms. The Jewish wisdom literature, like the wisdom movement of the ancient Near East, was fundamentally international, giving wisdom a timeless, non-historical quality that often transcended time and culture.

The Underlying Principle for Israel's Sages

What was the goal of Israel's sages? What did they hope to achieve by coining proverbs and formulating observations about the meaning of life? What were their concerns? What was the object of their search? One

---

5. Ibid., 43.
6. Anderson, *Old Testament*, 520–21.

means of discovering the self-consciousness of Israel's sages as a distinct group within society is to examine the carefully worded introduction to the book of Proverbs, where we find listed a cluster of words and phrases that characterize those who master the proverbial tradition: wisdom, instruction, understanding, intelligence, righteousness, justice, equity, discretion, knowledge, prudence, learning, and skill. Taken together, they constitute individual facets of the quest for "Life," what philosophers call "the good life." The canonical sages pursued the good life in all its manifestations: health, wealth, honor, progeny, longevity, and remembrance.

A study of four books central to the Jewish wisdom literature reveals different results in describing the object of the sapiential search:[7]

1. The book of Proverbs represents a quest for *practical knowledge*, an understanding about nature and human beings that enable people to live wisely and well. For the authors of Proverbs, finding "life" means not so much biologically but relationally, life with another. For the sage, "to live" means to live with wisdom, to banquet with her in her house.[8] According to Proverbs 9:4, living with wisdom is the opposite of living in ignorance. To live with wisdom requires "pondering," meaning that one must live with discernment. Living with the proverbs is like living in a house or a school of wisdom, where wise sayings are examined deeply. Hence the proverbial material is often couched in parables, allegories, riddles, and other enigmatic sayings, with emphasis on subtlety, paradox, and wordplay. Proverbial themes may appear simplistic or repetitive, but careful study reveals that details are important and vital to the meaning of the text.

2. The book of Job is not primarily a search for knowledge about how to cope with the enigmas of ordinary existence, but rather represents a quest for *God's presence*. The author, like the character of Job, acknowledges God's gracious presence in the past, and therefore cannot endure a God who is hidden in the present. Job searches the darkest depths of despair in pursuit of his God, and eventually risks death and even damnation to achieve restored communion. To Job, God is "Life," the highest good, and compared to that *summum bonum*, biological life pales.

3. The book of Ecclesiastes represents the quest for *meaning in a silent universe*. Like Job, Qoheleth cannot affirm biological life as the supreme good, but unlike Job, Qoheleth does not enter into dialogue with

---

7. The following segment is adapted from Crenshaw, *Old Testament Wisdom*, 62–65.

8. Clifford, *Wisdom Literature*, 64.

the living God. Lacking confidence in life's goodness, he searches in vain for some meaning that can enable him to endure his empty existence.

4. The book of Sirach represents the quest for Jewish *identity and continuity* in a Hellenistic world that esteemed quite different cultural and religious values. His intention is to convince Jewish youth that Greeks are not the only ones with a magnificent intellectual heritage. Highlighting the role of tradition for oneself and for one's community, his goal is tantamount to survival of the Jewish religion and way of life.

Each book, in addition to representing a different object of search, also provides a different temporal focus. The book of Proverbs looks to the distant past, when God established a pattern for the cosmos and for life. The book of Job, focusing on suffering, is concerned wholly with the present. Qoheleth is unable to discern any future worth living for, since death is the great leveler and silencer of hope. Sirach looks to Israel's glorious past in order to provide his generation the ability to resist cultural compromise in the present and thereby give a future to Diaspora Jews. Invariably, Israel's sages, whatever their goals, arrive at a closed door called Mystery, and none except God hold the key to this room. This understanding is what Proverbs 25:2 affirms when it declares that God's glory lies in the tendency to conceal essential reality.

There is a fundamental paradox in the Jewish sapiential tradition, for wisdom is both an object of search but also a gift from God. A relentless search oscillates between two extremes, trusting in one's ability to secure existence and dependence upon God's mercy. The latter, however, represents the final word, for the ultimate quest is that of a gracious God in search of humanity. For humans, the bottom line seems clear: self-discipline, coupled with trust, leads to joy: "When you get hold of [wisdom], do not let her go. For at last you will find the rest she gives, and she will be changed into joy for you" (Sir. 6:27–28).

Wisdom and Spirituality

A strong correlation can be found between the wisdom tradition and spirituality, particularly if spirituality represents the ability to live life authentically, for wisdom thinkers found ordinary human existence fascinating. Kathleen O'Connor, a Roman Catholic religious educator, views wisdom as a form of spirituality for the market place. Such spirituality represents the arena "where humans struggle to cope with the chaos of daily life, where Wisdom and Folly compete for human loyalties, and where the divine and the human meet."[9] A spirituality for the market place points equally to two aspects of the natural world; (a) a realm or sphere of life wherein humans might expect to meet God, and (b) a way of living in the world. Popular thinking often limits divine-human exchange to specifically religious activities and places, claiming that God is to be found primarily in the privacy of the individual soul. Wisdom literature provides a resource for a more holistic spirituality, one that perceives outer and inner life, individual and community life, and God and the world as inextricably intertwined. Understanding the realm of divine-human encounter to be ordinary human life, wisdom promotes the pathway of relationship.

The implications for such an understanding of spirituality are enormous. Wisdom spirituality leaves little room for dualistic thinking or living. Ordinary life and the life of faith are not separate or antithetical spheres, for all life exists in the presence of its Creator. From wisdom's perspective, the struggles and conflicts of daily life should not to be shunned or avoided as though they are evil, but rather embraced in full consciousness of their revelatory and healing potential. When Israel's wisdom literature focuses on mundane concerns, it is not ignoring but assuming faith.

Wisdom's focus on human concerns has caused some biblical interpreters to question the presence of this literature in the Bible, but these books should not be viewed as secular orphans next to their more theological siblings, the Law, the Prophets, the Gospels, or the Epistles. In defending wisdom's viewpoint by referring to it as "theological anthropology," Roland Murphy makes the point that by starting with the realm of human experience, wisdom writers are not excluding God from their world, but rather focusing on what it means to be human in the presence of God. Murphy maintains that the modern distinction between the realms of the secular and the sacred never existed in Israel. Wisdom does not impose God on life but assumes God's presence and activity in every facet of its existence. The various wisdom books all agree that to be wise is to live harmoniously with one's community, the earth, and the Creator.

Wisdom literature appreciates the ambiguity of human experience. It finds in ambiguity and confusion the opportunity for breakthrough into mystery. It struggles against rote religious answers to human problems.

---

9. O'Connor, *Wisdom Literature*, 14.

According to wisdom, life is not a simple set of truths to be followed indiscriminately, but a continual encounter with conflicting truths, each making competing claims upon the seeker. The subject matter of Proverbs, Job, Ecclesiastes, and the Song of Solomon is profoundly ambiguous and paradoxical. Opposing truths are set side by side and in some instances left unresolved. This is evident in the basic literary genre of wisdom, the *mashal*, a pithy saying, proverb, or riddle (see Proverbs 30:4, a riddle whose answer seems to be "God"; cf. Job 38:5–11). For the sages, life itself is a *mashal*, a world of ambiguity, a series of puzzles small and great. But the point of ambiguity or paradox is not to bring the individual to an intellectual impasse or a spiritual angst, but to lead one beyond the obvious into deeper understanding. Offering a spirituality of discovery, wisdom requires openness, discernment, and choice. Because wisdom views life as paradoxical, it also calls for patience, trust, and a glad heart.

According to Israel's sages, humans live in a moral universe. Discovering this "rational rule" enabled the sages to protect their existence by acting in harmony with the fundamental order that sustained the cosmos. One's conduct either strengthens the existing order or contributes to the forces of chaos that threaten survival itself. Once the sages discovered this moral or rational principle, it became their task to transfer it from the realm of nature to the human sphere. They accomplished this goal through analogy. Close observation of nature and the animal kingdom convinced Israel's sages that the world was truly a harmonious entity (see Prov. 30:19). The search for proper analogies had as its goal the securing of life. Those who successfully achieved correct knowledge purchased longevity for themselves, together with other indications of divine favor. Knowledge was therefore a means to an end, never an end itself.

Although most people today do not turn to the wisdom literature for prophetic inspiration, the wisdom method of reflection on life experience is gaining prominence. People are again recognizing that God is encountered *through* human experience.

The Influence of Wisdom on the Hebrew Scriptures

While Israel's wisdom literature stands by itself in the Jewish corpus, from a very early period the wisdom movement exerted a pervasive influence on Israel's historical, prophetic, and poetic literature. Certain passages in Isaiah (9:6; 11:2, 9; 28:23–29; 31:2) emphasize wisdom and understanding, so much so that some scholars consider Isaiah to have been a sage before he became a prophet. Similar conclusions have been reached concerning Amos, whose home town of Tekoa is said to have been a center of wisdom. By way of support, scholars point to his universalistic message (whereby all nations are subjected to God's judgment), his use of special vocabulary such as the word "right," his use of unusual rhetorical devices (such as the "woe" sayings), and linguistic phenomena such as numerical sayings, all of which place Amos squarely within clan wisdom. Similar arguments have led to the claim that Micah and Jonah wrote under the influence of the wisdom tradition. Within the historical literature, the Succession Narrative (2 Samuel 9–20 and 1 Kings 1–2) has been attributed to a wisdom writer who sought to illustrate the teachings of certain parables (see Nathan's rebuke of David in 2 Samuel 12) into his narrative, telling stories that embody eternal truths. The same goes for the Joseph Narrative in Genesis, which may have been written by a sage in the royal court to serve as a model for professional courtiers. The association of court stories and wisdom in the book of Esther has led some interpreters to conclude that the author was a sage who wished to emphasize the rewards that come to those who combine wisdom with integrity. The primeval history in Genesis 1–11 has been found to exhibit wisdom influence, particularly in references to a tree of knowledge and to the concept of the knowledge of good and evil. The entire book of Deuteronomy, which emphasizes retribution, life and death (see 30:15–20), and the importance of observing God's commandments, has been attributed to sapiential authorship. Some scholars argue that wisdom gave birth to apocalyptic, pointing to Daniel's association with the legacy of the sages, both Babylonian (1:4) and Israelite (12:3). Eventually, Israel's wisdom literature was fully integrated into Israel's historical faith, as evidenced by the identification of Torah and wisdom in a group of "wisdom psalms" and by the combining of familiar personalities and the events of Israel's history with the wisdom tradition in the later books of Sirach and the Wisdom of Solomon.

In their quest for wisdom, students of biblical wisdom literature will be encouraged to know that sacred learning—including study and intellectual questioning—is and always has been at the heart of true spirituality. Those who read this literature will be exposed to a set of core values necessary for vital citizenship and effective leadership at all levels of life. They will also obtain time-honored advice about how to deal with life's uncertainties in a holistic and pragmatic manner, because biblical wisdom is based upon theological tenets such as monotheism, God's providential care for humanity, the moral nature of the universe, and the notion of covenant. Such tenets promote the perspective that people who belong to communities of faith are related to God in patterns of worship, trust, love, obedience, service, protection, and grace. Surely here is "wisdom revealed."

PART I

Beginnings
CONVENTIONAL WISDOM

Chapter 1

The Book of Proverbs: A Quest for Practical Knowledge

Overview: The book of Proverbs is an anthology of traditional morality consisting of collections of instructions and aphorisms designed to inculcate trust in one's teachers and parents. Young people are asked to choose between two ways to live, following the advice of Lady Wisdom or Lady Folly. In Proverbs, the energetic search for wisdom is more important than learning specific things or acting wisely. The quest for wisdom brings prosperity and happiness because it orients one toward God and reveals the real structure of the world. Proverbs reflects two fundamental assumptions: that the universe is basically harmonious and that it has a moral structure characterized by retribution, whereby the good and just are rewarded and the bad or evil are punished.

Assigned Reading: Proverbs 1–5; 8–9; 10–13; 29–30; 31:10–31

Central Theme: The "fear of the Lord" is the beginning of wisdom.

Outline to Proverbs

I. Prologue 1:1–7

II. The Value of Wisdom 1:8—9:18

III. The Content of Wisdom 10:1—31:9

    A. First Collection of the Proverbs of Solomon 10:1—22:16

    B. Sayings of the Sages I 22:17—24:22

  C. Sayings of the Sages II 24:23–34

  D. Second Collection of the Proverbs of Solomon 25:1—29:27

  E. Sayings of Agur 30:1–33

  F. Sayings of Lemuel 31:1–9

 IV. Epilogue: Lady Wisdom as Wife 31:10–31

Contextual Analysis

In its broadest sense, wisdom denotes expertise or skill. Among the sages, however, wisdom came to denote expertise in life based on careful observation of God's created and moral order. Thus wisdom focused on practical success in everyday life, a goal at the heart of Proverbs (1:2–4). As previously noted, Israelite wisdom developed over a long time within the broader international wisdom traditions from Mesopotamia and Egypt. Despite formal attribution to Solomon (1:1), Proverbs explicitly identifies various other individuals or groups responsible for large portions of the book: anonymous sages (22:17; 24:23), Agur (30:1), Lemuel (31:1), and the scribes of Hezekiah (25:1). Ascribing Solomonic authorship to Proverbs gives the book the status of official teaching and credits the king with comprehensive wisdom.

  There is a possibility that the real royal authority behind the Proverbs is Hezekiah. Collections of proverbs could well have been compiled during the time of his religious reform, and it is equally possible that they received proper authority by their association with Solomon. While we do not have enough information to reconstruct this historical period, the book of Proverbs attests to both Hezekiah's influence (25:1) and Solomon's reputation (1:1; 10:1; 25:1).

  The book of Proverbs is an anthology or, more accurately, an anthology of anthologies.[1] Within the collections of proverbs the arrangement is often random. Sometimes proverbs are grouped according to theme or vocabulary; proverbs with a similar form, such as numerical sayings (Prov. 30:15–31), also occur in proximity. Because the book is an anthology, it contains repetitions (see 21:9 and 25:24). The individual proverbs are impossible to date with precision, since they lack reference to specific historical events, although those having to do with kings surely come from the monarchical period. Since there is little evidence of Greek

---

1. Coogan, *Brief Introduction*, 375.

influence or thought, scholars generally believe the collection itself was compiled during the Persian period, probably in the fifth or fourth century BC. While the book of Proverbs comes from an urban setting in the postexilic period, many sayings originate from diverse places years earlier, including the family farm (10:5; 14:4), home (13:24), city (11:10), and the royal court (25:2–7).

While the purpose of the book of Proverbs is to instruct youth in the life of wisdom, a secondary function is to entertain the audience by providing vignettes of humanity in all its foibles, flaws, and charms (see Prov. 27:14). The proverbs fall into two general categories: those that express some insight about human experience and those that have a religious dimension. Yet the two categories are not entirely separate. The religious dimension is for the most part one of divine justice in which God rewards the righteous and punishes the wicked. We must recall that the authors of the proverbs, like the ancient Israelites in general, did not have a fully developed belief in life after death, especially not in an afterlife where there was bliss for some and damnation for others. The reward for righteous behavior was in the present rather than in an eternal future.

While most of the proverbs depict the lives of the wealthy elite, especially in the royal court, the book of Proverbs testifies to some of the ideals of the prophets concerning social justice. Special attention is given to the poor and the needy, as well as to the rights of widows and orphans. Not surprisingly, the social world of Proverbs is essentially patriarchal, though the mother's status in the family is acknowledged occasionally (1:8; 10:1). The book ends with a famous acrostic poem celebrating the qualities of an ideal Israelite woman, though the ultimate reference is probably Lady Wisdom herself. Nevertheless, the values of the authors are for the most part conventional and patriarchal. The addressee of the book is also a male, as is indicated by nearly two dozen addresses to "my son" and by the advice to stay away from the "strange woman."

Like wisdom, the term "proverb" is difficult to define. The Hebrew word *mashal* has three meanings. (1) The root meaning derives from the verb "to be like" and points to the idea of "likeness" or "comparison." As a comparison, it usually consists of two parts in some kind of poetic construction. The sentence (see 10:2), the purest form of the proverb, is distinct from the instruction (22:17–29), which is a much longer unit, sometimes almost a short essay. Sentence and instruction alike, however, are expressed in poetic form, the two parts being either compared or contrasted in parallel balance. There are three major types of parallelism.

The simplest is called synonymous parallelism, where the second half of the line repeats the thought of the first with a slight variation (4:11). Antithetic parallelism contrast ideas (10:7) while the third type, synthetic parallelism, advances an idea and moves it toward a new concept (16:31). It is important to appreciate the prominence of poetry in the Bible. The Israelite elite, whether scribes, priests, prophets, kings, or sages, did not casually choose to express themselves in poetic form. Their very perception of reality was poetic. The modern word of science and logic does not always grasp, much less appreciate, the perspective of the ancient world. We insist on precision because we tend to perceive reality scientifically. Ancient Israel did not. Its encounter with reality was aesthetic and, therefore, it expressed itself in artistic thought patterns and literary forms. This does not minimize the validity of its perception and the truthfulness of its expression, nor does it minimize modern sensibility. They are simply two very different ways of looking at reality and talking about it.

In such cases the pupil is not instructed by rote or through dogma or commands, but by comparing the good with the bad, the wise with the foolish. Proverbs do not command, they persuade. Their purpose is not to indoctrinate, but to educate. They are not precepts that call for obedience, but adages that invite prudent response. They do not dictate what must be done, but rather they describe how things work. While the book of Proverbs insists on the importance of living an ethical life, the ethics it promotes issue from reflection on life rather than from conformity to law.

(2) The second sense of *mashal* derives from the verb "to rule over," meaning that another purpose of the proverbs is to help individuals cope with or "rule over" the chaos and uncertainties of life. On the surface of things, life is chaotic and unclear. Proverbs can shed light on our path and on our decision-making by providing insight into a situation. (3) A third meaning of *mashal* is "riddle" or "puzzle." The sayings actually require imagination to uncover their secrets. Two concepts seem to be implied in the use of riddles: the ambiguous nature of life and the importance of human freedom. Underlying this function of the proverbs is the belief that wisdom, though present in the world, often remains hidden.

The proverb itself serves two important functions. It depicts a situation from the past and from this depiction suggests a way of acting in the future. Understanding how this literary form works should help us grasp the dynamics of the wisdom tradition. Wisdom is not a blueprint for life, a collection of quaint catchy phrases that guarantee favorable results if we simply follow the directions. Proverbs are artistically honed images that direct our attention to the commonplace, and usually by some type of comparison or contrast, provide us with an opportunity to gain insight into the complexities of life. Different proverbs do this in different ways. The wise person is the one who understands life from more than one proverbial point of view and can discern appropriate forms of response.

Literary Analysis

The size and scope of the book of Proverbs is striking. Compared with ancient Near Eastern literature, the inclusion in one book of so many different genres on such a grand scale is impressive. Proverbs incorporates instructions, speeches, and collections of saying into a volume of thirty-one chapters. The wide array of material can be divided into four extensive collections and five short ones:

1. First Major Collection (Proverbs 1-9): Instructions on Wisdom;

2. Second Major Collection (Proverbs 10:1—22:16): First Solomonic Collection

    a. 10:1—15:33 (mostly antithetic parallelism);

    b. 16:1—22:16 (much synonymous and synthetic parallelism);

3. Third Major Collection (Proverbs 22:17—24:22): "Sayings of the Wise" (modelled on the Egyptian *Wisdom of Amenemope*);

4. First Minor Collection (Proverbs 24:23-34): More "Sayings of the Wise";

5. Fourth Major Collection (Proverbs 25-29): Second Solomonic Collection (transcribed by the men of Hezekiah, king of Judah);

6. Second Minor Collection (Proverbs 30:1-9): Sayings of Agur (a dialogue between a skeptic and a believer, 30:1-6, to which a prayer has been added, 30: 7-9);

7. Third Minor Collection (Proverbs 30:10-33): Anonymous Sayings (many in the form of numerical sayings);

8. Fourth Minor Collection (Proverbs 31:1-9): Sayings of King Lemuel, which his mother taught him;

9. Fifth Minor Collection (Proverbs 31:10-31): Ode to a Virtuous Wife (an anonymous acrostic poem, alphabetically arranged).

A brief prologue (1:1–7) provides the title (v. 1), objectives (vv. 2–4, 6), audience (vv. 4–5), and primary theme of the book: the key to genuine wisdom is one's relationship to the Lord ("fear of the Lord," v. 7). Form and content then divide the book into two halves.

The first half of the book (1:8—9:18), which links individual sayings together loosely, makes use of the short essay, generally in the form of speeches from a father to a son. As a result, certain themes surface, particularly the dangers posed by an adulteress (two of the extended poems, chapters 5 and 7, deal with the wily seductress and the gullible young male). In addition, poetic personifications function pedagogically. Various passages feature Lady Wisdom personified as a woman (1:20–33; 3:13–18; 4:5–9; 8:1—9:6). Lady Wisdom woos her followers, inviting them to a banquet in her home (9:1–6), whereas Lady Folly lurks in the night, actively seducing simpletons to their ruin (9:13–18). The cumulative aim of this collection is to convince the reader of the importance of choosing wisdom as a way of life, a choice between life and death.

The second half of the book (10:1—31:9) presents the content of wisdom through individual sayings that describe wise and foolish behavior. Seven sections or collections provide minimal structure to these diverse proverbs. The first and longest is a collection of "the proverbs of Solomon" (10:1—22:16) that has little discernable internal order other than beginning with a large group of antithetical proverbs (10:1—15:33). The brief maxims in the remaining section (16:1—22:16) cover a wide range of everyday occurrences, offering astute observations on the folly of pride, laziness, passion, deceit, gossip, and similar vices and speaking in favor of virtues such as generosity, faithfulness, self-control, industry, and sobriety. The second and third collections in this half of the book derive from anonymous sages (22:17—24:22 and 24:23–34). Unlike the First Solomonic Collection, the second section rarely employs the various types of parallelism by which Israel's sages expressed their teaching. This section includes a brief essay on the plight of drunkenness, described with extreme pathos (23:29–35). One other feature of this section of foreign extraction is the use of exquisite metaphors, indicative of an advanced stage in poetic reflection. The third section (24:23–34) shows an unusual relationship with Proverbs 1–9, inasmuch as a single proverb from that extensive collection (6:10-11) has been taken over and used as the basis for a brief essay on laziness.

The fourth section, attributed to Solomon, was preserved by Hezekiah's scribes (25:1—29:27), who either inherited or arranged some of their materials according to theme. This material resembles the first Solomonic collection in its fondness for antithetic parallelism, but makes lavish use of comparative statements. Proverbs credits the fifth and sixth sections (30:1–33 and 31:1–9) to non-Israelites: Agur and King Lemuel, though stylistically and thematically, 30:1–9 and 30:10–33 consist of separate collections. Proverbs 31:1–9 takes the form of advice offered by a Queen Mother to her young son.

An acrostic poem regarding the woman of noble character comprises the epilogue to the book (31:10–31). Although this poem describes an ideal wife, it is more likely that the woman is personified Wisdom from chapters 1–9. Earlier the sages had urged the son to pursue and marry Lady Wisdom (4:5–9); now they present the benefits of having chosen wisdom as one's life partner.

While the nature of this proverbial literature makes it extremely difficult to date, generally scholars consider the "Solomonic Collections" (10:1—22:16 and 25:1—29:27) to be the oldest sections of the book. Some may date back to Israel's "Golden Age," the period of David and Solomon, particularly those that give the impression of moral neutrality (11:24; 20:29). The first nine chapters and the thirty-first are considered postexilic, added to the older collection in the early Persian period, after the return from the Babylonian Exile. Various versions of the book existed during the Hellenistic period, as evidenced by the Septuagint, with its different ordering of the last sections and its additions to and deletions from the Hebrew text.

Thematic Analysis

Life

At the heart of the sage's search for knowledge lay the ultimate value: life. If death represents the end of life, then all that supports longevity of life—good health, abundance of friends, many children, safety, and adequate resources—constitute the blessings of life. This helps to explain why images like "tree of life" and "fountain of life" recur with such frequency in the sayings. Lady Wisdom is even depicted with long life in her right hand, riches and honor in her left (3:13–18).

Path or Way

Another prominent image in the vocabulary of the sages who composed the book of Proverbs is the "path" or "way" to life. The significance of this terminology depends upon the double sense with which the word for "way" is used: (a) the mysteries of nature, and (b) path. The first meaning is found in Proverbs 30:18–19: "Three things are too wonderful for me; four I do not understand: the way of an eagle in the sky, the way of a snake on a rock, the way of a ship on the high seas, and the way of a man with a girl." The incomprehensible feature of the four movements concerns the lack of any "tracks" or trail evident in the various activities. The notion of a path was particularly appropriate in the thinking of Israel's sages, for at birth everyone embarks on a journey that leads either to full life or to premature death. Children and adolescents often stray and need to get back on track. In ancient times few maps existed, but they were invaluable on the winding foot paths. Youth needed instruction on the paths before them, literally and symbolically. Useful road maps exist, but they are the fruit of long effort. Those who rely upon their own ingenuity soon become hopelessly lost. Sometimes human plans get interrupted; often they fall short. From this encounter with human finitude, sages learned an important lesson, that ultimately God is the guide: "All our steps are ordered by the Lord; how then can we understand our own ways?" (20:24).

Wisdom and Folly

On the path of life two distinct groups of pilgrims—the wise and the foolish—pursue different goals. Everyone falls into one or the other category. For the authors of Proverbs, there is no middle ground, and one cannot walk both paths simultaneously; one either participates in wisdom or in folly. Moreover, an ethical quality prevails: the wise are righteous and fools are wicked. This surprising conclusion, simplistic in appearance, arose from the operative assumption that those who strengthen the order upholding the universe represent God's ways (and are therefore blessed by the Creator), while those who undermine this harmony are enemies of the Creator.

Although the sages did not allow for a middle ground between wisdom and folly, they coined a rich vocabulary to distinguish among fools. Eight different terms for "fool" occur within the Proverbs: (1) one who is naïve; (2) one who is innately stupid, (3) one who is obstinate; (4)

one who persists in folly, (5) one who is crude, (6) one who is cruel, (7) one who is insane, and (8) one who is overly opinionated.[2] While there is variance between these categories, meaning that some such persons are not beyond help, most fools are viewed as rebellious and therefore as objects of contempt.

If all humans belong to one of these two camps, then it follows that they represent two different lifestyles. One pattern of behavior—that of the wise person—secures existence, and its opposite—that of the foolish person—leads to destruction. For the authors of Proverbs, the prerequisite for wisdom is *humility*. To be wise is to have an open mind. Some people are incapable of learning, not because they lack intelligence, but because they lack humility. Such people are disruptive, because they are unable to learn from others (13:10). People who are humble are adaptable and teachable (10:8). For the humble, life is a quest for the truth that must be pursued continuously in the changing circumstances of human existence. In Proverbs, humility is desirable, not merely for practical reasons, but because it is paired with the greatest virtue of the wise: the fear of the Lord (22:4).

In the book of Proverbs, wisdom is spirituality, a stance toward life that incorporates a broad range of chosen attitudes and behaviors, often called "virtues." While virtues can be passed on from one generation to the next, proverbial wisdom assumes that people are free to choose, indeed, that they must choose their own course of action in life. The reason is clear: life is ambiguous and multivalent, and no predetermined code or blueprint can prepare us for all the turns and permutations of life. While some of the proverbs appear prescriptive and dogmatic, few teach behavior that is universally applicable. This explains why for every clear statement about how one should act, there is another statement affirming its opposite: "do not speak harshly" and "do not refrain from rebuking"; or, "never lend money" and "lend money to the poor." It is not blind obedience that the sages desire, but flexibility of mind in determining which approach to a given situation is appropriate. Ahead of each person lies a lifetime of choices: to cope with life—sensibly, morally, judiciously—is to make wise choices.

In the book of Proverbs, certain qualities are said to secure existence:

1. *Fidelity* in relationships. This includes (a) loyalty to parents, which is of central importance for society in that it maintains stability in

---

2. Crenshaw, *Old Testament Wisdom*, 79–81.

the social order (this respect is integral to the fifth commandment in the Decalogue: "Honor your father and your mother, so that your days may be long in the land that the Lord your God is giving you"; Exod. 20:12); (b) faithful friendship (17:17; 20:6); (c) proper treatment of neighbors; and even (d) proper treatment of enemies (24:17–18, 29). Wisdom is relational, and respectful behavior should be part of all human interaction. (The opposite of fidelity is disloyalty and disrespect.)

2. *Diligence* in one's endeavors. Fundamental to this virtue is the willingness to channel energy into one's responsibilities. Diligent people persevere single-mindedly, like the oxen (14:4). They are steady, dependable, and regularly maintain momentum. The opposite of diligence is laziness or careless action (10:4). While laziness produces poverty, diligence yields prosperity. In the world of conventional wisdom, where cause and effect are organically joined, timely, persistent hard work inevitably produces wealth and power (12:24; 21:5). Diligence extends to all of life's endeavors, even to parenting, as we learn from the well-known maxim: "spare the rod, spoil the child," taken from 13:24: "Those who spare the rod hate their children, but those who love them are diligent to discipline them."

3. *Prudence*. Diligence must be balanced by other virtues, because by itself diligence can lead to excess or degenerate into obsession. Like every human activity, diligence is valuable only when governed by prudence. The term "prudence," once common in English parlance, seems archaic and even alien to modern Americans. Kathleen O'Connor's definition highlight's the term's usefulness: "Prudence is the guiding intelligence which dictates what action or withdrawal from action is appropriate in a specific situation."[3] Prudence is akin to discernment. The prudent know when to act and when to resist action (12:16; 27:12). Prudent timing is the secret of wise speech (25:11). Prudence is the essential mark of the wise person because life is often ambiguous, confusing to interpretation. The opposite of prudence is carelessness.

The book of Proverbs emphasizes the prudent use of the tongue, devoting over sixty sayings to the topic of speech. Prudence in speech was particularly critical in antiquity because speaking was the only form of communication available to most people. In Western society speech is often uttered carelessly, but today we must all learn prudence in our use of emails, text messaging, posting of photos, and in all use of media.

---

3. O'Connor, *Wisdom Literature*, 43–44.

What one says cannot be retracted. As a result, a person's speech must be utterly reliable, and it must be appropriate to the occasion. It is these skills that enable a wise person to "rule over" (one of the meanings of *mashal*, the Hebrew word for proverb) those situations in life that require insightful understanding. For example, we have all heard the maxim, "silence is golden," but as we learn in Proverbs, silence is not always the better choice. While false speech can harm the community, "Better is open rebuke than hidden love" (27:5). Prudent timing is the secret of wise speech (25:11).

4. *Self-mastery* (discipline). The book of Proverbs accentuates the significance of self-discipline or self-control, for in the estimation of Israel's sages, self-mastery deserves high praise. Though Proverbs extends discipline to many facets of daily life, a number of sayings address anger. While anger is not considered bad in itself, it must be under control: "one who is slow to anger is better than the mighty, and one whose temper is controlled than one who captures a city" (16:32). The sayings about anger teach that discipline is essential to wise living. Like the other attributes of the wise, self-mastery is useful only when practiced in a balanced fashion and appropriately. Without discipline, a person lacks focus and therefore integrity. Such persons lack discretion, and their behavior is often reckless. Mature people are characterized by profound honesty about themselves and the world. Such people are particularly secure, perhaps because they have nothing to hide and, ultimately, nothing to lose. Because of these qualities, people of integrity are able to be responsible and loyal in human relationships, the arena where all the virtues of the wise are employed.

5. *Generosity*. The sages valued wealth, seeing it as a sign of divine favor. However, even good things are sometimes ambiguous. This is the meaning of Proverbs 30:7-9, which includes the petition "give me neither poverty nor riches" (v. 8). Abundance should always be tempered with liberality, for those who are kind to the needy honor God (14:31). Sayings about the poor and the wealthy abound in Proverbs. Some proverbs blame the poor for their victimhood, deriding the poor as lazy. The formula seems simplistic: hard work brings profit, laziness brings poverty. According to conventional sages, wise living is accompanied by material gain. However, these ancient teachings are not as crass as they first appear. Then as now, wealth was highly valued because it provided security in the face of uncertainty. The purpose is not to deride the poor but to warn the young, exhorting them to prudence, vigilance, and effort. Some

of the sayings speak sympathetically about the poor and their plight. A number of proverbs exhort the rich to share their wealth: "All day long the wicked covet, but the righteous give and do not hold back" (21:26). Generosity blesses the giver as well as the recipient (11:25; 22:9). The true motivation for generosity, however, is not blessing, but equality: the poor and the rich are seen to be equal before God (22:2). In one saying God is identified with the poor, making actions toward the poor equivalent to actions toward God: "Those who oppress the poor insult their Maker, but those who are kind to the needy honor him" (14:31; cf. Matt. 25:31–46). Poverty is not always the worst tragedy in life. A greater tragedy is to lose one's integrity (10:2; 20:7; 21:6).

As some conduct leads to wisdom, other conduct leads to destruction:

1. *Adultery and promiscuity.* The vivid descriptions of "the adulteress" in the first major collection of Proverbs leave no doubt that her way leads to shame, loss of wealth, dread disease, and other consequences, together called "death" (2:18–19; 5:5; 8: 36; 9:18).

2. *Drunkenness.* Like promiscuity, excessive wine and strong drink are said to bring ruin without delay (23:29–35).

3. *Laziness.* Numerous sayings denounce sluggards and describe the dismal lot that befalls lazy persons (6:10–11; 10:26; 26:14). Sometimes an element of ridicule is introduced, as in the observation that a sluggard is too lazy to lift a spoon to his mouth (19:24). Israel's sages tried their utmost to reduce the possibility that sluggards could blame their miserable life on unexpected circumstances.

4. *Lying.* The most important bodily organ in Proverbs is the mouth (or "tongue"), for through speech teachers communicate instruction, knowledge, and wisdom. Speech must be truthful and reliable; lying is vehemently denounced (17:4; 19:22; 30:6), particularly lying in a court of law (6:19; 12:17; 14:5, 25; 19:5, 9, 28; 21:28).

5. *Gossip.* The book of Proverbs attends particularly to prudent use of the tongue, probably because careless or vicious speech was a major problem in ancient Israel. In oral societies, what one says is remembered and profoundly affects the life of the community. To encourage proper speech, Proverbs instructs the wise in its power. The mouth of the wise is a "fountain of life" (10:11), but the speech of scoundrels "is like a scorching fire" (16:27). The speech of a wise person "is a tree of life" (15:4), whereas "whoever utter slander is a fool" (10:18), whose babbling results in ruin (10:14). The list of seven vices in Proverbs 6:16 concludes with

"a lying witness" and "one who sows discord in a family," both related to gossip.

Despite attention to vices, the focus in Proverbs is on positive action. It is good to remember that aphorisms were written not in order to motivate the foolish and lazy to change their ways but to motivate the virtuous to action. How does one defeat these vices, foes to Life? While self-reliance and self-mastery are emphasized, the authors of Proverbs favor dependence upon God, the author of Life: "Trust in the Lord with all your heart, and do not rely on your own insight. In all your ways acknowledge him, and he will make straight your path" (3:5–6).

Essay 1: The Personification of Wisdom—Lady Wisdom and Lady Folly

At the center of Israel's wisdom literature stand two women: the alluring female dubbed Lady Wisdom and her counterpart, Lady Folly. Lady Wisdom is the most striking biblical personification. While personification as a literary device enlivens a text, it also fits well with the Israelite tendency toward anthropomorphism. In the case of biblical wisdom, however, the extent and the significance of the personification are so great that she appears as more than a literary character. In Proverbs 1–9 and implicitly elsewhere in the book, we find reference to wisdom as a figure who speaks frequently in the first person and identifies herself not just as the divine companion but also as the source of order in society and success in life (8:15–21). In Proverbs 8:22–30, wisdom speaks of herself as having been created before anything else and as God's companion and even assistant at the creation of the cosmos. The same language is found in Sirach 24 and Wisdom of Solomon 7–9. In these texts, wisdom is depicted as a divine being, but scholars disagree about her exact status. For many interpreters, she is a hypostasis, a divinized personification of an abstract quality, like Victory or Justice. The language of Proverbs 8 is highly mythological; it also has sexual overtones, an intriguing appropriation of the common ancient polytheistic view that male deities had female consorts.

The personification of wisdom in Proverbs is so distinctive that it has stimulated scholars to search for its origins. While some scholars have located its source in other cultures, the usage can be explained biblically. In addition to grounding its practical teachings in reverence for the

Lord, Proverbs also asserts an authority for wisdom rooted in creation itself. Wisdom is personified as a principle associated with the creative process, present with God from the beginning (3:19–20 and 8:22–31). Wisdom is here heralded as the life-giving principle of cosmic order. This gives a theoretical foundation to the claim that wisdom is the order for everyday living. The personification of wisdom in Proverbs introduces a type of speculation that we will encounter in the New Testament, particularly in Christological contexts, as well as in later Christian theological discussion of the three persons of the Trinity.

Whatever associations wisdom may have had in other cultures, she is best understood in her biblical expression as a communication of God. Israel's covenant language teaches blessing for obedience and curses or punishment for disobedience. Jews believed they lived in a moral universe, a perspective affirmed by Israel's traditional sages and enacted by the principle of retribution. The silence of heaven on vital topics, such as calamities and suffering, as well as uncertainty about such things as one's destiny and the will of God, called out for divine mediation. Personified wisdom achieved that purpose for Israel's sages.

The figure of wisdom might also have been created by the authors of Proverbs as a foil to the "strange woman" (which we are calling Lady Folly). As stories of seductive women exist in all societies, perhaps Lady Wisdom was created as a literary contrast, her sex appeal having didactive power. The highly erotic language associated with her would certainly capture the attention of young males, the primary audience of the text. The figure of Lady Folly may also represent the allurement of foreign culture and even foreign religion. Nevertheless, what is important for our purpose is the function of these women in Proverbs, not the origin of their character.

Wherever Lady Wisdom appears in the text, her primary mode of being is relational. Her connections extend to every part of reality: the natural world, God, and humanity. No aspect of reality is closed off from her. To follow Lady Wisdom is to awaken and participate fully in this matrix of relationships.

In the collected sayings of the second half of Proverbs (chapters 10–29), the decision to become wise is presented as a continual series of practical choices, made throughout life, whereas in chapters 1–9 this choice is portrayed as the single major decision of a lifetime. The setting here involves a young man deliberating between two women, one of whom he must choose for a life's companion. One is the seductress—Lady

Folly—whose friendship leads to death; the other is Lady Wisdom, whose intimacies bring blessing, life, peace, and relational joy. Each woman symbolizes both a stance toward life and the world and the consequences of taking that stance. The image of a young man choosing a marriage partner for life underscores the seriousness of choices regarding wisdom. It also points to the covenant relationship underlying Israel's self-understanding—Israel as married to God, with consequent fidelity to that vow. Faithfulness to Yahweh (monotheism) is represented by covenant loyalty, whereas compromising with polytheistic cultures and values is unfaithfulness to the covenant, represented in the Bible as adultery. The two ways are set forth clearly in Deuteronomy 30:15-20, a text every ancient Israelite surely knew by heart: "See. I have set before you today life and prosperity, death and adversity. . . . Choose life."

The personification of wisdom and folly in female figures appears at first glance to offer women a place of their own in the biblical tradition, which was overwhelmingly patriarchal. But even in Proverbs, both women remain idealized images created by men. Furthermore, they are male projections of opposing aspects of the human condition onto the female figure. These are not women as they existed in Israelite society or in other ancient societies, nor are they women as they exist today. They are stereotypes of womanhood as men envisioned it. One represents everything good, desirable, and profitable for men; the other is everything harmful to men. No woman, no human being, is all that good or all that bad. Both images are idealized, and both are harmful to women. No woman should be portrayed as Madonna or as whore, as the cause of good or of evil. In real life, men and women are good and evil; both are responsible for their own choices, and neither sex can be totally blamed or totally excused.

We must approach wisdom literature and all biblical literature with caution, because much of it reinforces gender stereotypes. Many views of women in the wisdom literature are unfortunately misogynist, such as Sirach's view: "From a woman sin had its beginning, and because of her we all die" (25:24). Passages like these led to the danger of blaming original sin on Eve, finding their way ultimately into the New Testament literature (see 1 Tim. 2:14-15) and eventually into popular Christian notions that see the Virgin Mary as the counterpart of Eve and therefore as the progenitor of salvation.

Poetry creates imaginative worlds of beauty and response. That Lady Wisdom is a figure of poetry means that she can and should be understood on many levels of meaning. As a poetic character she represents insights into the nature of reality designed to evoke emotional and intellectual responses from the readers. This means that she cannot be reduced to a list of functions that she performs in the cosmos, though that can be given. Though such lists appear, wisdom is more than what she does. She brings with her a haunting series of allusions and revelations about the world and about God. In the riddle her identity poses, she is a metaphor leading us into deepest mystery. What would happen if we were to view religion and morality as we do Lady Wisdom, as poetry to be imagined and interpreted aesthetically and holistically?

Proverbs 8:1—9:5

The remainder of this essay examines two extraordinary poems in Proverbs: 8:1—9:5 and 31:10–31. Proverbs 8 presents the fullest biblical personification of Lady Wisdom, including (1) the location for her proclamation (8:2–3; cf. 1:20–21), (2) her audience (8:4–9), (3) the necessity of choice (8:10–11), (4) the qualities of wisdom (8:12–21), and (5) wisdom's origins (8:22–31). The poem ends with an appeal to wait at wisdom's door (8:32–36). Love language is used, underscoring wisdom's desire for disciples. Save 8:36, all is promise. Chapter 9:1–5 describes an invitation to wisdom's feast.

1. Concerning the *location* for her proclamation (8:2–3; cf. 1:20–21), wisdom is said to appear wherever people gather (at the crossroads, in the marketplace, at the gates, at the top of city walls), in their daily routines, and in the struggles of ordinary people to survive. Her invitation is audible and palpable; it gets our attention, because wisdom is practical.

2. Wisdom's *audience* is inclusive, including the simple and the foolish; it is also universal, for everyone is invited to accept her promises. In 8:6–9 she promises nothing but straight talk.

3. In the third segment of the poem wisdom claims that her message is of greater value to people than silver, gold, or anything else desirable. The Hebrew word translated "take" at the beginning of verse 10 ("take my instruction") means "choose," underscoring the *necessity of choice*, for wisdom cannot be inherited or passed on involuntarily.

4. The poem withholds a precise description of the *qualities of wisdom*, though verse 12 mentions prudence (balanced reasoning or discretion), knowledge (which in proverbs is not a reference to knowledge but to the ability to apply information practically), and discretion (good

sense). These terms overlap and may even be synonymous, for the key to Hebraic proverbial wisdom is always its practical implementation. While the claims of this woman are extraordinary, the poem does not so much offer a list of benefits as tell us that wisdom wishes to give herself, a self-gift accompanied by promises for human happiness and prosperity.

5. That Lady Wisdom is no ordinary human is clear from the traditions about *her origins* in 8:22–31. Speaking in the first person, she goes on from her beginnings to describe the wondrous events of God's subsequent creation of the universe. The poem, with its literary structure, is quite mystical. Several statements can be made about this remarkable poem. First, wisdom is said to have existed forever (the Hebrew word *'olam*, translated as "long ago" in 8:22, literally means "from eternity"). By placing her birth before creation, the author gives wisdom unquestionable authority to speak the truth. Second, wisdom is said to be the enduring principle of all creation, for creation was made with wisdom and thus serves to explain why signs of the Creator are visible in nature. Wisdom has a distinct relation with the world, not as a passive observer of God's work, but as chief artisan or executor of the architectural plans of the Creator. Third, wisdom is not explicitly called God's daughter, but the poem verges on that meaning. Fourth, wisdom is portrayed as God's companion, indeed with God in the beginning, but not as co-eternal with God, for as "the first" of God's acts, she remains subordinate to God. Fifth, the language is metaphorical, as is all God-language. This poem breaks out of masculine metaphors that dominate much of scripture and creatively utilizes feminine imagery. Sixth, her origins, her intimate part in creation, and her relationship of love with its Creator are but preludes to her current occupation: rejoicing in the inhabited world and delighting in the human race (8:31). It is to this announcement that the poem presses: humans and the world they inhabit are wisdom's interests, her primary role.

The threefold cause of her rejoicing—God, the world, and humanity—make her the center of a matrix of relationships. It is wisdom who communicates among them; it is wisdom who acts as the mediator between God and humans; it is she who reveals to humanity the world and God in their mystery and wonder. From her comes understanding of reality and of humanity's place within it. Wisdom is the key to human enlightenment.

Who is Lady Wisdom, this alluring figure of poetry? Is she merely a literary fiction? Is she a personification of the order and harmony in the universe? Is she a personification of Torah, or of an attribute of God? In the Hellenistic period, Jews began to think of wisdom as the Word of God (Sir. 24:3), and therefore, like Torah (Sir. 15:1; 19:20; 24:23), indistinguishable from God's mind, will and love. She is the thread that ties together all of reality. In the Wisdom of Solomon, the last of the Jewish wisdom books, her identification with God is made more explicit. She is described as "the fashioner of all things" (7:22) and equated with God's Spirit (7:22–27; 9:17). To follow wisdom, to embrace her and to live with her is, finally, to live with God. Such living recognizes, collaborates, and is transformed by the harmony, beauty, and order of God in this world. This is what it means to become wise.

It is not a big leap from here to the Christian understanding of the Holy Spirit or to Christological passages in the New Testament, such as the connection of the divine Logos to Jesus (John 1:1), the Word of God, or to Jesus, the "firstborn of all creation" (Col. 1:15).

Proverbs 31:10–31: Ode to Lady Wisdom

The thrust of the poems concerning intimate relationship with Lady Wisdom culminates in Proverbs 31:10–31, often called the "Poem of the Good Wife." Many view this popular piece to be about the ideal wife whom the wise young man should choose to enhance his future. However, recent scholarship takes a different view regarding this passage. Rather than supplying the image of the correct marriage partner, this alphabetic poem has been likened to the acrostic Psalm 112, which describes those who fear the Lord. In this passage the fear of the Lord—meaning that which every human owes the Creator—amounts to religious devotion as we understand it today. Reverential disposition toward God, living life well and right in the light of the existence of a sovereign God, is central to Proverbs as well (1:7; 9:10; 31:30), making the "Ode to Lady Wisdom" a summary of the entire book.

Who is this woman, described in 31:10 as "capable wife" but also translatable as "strong woman"? (The adjective "capable" is the same Hebrew word translated "strength" in 31:3 and "noble things" in 31:29.) Is she the female counterpart to "capable men," persons who in the Bible approach a variety of tasks with wisdom, competence, and vigor? The focus throughout the poem is on the woman's wise and energetic activity. This female character, central to Proverbs, is no ordinary woman but rather is

Lady Wisdom herself. Drawing from images of the young man choosing between Lady Wisdom and Lady Folly found in Proverbs 1–9, this poem demonstrates what life is like once one has chosen to live with wisdom. That this woman is not a real person is evident from her role. No woman of ancient Israel held such a high place in family, society, or economy as the poem imagines. No woman held such authority or was granted such responsibility, not even as the ideal. In ancient Israel, this woman would have been unimaginable as a real woman. The answer to the rhetorical question, "A capable wife who can find?" (31:10), is negative. No one can find her because she is not human.

The benefits of life with the "strong woman" are precisely the gifts Lady Wisdom promises to all who seek her. If you find this woman, marry her! This is what is urged on the reader of the book of Proverbs. Why? Because wisdom is God![4]

Questions to Ponder

1. Proverbs 1:2–5 identifies twelve qualities that are associated with those who master the proverbs. In your own words, define each term or concept. Which do you find most desirable? Support your answer.

2. Proverbs 4:1–5 speaks of wisdom as a legacy transmitted from parents to children. What role did your father and mother play in transmitting this legacy to you? (See Sirach 8:8–9.)

3. In Proverbs 1:7, what is meant by the phrase "fear of the Lord"? (cf. Job 28:28 and "Fear God" in Ecclesiastes 12:13).

---

4. The biblical concept of wisdom is, of course, complex. Wisdom in some cases is said to be an attribute of God, in other cases an attribute God has bestowed on creation, and in some cases a gift God gives to humans. There is a big difference between personifying one attribute of God and talking about God in all God's attributes. By saying that wisdom is God, I do not mean to say that she is all of God. The view that Lady Wisdom is a personification of God's total self is not supportable in Proverbs, since it is clear that Lady Wisdom, like Lady Folly, is an abstraction. Furthermore, in the text of Proverbs 8 clear distinctions are made between God and wisdom. Elsewhere, such as Job 28 and Sirach 24, one hears of God searching for wisdom. None of these texts encourage one to think that the authors were identifying God and wisdom. However, since only God can be said to have existed before creation, and wisdom is said to have existed before all things, it seems possible to postulate—if only metaphorically—the direct connection of wisdom with God's own self.

4. Glance through chapters 10 to 16 of Proverbs and note the pervasiveness of the use of antitheses. Note also the use of "two paths/ways" in Proverbs 2:13 and 4:10–19. This one-dimensional approach seems to bypass the importance modern people place on subtlety, ambiguity, complexity, and the "grey areas" of morality. Is the notion of opposites in Proverbs (good/evil; right/wrong) too simplistic?

5. Read Proverbs 10 and make a list of the virtues and vices you detect in the passage.

6. Why is wisdom personified as female in Proverbs? (See 8:1—9:12 and 4:6–9).

7. In Proverbs 8:22–31, why is wisdom portrayed as the first of God's creation?

8. In your estimation, what is the meaning in Proverbs 31:10–31 of the metaphor of "the capable wife"?

PART II

Unconventional Wisdom

Chapter 2

The Book of Ecclesiastes: A Quest for Meaning

Overview: The book of Ecclesiastes (Qoheleth) depicts the folly of seeing life solely from an earth-bound perspective, that is, from "under the sun." This short work is said to contain the reflections of a great king in his maturity, reflecting on what he has learned about life. The uncertainties of life and the inevitability of death have made him skeptical toward traditional wisdom and led him to advocate enjoying the present moment. While the notion of retribution and the understanding of justice found in Proverbs are challenged in both Job and Ecclesiastes, all three books reflect a theology of creation. Wisdom is inherent in creation, and therefore creation is to be reflected upon and its lessons learned. One result of the examination of creation is discovery of the limits of human knowledge. Though humans may uncover inklings of a moral order that is good, true, and beautiful, they are unable to see the larger design of God.

Assigned Reading: Read Ecclesiastes 1–12

Central Theme: Life should be lived with enjoyment; all else is futile.

Outline to Ecclesiastes
   I. Superscription 1:1
   II. Framing Verses 1:2–3
   III. Poem on Cosmology 1:4–11
   IV. Qoheleth's Quest for the Meaning of Life 1:12—6:9

    A. Three Experiments 2:1—2:26

        1. The Futility of Pleasure 2:1–11

        2. The Futility of Wisdom 2:12–17

        3. The Futility of Toil 2:18–26

    B. Musings on Time 3:1–22

    C. Musings on Human Activity 4:1—6:9

        1. Society, Toil, and Friendship 4:1–16

        2. Advice on Religious Duties 5:1–7

        3. The Enjoyment of Life (chiastic structure) 5:8—6:9

V. Qoheleth's Conclusions 6:10—11:6

    A. Transitional Comments 6:10–12

    B. A Collection of Proverbs on Human Limitations 7:1–14

    C. Moderation and the Doctrine of "The Golden Mean" 7:15–29

    D. Wisdom and Earthly Power 8:1–9

    E. Wisdom and the Problem of Retribution 8:10–17

    F. Life and Death 9:1–10

    G. Living with Risks 9:11—10:15

    H. Living with Political and Economic Risks 10:16—11:6

VI. Poem on Youth and Old Age 11:7—12:7

    A. Framing Verse 12:8

    B. Epilogue 12:9–14

Contextual Analysis

Counter-Order (Unconventional) Wisdom

The distinctive teaching of Israel's conventional sages was that wisdom is a gift of God rather than a human achievement (Prov. 16:1). Though the sages were aware of the limits of the human quest, they firmly believed that wisdom, when based upon "the fear of the Lord," provides the key to knowing the right course of action and leads to a reliable understanding of the basis of reality. In this respect, the book of Proverbs reflects two fundamental assumptions, (a) that we live in a harmonious universe, ordered and upheld by God, and (b) that the universe has a moral structure. Underlying these assumptions is the conviction that God made the world in such a way that good actions are rewarded and evil actions are punished. Obtaining wisdom means understanding this world view and behaving in ways that result in happiness and prosperity. In preexilic Israel, it is clear that biblical authors expected rewards and punishments to take place in the temporal sphere, since there was as yet no real doctrine of an afterlife: "If the righteous are repaid on earth, how much more the wicked and the sinner!" (Prov. 11:31). So long as one approaches the exhortations in the book of Proverbs with the understanding that they promote wise behavior, then the moral advice works, but when those exhortations are mistaken for unbending rules by which outcomes can be predicted, then they strike us as rather naïve, and it would be easy to become cynical. As we all know, sometimes the wicked are clever enough to prosper; in addition, there are natural disasters, sickness, accidents, and mistakes, most of which are not easily rectified, if at all.

Such a set of problems gave rise to a second stream of biblical wisdom literature found in books like Ecclesiastes and Job. At one level, these books seem to doubt or even to repudiate the conventional wisdom we find in Proverbs. It is helpful to understand this tension through the biblical concept of the covenant, one of the most important concepts in the Bible. By "covenant" we mean the idea that God has made solemn agreements with chosen people, whether Jews or Christians. This idea embraces the entire covenant tradition called Torah, which includes the relationship between God and the covenant community. While the covenant that God made with Moses and with the Israelites is prototypical, the Bible presents a series of such agreements, including with Adam and Eve, Noah, Abraham, and David. The prophet Jeremiah speaks of a new covenant (31:31–34), one that Christians believe to have been fulfilled in the person of Christ.

The idea of the covenant was the perspective of Israel's conventional sages, found in the books of Proverbs, in the wisdom Psalms, and also in deuterocanonical books like Sirach and the Wisdom of Solomon. These sages were deeply committed as well to the idea that the essence of wisdom resides in Torah, God's supreme gift of law and the basis of covenant made at Sinai. At the center of these ancient covenant traditions is the notion of obedience to stipulations. In the case of Adam and Eve, there is a clear command that they are to obey. They may eat of any of the trees in the garden except the tree of the knowledge of good and evil, lest they die. As we know, the story of Adam and Eve, with the tree of life and the tree of the knowledge of good and evil, is a wisdom story par excellence. In that account, actions have immediate consequences, and the consequences of disobedience are clear: "In the day that you eat of it you shall die" (Gen. 2:18). The entire story is based upon retribution; those who disobey are expelled from the garden.

In the story of Noah, the pervasiveness of moral evil stirs the Lord to send the deluge. But a careful reading of the flood narrative, while utilizing explicit covenant language, also offers new options: the appearance of the rainbow indicates that God will never again destroy all life in this manner (Gen. 8:21–22; 9:9–17). Such a promise can be taken to mean that there will no longer be an immediate reward for virtue and an immediate punishment for vice. Rather, by saying that the rain will fall on the just and the unjust alike, we can understand, as Matthew indicates in Jesus' discourse on the Sermon on the Mount (Matt. 5:45), that God will allow the good and the wicked to live together.[1] In this alternative way of understanding the covenant, the Lord withholds "his wrath at injustice and instead instruct his people in the ways of wisdom, so that they may by their free choices learn to please him. Seen in this way, the covenant with Noah explains at least something about why bad things happen sometimes to good people, why the wicked sometimes prosper and why the innocent sometimes suffer. Paradoxically, the tragedy of innocent suffering is the result of the mercy of God in not insisting upon immediate retribution by another world-destroying flood."[2] Put philosophically, God's self-imposed distance enables what we call human freedom. How we live in a world where evil (wickedness) is allowed to thrive is a problem that the sapiential tradition faces directly in Ecclesiastes and Job. These books address the inequities of life and present the beginning of a "counter-order" or unconventional wisdom in early Judaism. Here we see the first hints of an emergence of a doctrine of an afterlife to deal with the lack of adequate justice or retribution in this life. Another central issue or theme in these wisdom books is an acknowledgment on human limits. Though humans can see glimpses of a moral order, they are unable to see the larger design or the purposes of God.

---

1. The Sermon on the Mount, found in Matthew 5–7, is almost entirely made up of wisdom material.

2. Koterski, *Wisdom Literature*, 1:79.

Authorship, Date, and Historical Setting

A Jewish tradition claims that Solomon is the author of three biblical books. When he was young and in love, he wrote the love poems in the Song of Songs; when he matured and turned to making a living, he wrote the practical wisdom found in the book of Proverbs; when he grew older, he gave voice to the feelings of cynicism and futility that we find in Ecclesiastes (having one thousand wives and concubines can have that effect!).

The book is basically the work of one author, although at least two epilogues are readily discernible (12:9-11 and 12:12-14), added later, possibly by disciples of Qoheleth. The first epilogue praises the sage for the genius displayed in studying and arranging proverbs, while the second cautions readers to take the teaching with a grain of salt, for "of making many books there is no end, and much study is a weariness of the flesh" (12:12). The book contains variations in mood, contradictions in thought (for example, 2:2 and 7: 3 deride laughter and joy, whereas 8:15 praises joy), and perspectives ranging from cool skepticism to orthodox affirmations. Some scholars argue for multiple authorship, but the best solution is single authorship, coupled with the awareness that the work contains numerous proverbs and quotations that the author collected and embedded into original material. The author clearly blends unconventional wisdom (his own skeptical perspective) with conventional wisdom, occasionally relying on traditional vocabulary and thought, which he uses in his own way. Qoheleth's bold challenge to Judaism, with its doctrine of rewards and punishments, surely offended the religious sensibilities of traditionalists. Some of the contradictions may be attributed to later editors, who reworded certain passages to make them more acceptable to conservatives.

The title Ecclesiastes takes its name from the Greek translation of the Hebrew name Qoheleth, meaning "one who assembles people."[3] The NRSV translators replaced the traditional English translation "Preacher" by the more appropriate term "Teacher" in the superscription (1:1), for the author is less a religious figure who sermonized than a teacher who assembled his pupils for instruction. Since the book contains no sermons and since its thesis—the vanity of all things—strikes many as unorthodox, perhaps the best approach is to view the author as a *hakam*, a sage who gathers pupils and renders counsel at the city gate. Some commentators read biographically the account in 9:13-16 of a poor *hakam* who saves a

---

3. In Jewish literature the term is spelled Koheleth (or Kohelet).

city from a threatening foe. If the subject of that vignette, never thanked and quickly forgotten, were Qoheleth, that might help explain the book's negative tone. Nonetheless, viewing Qoheleth as a teaching sage makes better sense than turning him into an ecclesiastical figure. The author was not Solomon, though the persona of Solomon clearly inspired the book, as indicated by the royal testament in 1:12—2:26. The literary fiction of Solomonic authorship soon disappears, and elsewhere Qoheleth, reflecting about kings from the position of a subject (8:2–4), writes from the standpoint of one who lacks power to correct human oppression.

While Ecclesiastes gives tantalizingly few hints about Qoheleth's personal life, the book can be read autobiographically, for no other book within the Bible is as intensely personal and existential in mood. Though interpreters disagree on the passages they read autobiographically, the following key points appear relevant.[4]

1. The detailed description of luxury in chapter 2 suggests that Qoheleth was a wealthy aristocrat, though it may be that the author was merely adopting the role of King Solomon as a literary device to emphasize the inadequacy of wealth and wisdom as absolute goals.

2. All signs indicate that Qoheleth lived in Jerusalem (1:1, 12; 2:9), for the sophistication that characterizes the book is best explained by a great cultural center like the capital city. The references in 5:1–2 suggest that the Temple and the sacrificial cult are nearby.

3. The content and form of his book indicate that Qoheleth was a teacher in one of the academies in Jerusalem, which served the educational needs of upper-class youth. The internal evidence is backed by the testimony found in the epilogue (12:9–10), written by a colleague who knew him personally. These verses indicate that Qoheleth not only taught but also carried on literary activity, collecting and composing proverbs and other literary material.

4. As a wisdom teacher Qoheleth would have been identified with the Jewish elite by vocation. If he had been lower-class by birth, we would expect more sensitivity to social injustice and oppression than we find in the book, though there is certainly some concern with the topic (3:16; 4:1; 5:7). It seems most likely that Qoheleth belonged to the upper classes by birth and position, for he displays the benefits of such a position in his education and in the opportunities available to him.

---

4. The following autobiographical ideas are adapted from Gordis, *Koheleth*, 75–86.

5. While his range of knowledge does not equal that of the author of Job, Qoheleth was cultured and well-informed. He draws upon history, contemporary affairs, and current scientific knowledge to express his worldview. He demonstrates familiarity with at least some of the fundamental ideas of Greek philosophy, such as the four elements (1:4–7) and the doctrine of the golden mean (7:15–18). In the same manner he demonstrates an original application of key concepts in the Torah and in the historical books of the Hebrew Bible.[5]

6. Qoheleth was probably a bachelor, or at least a man without children, since he is vexed over the fact that when a man dies he must leave his wealth to strangers (6:2; see also 4:8).

7. That Qoheleth is writing as an old man is clear from the deeply felt Allegory of Old Age in 12:1–7. This is also demonstrated in his nostalgic stress upon the joys of youth and on his obligation to live with vigor before it is too late (11:9; 12:1; see also 9:10).

Though nothing more is known definitely of the external events of Qoheleth's life, the book permits us to reconstruct three principal phases of his spiritual journey, each leaving its mark upon his philosophy of life. During his youth, Qoheleth's life was marked by (1) *zest for life*. As a boy and young man, he seemed to have had a passionate love of life, energized by its good things, including the joys of nature (11:7; 12:1). He seemed to appreciate women deeply (9:9), whether he was married or not. He also valued material comfort and beauty, including the coolness of gardens and orchards, good food, and fine wine.

As a Jew, he would have been reared in the rich religious tradition of Israel, embodied in the books of the Torah and the Prophets, which were in his day already recognized as sacred scripture. His life was marked by (2) *zest for justice and righteousness*, the hallmark of the legal, prophetic, and sapiential Jewish tradition (see Prov. 14:34). He became sensitized to human wickedness and injustice (Eccl. 3:16), which led him to question the unshakeable faith of the prophets in the ultimate triumph of the good and the right. Wrongdoing and corruption, he felt, were eternal, inherent in the scheme of things (5:8). Yet Qoheleth did not react to human suffering with easy cynicism (4:1–2). As he matured, the happiness of a carefree and joyous existence was overshadowed by a vision of a world in agony. He became a cynic, not because he was indifferent to human

---

5. See, for example, Genesis 3:19 and Ecclesiastes 12:7; Deuteronomy 4:2 and Ecclesiastes 3:14; Deuteronomy 23:22–25 and Ecclesiastes 5:4–7; and 1 Samuel 15:22 and Ecclesiastes 4:17.

suffering, but, on the contrary, because he was acutely sensitive to human cruelty and folly.

But Qoheleth had not yet plumbed the full depth of despair. Stronger even than his love of justice was his (3) *zest for truth*. Possessing a keen mind and a lively curiosity, he sought fundamental insight into the world and its meaning. Like other sages, he strove to know God's mystery underlying the cosmos (Prov. 3:19; Job 28:20). Qoheleth sought to probe the mysteries that the more prosaic Ben Sira would later advise leaving alone, perhaps because he knew the perils that lurked in the quest: "Neither seek what is too difficult for you, nor investigate what is beyond your power. Reflect upon what you have been commanded, for what is hidden is not your concern. Do not meddle in matters that are beyond you" (Sir. 3:21–23). When Qoheleth reached the same realization, that the wisdom of the universe was unattainable (8:17), a deep cynicism settled upon the youthful enthusiast. Justice he had sought, but it was nowhere; wisdom he had pursued, but the phantom had vanished. All life was meaningless and futile, and his judgment upon it was devastating: "Vanity of vanities, says Qoheleth, vanity of vanities! All is vanity" (1:1; 12:8). Three great ideas had ignited his way in the world, but the yearning for justice and wisdom brought him only sorrow and disillusionment.

Ecclesiastes is fundamentally the work of one sage who wrote during the late postexilic period, perhaps between 300 and 200 BC. Several factors favor a rather late date for this book: (1) the language resembles the latest Hebrew in the canon, including Persian loanwords plus a large number of Aramaisms; (2) its tone seems definitely postexilic, reflecting the pessimism and even cynicism of the age; (3) the individualism of the book plus familiarity with Greek ideas reveal the influence of Hellenism. In addition, Qoheleth's focus on the achievement of happiness in an indifferent world and his use of sensory experience as the ultimate arbiter of what is real and true reflect Epicurean perspectives. (4) Instead of a purely private or personal crisis as the motivation for writing the book, some scholars argue that Qoheleth may have been reacting to a sort of cultural malaise or crisis (see 4:1 and 5:8), indicative of conditions during the third century BC. For example, taxes are being levied by outside forces, making life difficult for both peasants and aristocrats; the economy is based on money and coinage (7:12); and aristocrats are required to perform tasks that are alienating them from other groups in society (10:20).

By way of summary, we can say that the book of Ecclesiastes was written in Hebrew by a Jewish sage in Jerusalem who knew Aramaic but not Greek, though he was familiar with basic Greek ideas. The date of his book, which coincided with the last years of his life, falls in the middle of the third century BC (about 250 BC, during the Ptolemaic or Seleucid period).

The Place of Ecclesiastes in the Sacred Jewish Canon

Because of its unorthodox views, the book of Ecclesiastes was controversial in ancient times. Early in the Common Era, when rabbinical authorities debated the books that should be included in the Writings (the third part of the Hebrew scriptures), they disagreed about whether the book should be included in their Bible. The rabbinic school of Shammai rejected Ecclesiastes on what they regarded as its inconsistency and possible heresy. On the other hand, the school of Hillel offered an orthodox interpretation, a view that prevailed. That the book contained proverbial material and traditional religious vocabulary such as "pleasing God," "sin," "wise," "command," and the editorial addition "fear God and keep his commandments" (12:13) made it acceptable during canonical debates. Ancient readers probably missed some of Qoheleth's subtleties, while rabbinical authorities approved of contradictions and inconsistencies in biblical texts, reconciling them allegorically. Had it not been for pious revisions and the tradition that ascribed authorship to Solomon, the book might not have been included in the Hebrew canon.

In the post-Talmudic period (between the eighth and tenth centuries AD), Ecclesiastes came to be classified as one of the Five Scrolls, alongside Ruth, Esther, Song of Songs, and Lamentations, each of them read annually at a Jewish religious festival. Ecclesiastes is read on Sukkot (also known as the Festival of Booths), which celebrates the completion of the fall harvest and represents the completion of the yearly cycle of Torah reading. Sukkot is known as the Season of Rejoicing (Deut. 16:13–15), and Jewish religious authorities associated Ecclesiastes with Sukkot by recognizing the book's basic theme as *simhah*, the enjoyment of life.[6]

---

6. The author of Ecclesiastes might have been shocked and perhaps also amused that religious authorities attributed such a positive thesis to his book and that his notebook was canonized as part of sacred scripture.

Literary Analysis

Style

Like Proverbs, the book of Ecclesiastes is a collection of disparate items, including maxims, aphorisms, and admonitions. Lying somewhere between a treatise and a collection of sayings, the book alternates sayings and admonitions with lengthier meditations. Ecclesiastes also contains a literary form not found in Proverbs, designated "reflection" by Roland Murphy. A reflection generally states a thesis, which is then developed through sayings and observations. Reflections are frequently introduced by formula phrases such as "I gave my heart to know" (1:13, 17; 8:16) or simply "I know" (3:12, 14). Sometimes Qoheleth utilizes an "example story" to make his point (4:13–16; 9:13–16). Extended discussions on a single topic are also found in 6:10—7:14 and 11:9—12:7. Another characteristic of Qoheleth's style is his use of proverbial quotations (7:1–13; 8:1; 10:1–4; 10:8—11:4). Since these sayings lack quotation marks or even introductory formulas, it is often difficult to determine when quotations begin or end.

The author uses twenty-seven words repeatedly, which together comprise one-fifth of the book. The most common term is *hebel*, variously translated in English as "absurd," "vanity," "futility," "toil," and "emptiness," which occurs thirty-seven times in the book and is perhaps the major theme. Key phrases include "pursuit after wind" and "under the sun," while key word pairs include "good/evil" and "remember/memory."

The recurrence of themes, reinforced by Qoheleth's technical terminology, underscores the author's literary style, a "leisurely, self-conscious, ruminative process in which Koheleth is engaged, meandering through, around, and back to his favorite issues, considering them first from one angle, then from another."[7]

Structure

Despite a growing recognition among scholars of the work's basic unity, there is no general agreement on its structure. A frame ("Vanity of vanities, says the Teacher; all is vanity") surrounds the book, as 1:2 is repeated in 12:8. The assertion in these verses that everything is futility reflects what may be considered the book's fundamental theme. Within that

---

7. Machinist, "Ecclesiastes: Introduction," 1604.

frame are a variety of smaller units, defined by formal markers, often repetitions of certain nouns or verbs. The catalogue of polarities in 3:1–8 is an obvious example of such a unit, with opposites arranged as parallels.

In addition to the framing verses, there is a general recognition that envisions two fundamental units (1:12—6:9 and 6:10—11:6), preceded and followed by a poem in 1:4–11 and 11:7—12:7. Linguistic evidence seems to support this division, as the two main sections employ different refrains. Whereas the first uses "vanity" and "chasing after wind," the second is characterized by "find/not find" and "know/not know." Further support for dividing the text at 6:9 comes from numerological evidence. There are 222 verses in the book, with 111 verses each before and after the break at 6:9. Furthermore, according to the ancient practice of gematria, where each letter of the Hebrew alphabet is equivalent to a number, the numerical value of *hebel* ("vanity") is 37, which is the number of times the word appears in Ecclesiastes (excluding the repeated *hebel* in 9:9, omitted in many English translations). In addition, *hebel* is repeated three times in 1:2, yielding the number 111, the same as the number of verses at midpoint. The presence of a chiastic structure in the final section of the first half of the book (5:8—6:9) makes convincing the division at 6:9.

Textual Analysis

The expression "vanity of vanities," found in the framing verses, is the leitmotif of the book, something the author repeats in a variety of ways (as in the clever expression "chasing after wind"; 1:14, 17). The term *hebel*, from its literal meaning "air" or "breath," is translated "vanity" or "futility," meaning (a) temporal (short-lived) or (b) absurd (meaningless). The use of the superlative in 1:2, *hebel hebalim*, suggests absolute futility or total absurdity. The expression points to the reality of death and the uncertainty of meaning beyond death. There seems to be incongruity between faith in God and a moral order in the universe with the fact that everything points to death as the end of life. Life without justice and fairness, without just reward and punishment, seems meaningless and absurd.

The cosmological poem in 1:4–11 views the cosmos as a stage for human life. In verses 3 and 4, Qoheleth raises a question that he answers eventually: What does a person gain from all his or her toil "under the sun"? The answer seems to be, little or nothing. Human generations come and go but only the earth remains forever. In introducing the four elements of creation (earth, sun, wind, and sea), Qoheleth uses familiarity with the primal elements of Greek cosmologies (earth, wind, fire, and water) to emphasize that life, including human life, is cyclical, not linear. All things come and all things go; only the earth remains forever. Hence there is nothing new under the sun. By accommodating to a view of nature that is going nowhere so far as a purpose or goal is concerned, Qoheleth seems to have capitulated to the idea that human life lacks meaning. Verses 10 and 11 inject a pessimistic tone; things appear new only because the past is forgotten. In actuality, "there is nothing new under the sun" (1:9).

In 1:12—2:26 Qoheleth appears in the guise of the king. Acknowledging he has increased in wisdom and knowledge, he finds that these do not bring greater prosperity and longer life, the things promised in Proverbs. In fact, increase in wisdom brings a surplus of trouble as well (1:18). Chapter 2 consists of two test cases, the pursuit of pleasure (2:1–11) and of wisdom (2:12–17). Immersing himself in the pursuit of pleasure or joy (the term *simhah* has a broad range of meaning in Hebrew, from religious ecstasy to sexual excess), Qoheleth concludes that such pursuits finally gain one nothing of lasting value (2:11). The second test case involves wisdom and folly. The former is decidedly better, like light is better than darkness, but both have the same *miqreh* ("fate"; the term is one of Qoheleth's favorites). *Miqreh* does not refer to an impersonal force but rather "what chances to happen to someone." In the end, the same fate befalls the wise and the foolish: death. This is the first of four negative conclusions in this passage, all of which contradict the teachings of conventional wisdom: (1) that what befalls the foolish will not befall the wise (contradicted by 2:15); (2) that the wise will be long remembered (contradicted by 2:16); (3) that "life" is the highest value (contradicted by the shocking statement "I hated life" in 2:17, a sentiment seemingly impossible for a sage to make); and (4) that work is beneficial (contradicted by 2:23).

Qoheleth's preliminary conclusion in Ecclesiastes 2:24–26 brings readers to an important stop in their journey. The message, "enjoy yourself," is one of the author's most important points of advice, repeated time and again (3:12–13, 22; 5:18–19; 8:15; 9:7–10; 11:9–10). Qoheleth's advice does not address what is *good* in a flawed world—there is no *summum bonum* here—but rather only a "better *bonum*," what is *better* than the alternative. It is better to eat and drink and to find some satisfaction in one's work. Verses 24b–26a add a traditional proviso, that life is a gift from God, and that wisdom and happiness also come from God. However, the passage ends pessimistically: "This also is vanity and a chasing after wind."

Ecclesiastes 3 contains the book's best-known passage, with its theme "timing is everything" (3:1–8). Because the sages believed there was a right time and a wrong time for everything, these verses represent conventional wisdom, which is then critiqued in 3:9–15, where limits are placed on human understanding. The list in verses 1–8 involves a series of merisms (where the totality of a set is represented by its extreme members). While the sense of a "right" time may be true from God's perspective, verse 11b emphasizes that humans cannot know such timing, merely receive it when it comes.

In 3:16–21 Qoheleth is deeply disturbed because the law of retribution does not seem valid. Rather, wickedness is present even in the courts, the place of judgment. In a world of evil and oppression, humans are little better than animals, and in some cases worse. God tests humans to show them how similar to animals they are. Both live and die, and God gives the same animating life force to both. Although he is far from sure, Qoheleth surmises that the human spirit, unlike that of animals, rises to God. He finds it pointless to speculate about the afterlife. Curiously, the Septuagint translators, acknowledging belief in the afterlife, change Qoheleth's "Who knows whether the human spirit goes upward?" (3:21) to a statement of certainty: "The human spirit does rise." Whether Qoheleth entertains the idea of a positive afterlife beyond Sheol, he places hardly any confidence in such a possibility.[8] Since human history is predetermined (3:15, 17), and because human knowledge is inadequate, Qoheleth advises enjoying the present moment (3:12, 22).

Chapter 4 continues the themes of injustice and the horrors of solitary existence. Some scholars interpret the statement "I saw all the oppressions" of 4:1 as indicative of pervasive social instability, of dark days for the entire community rather than an isolated case of suffering. Verses 3–6 introduce a series of "better than" sayings, which continue in 7:1–8. Verse 4 states the principle that human efforts grow out of envy and even jealousy, and that competition and rivalry are inseparable from work and striving for success. Verses 5–6 contain quotations that are diametrically opposed. Here Qoheleth is looking for a compromise between

---

8. The idea of a positive afterlife is found only in late Jewish documents; see Daniel 12:2–3 and Wisdom 3:1–8.

two extremes, a life of idleness, which leads to ruin, and a life of striving, which produces anxiety. Qoheleth's solution is the path of moderation: be satisfied with what amounts to enough. In verses 8–12 Qoheleth lauds the virtues of companionship and family. The passage ends with the famous analogy between a rope with three strands that is not quickly broken and the value of teamwork (4:12). It is important to note that there is no reference to "vanity" in this affirmation of companionship. The chapter ends with a restatement of proverbial material (4:13–16).

Chapter 5 begins with advice on religious duties (5:1–7). The reference to "the sacrifice offered by fools" in verse 1 speaks of nominal believers whose piety is mindless and rote (see Prov. 15:8). The caution against "going through the motions" in worship is coupled with a further caution against lengthy prayers and other forms of religious insincerity (5:2–6). The injunction to "fear God" in 5:7 points to the conventional adherence to institutional religion that characterized upper-class piety. Such piety is based upon the distinction between God as sovereign Creator and humans as mortal creatures.

The final unit in the first half of the book (5:8—6:9), is concerned with one of the two basic themes of the book: the duty to enjoy life to the full. It also contains a warning against excessive greed, which increases wealth but decreases its enjoyment. This unit is characterized by a chiastic structure, a basic V pattern characteristic of sapiential literature, in which clauses or verses are related to each other through a reversal of structure in order to make a larger point. The basic ideas of this unit have appeared earlier, but the chiasm puts them into a fresh setting. When applied to the seven segments, the topic of scene one (5:8–12) corresponds to that of scene seven (6:7–9). This means that scene two (5:13–17) is related to scene six (6:3–6), as are three (5:18–19) and five (6:1–2). This structure draws special attention to 5:20, the fourth and pivotal point in the chiasmus. The topics of the chiasmus correlate as follows:

A (5:8–12) lists people who cannot be satisfied
A' (6:7–9) restates the theme of dissatisfaction
B (5:13–17) provides an example
B' (6:3–6) provides a similar example
C (5:18–19) tells what is good = enjoy
C' (6:1–2) tells what is bad = no enjoyment
D (5:20) advises people on enjoying what they have and on taking pleasure in their work; in other words, one should not overanalyze life, but should simply enjoy and appreciate its benefits.

The first half of the book ends with Qoheleth's motto and verdict for life: all is vanity and futility. But there is a glimmer of hope in his closing exhortation: "Better is the sight of the eyes than the wandering of desire" (6:9).

Scholars disagree on the structure of the second half of Ecclesiastes (6:10—9:6), which I have divided into eight segments, but some consider to be one unit. The entire section can be seen as a critical review of conventional proverbial wisdom. Some scholars divide the unit according to the fourfold repetition of the concluding phrase "find out" or "find," which suggests four sections (7:1–14; 7:15–24; 7:25–29; 8:1–17), and the recurrence of the phrase "I have observed," though it is not clear that these markers are structurally significant. Ecclesiastes 6:10–12 can be read as an independent frame, marking the transition to a new section. Qoheleth's literary intention is rather obvious at times, for the end of a section is often identified by reference to one of the book's fundamental ideas. Most sections conclude with one of four concepts: (a) the weakness and impermanence of human achievements (1:11; 4:16; 10:1); (b) the uncertainty of one's fate (8:9; 9:3; 9:12; 11:6); (c) the impossibility of attaining true knowledge and insight into the world (3:15; 6:12; 7:14; 7:25); and (d) the need to make joy the goal of one's efforts (2:26; 6:9).

Ecclesiastes 7:1–14 consists of a collection of proverbs; some use synthetic parallelism, some antithetical, and others lack logical correspondence. The material in this collection bears Qoheleth's personality and perspective. Seven of the sayings begin with "good" or "better than," with a conclusion that leads to a carpe diem philosophy: enjoy the good times when they come and in the bad times be reflective about the divine mystery of it all. Chapter 7:15–25 urges the doctrine of the "golden mean," a characteristic idea of Greek philosophy probably part of the intellectual climate of the mid third-century BC, but in a way or from a point of view uniquely Qoheleth's. Knowing that wickedness violates the accepted norms of society, Qoheleth appears realistic, advocating moderation (7:18). The section concludes with ideas some interpret as misogynistic (7:26–29), but despite the negative tone, it seems more likely that Qoheleth is referring here to Lady Folly, the temptress who leads fools to sin, rather than to Lady Wisdom, mentioned in the book of Proverbs as the revealer of the secrets of God. Verses 28–29 are negative about humanity in general, with women perhaps one step below the male's rather abysmal evaluation. Verse 29 exonerates God from human sin.

Chapter 8 consists of two sections, 8:1–9 and 8:10–17. The first deals with the limits of human power, arriving in verse 8 at a perception that is fundamental to Qoheleth's outlook, namely, the essential ignorance of individuals regarding life and their own destinies. Ecclesiastes 8:10–17, a section that possibly extends to 9:3 and beyond, deals with the failures of the process of retribution. Verses 11–13 are difficult to reconcile with the perspective in chapters 6–7, so it is helpful to remember that Qoheleth affirms two opposite notions: he disagrees with traditional wisdom in the certainty it places on retribution while also refusing to give up completely on conventional wisdom. Qoheleth does not believe that evil always triumphs (see 7:17, 25; 8:8d) or that the righteous always fail. Thus, 8:14 should read: "There are [some] righteous people who are treated according to the conduct of the wicked." While affirming that the same fate awaits both the good and the evil (9:3), Qoheleth also affirms the possibility that it will go better for the one who fears God (8:12–13). Verse 15 again commends enjoying life (each time Qoheleth commends enjoyment, he seemingly does so with increasing vigor).

Ecclesiastes 9:1—11:6 may be treated as a unit. Chapter 9:1–10 promotes two themes: the inevitability of death (9:4–6) and the supreme duty of humans to derive the most from life (9:7–10). Verse 5 states a rather common view of Sheol, that the dead are like shades, knowing nothing (cf. 9:10b). Verses 7–9 revisit the topic of enjoyment of life, a common theme found in much of the ancient literature of the world. Ecclesiastes 9:11—10:15 address the theme "living with risks," a topic that continues in 10:16—11:6. This section consists of three sub-units (9:11–12; 9:13—10:4; 10:5–15), all introduced by the formulas "I have seen" or "I have observed." Qoheleth is speaking from personal experience to counter traditional wisdom's emphasis on the law of retribution. Chapter 9:13–14 contains a short story to illustrate his point. Chapters 10–11 are essentially a collection of maxims sages would have taught upper-class youth; those in chapter 10 point out incongruities in life, such as the statement in 10:1, "a little folly outweighs wisdom," which sounds like the modern statement about the "fly in the ointment" or the "rotten apple in the barrel." The subject of folly in this chapter is not simply the action of the ignorant, but more that of the morally deficient. In 11:5–6 the practical uncertainties of life recall the great mystery of existence, including two unexplainable things to ancients: the path of the wind (11:4) and the formation of the fetus in the womb (11:5). These verses serve as a coda, reiterating an earlier point that the work of God, like God, is impossible to understand; it too is a mystery.

Ecclesiastes 11:7—12:7 address the topic of youth and old age, concluding with a remarkable poem on old age (12:1–7). Three times Qoheleth states his theme, that the enjoyment of life is imperative (11:7–8a; 11:9; 11:10). The concluding poem may be interpreted as an allegory of old age or as a reference to death itself (including a funeral); perhaps both are intended. The text reads:

> (1) Remember your creator in the days of your youth, before the days of trouble come, and the years draw near when you will say, "I have no pleasure in them"; (2) before the sun and the light and the moon and the stars are darkened and the clouds return with the rain; (3) in the day when the guards of the house tremble, and the strong men are bent, and the women who grind cease working because they are few, and those who look through the windows see dimly; (4) when the doors on the street are shut, and the sound of the grinding is low, and one rises up at the sound of a bird, and all the daughters of song are brought low; (5) when one is afraid of heights, and terrors are in the road; the almond tree blossoms, the grasshopper drags itself along and desire fails; because all must go to their eternal home, and the mourners will go about the streets; (6) before the silver cord is snapped, and the golden bowl is broken, and the pitcher is broken at the fountain, and the wheel broken at the cistern, (7) and the dust returns to the earth as it was, and the breath returns to God who gave it.

Treated as an allegory of old age, the reference to "house" (v.3) is to one's body; the "guards of the house" (v. 3) are the hands that may tremble when one gets old; "the strong men are bent" (v. 3) refers to bent legs; "the women who grind" (v. 3) are the teeth that stop working because they are few; "those who look through the windows" (v. 3) are the eyes that grow dim with age; "the doors on the street are shut" (v. 4) refers either to the ears or eyelids closing; "one rises up at the sound of a bird" (v. 4) refers to the elderly who are light sleepers; "the daughters of song are brought low" (v. 4) refers to the loss of the ability to sing due to weak vocal chords; "one is afraid of heights" and "terrors are in the road" (v. 5) may refer to the old being afraid of heights and to being ambushed in the street due to feebleness; the "almond tree blossoms" (v. 5) refers to white hair on the head; and "the grasshopper drags itself along and desire fails" (v. 5) refers to the loss of appetite and of sexual desire.[9]

The remainder of the poem addresses death directly, speaking of mourners in the streets and providing graphic images of death (a smashed bowl, a jar thrown into a pit like a body placed in the ground, and the reference to the breaking of the pitcher at the well, when the pulley by which it is usually raised is shattered). Following the allegory of ailing body parts, the "silver cord is snapped" (v. 6) could refer to the spine or to the soul; "the golden bowl is broken" (v. 6), a symbol of life, seems to speak specifically of the head or the marrow; "the pitcher is broken at the fountain" (v. 6) may be about the failure of vital organs such as the gall bladder, the stomach, or the heart; and "the wheel broken at the cistern" (v. 6) may refer to the eye or to the body as a whole.[10]

Such detailed identifications are of course, conjectural, not only because they are far from conclusive, but because they make the passage exceedingly prosaic. Since 12:5 speaks of "their eternal home," those who avoid allegorizing the passage find that it seems to describe death and dying generally, rather than refer to specific details. The reference in 12:7 to the body decaying and the breath of life returning to God implies that something survives death, though it is not clear that Qoheleth has more in mind here than a trip to Sheol, with Genesis 2:7 and 3:19 providing the textual background. Ecclesiastes 12:1 and 12:7 frame the poem: the Creator gives life, and to the Creator life returns. The writings of Qoheleth end with 12:8, a reiteration of the original leitmotif that life is ephemeral.

Ecclesiastes 12:9–11 comes from a colleague or more likely a student and admirer of Qoheleth. By referring to Qoheleth's sayings as "goads" (12:11), the editor means that the words are like cattle prods, pricking and prodding readers out of lives marked by routine, comfort, or stagnation. Also "like nails firmly fixed" means that Qoheleth's words are reliable, firmly embedded and reliable, able to hold things together. Ultimately, says the editor, wisdom goes back to one source, one shepherd. Enough said, advises a later editor (12:12–14); more words are not needed. While the admonition to "fear God" in 12:13 is consonant with an earlier theme (7:18; 8:12; cf. 3:14), verse 14 ("For God will bring every deed into judgment") seems to go against Qoheleth's doubts about retribution (cf. 8:9—9:3). It is interesting that the Masoretes, scribes who

---

9. Whybray, *Ecclesiastes*, 163–65. See also Witherington, *Jesus the Sage*, 70.
10. Gordis, *Koheleth*, 348.

gave finality to the Jewish text of the Bible, did not like to close a book of scripture on a negative note and so, as they did with the text of Isaiah, Lamentations, and Malachi, they reversed the final verses. In actuality, 12:13 is repeated after 12:14 as a refrain in the Tanakh (Hebrew Bible).

It is important to view the entirety of Ecclesiastes as a *mashal* (cf. 12:9) created by Qoheleth, using contradictions, approximations, and analogies to force pupils to the heart of the matter. A *mashal* is a comparison, as is Ecclesiastes. The book contains two contradictory pictures of life: one picture presents human existence as bleak, dismal, and empty; the other views life as beautiful, simple, and filled with causes for joy and delight. Some interpreters stress the book's negative vision, others the positive affirmations. The student or colleague who penned the first epilogue saw the book's many points of tension as a way of imparting knowledge to others, as an approach to truth. "True wisdom and false wisdom are set side by side to create deliberate contradictions. . . . The purpose of paradox, however, is not to leave us at an impasse, but rather to engage the imagination by forcing the reader to press beyond the contradictions into the world of mystery. Qoheleth, like Job, leads the reader through conventional thinking and then beyond it to insight about realities that cannot be articulated one-dimensionally."[11]

Thematic Analysis

As we noted earlier, biblical sages understood that the qualities that constitute "wisdom" are accessible in three primary forms: wisdom taught by God, wisdom taught by nature, and wisdom that arises from reflection on human experience. In the case of Qoheleth, he came to his conclusions existentially, through experience and by experimentation. In speaking of his quest for the meaning of life, Qoheleth focuses on several candidates: knowledge, pleasure, power, wealth, love, and life itself. He presents evidence for rejecting each of these as adequate and remains skeptical about easy answers. After a lifetime of investigation, he concludes that life is nothing more than a meaningful series of unrelated events. The task of wisdom, as Qoheleth sees it, is to clarify its own limits, to understand what can and what cannot be known. Qoheleth's answer to the questions he raises is to emphasize the limits of human wisdom, not to not deny that

---

11. O'Connor, *Wisdom Literature*, 131.

God is in control. Hence the famous theme: "Vanity of vanities," which means that humans cannot know with finality what they wish to know.

Despite the limits of human understanding, despite uncertainty about the future and one's destiny, there is a sense in which Qoheleth is encouraging us to keep faith during confusion, to live fully and make wise choices despite uncertainty. Amidst the contingencies of life, the best we can do is fear the Lord and avoid folly. A crucial part of the Jewish religion—and of Christianity as it emerged from Judaism—is the importance of human freedom and a profound sense of the responsibility that comes from our choices.

Some see Qoheleth espousing a philosophical perspective akin to Epicureanism (enjoy life) or Stoicism (indifference to what one cannot control), but such an approach surely falls short of the author's intention. In this respect, a distinction must be made between "truth" and "certitude." Philosophically, truth refers to whether what one believes corresponds to reality, whereas certitude refers to how sure one can be about that correspondence. Qoheleth is profoundly connected to the wisdom tradition, only with his own point of emphasis. He has faith in divine providence (11:5); "trust God," he seems to say, as the ultimate source of trustworthiness. But in so doing, he is not merely paying lip service to the goodness of divine providence, for he clearly avoids presumption about God, retribution, and divine judgment. In temporal matters, such as what the future holds or what heirs will do with their inheritance, he has little certainty.

The noted biblical scholar Roland Murphy finds in Ecclesiastes two thematic affirmations seemingly antithetical to each other: (1) The futility of life (underscored by the superlative use of the term *hebel* at the beginning and end of the book), and (2) the need to fear God and keep his commandments (despite being an editorial addition, the exhortation provides a basic orientation to the work). To resolve the paradox, Murphy suggests a third thematic possibility: (3) the need to enjoy life (9:7–9). He then discusses six key words that are used repeatedly in the book, functioning as road markers along life's journey: vanity, joy, wisdom, fear of God, retribution, and God (the book does not disclose a personal or intimate understanding of God, but rather speaks of God as Creator, whose gifts include the gift of life).[12]

---

12. Murphy, *Tree of Life*, 52–59.

Peter Kreeft, Professor of Philosophy at Boston University, examines Qoheleth's message under the concept of "toil," by which he means not simply "work" but all human pursuits. Qoheleth experiments with five toils, valued universally as worthy aims of life, evaluating each as a candidate for life's *summum bonum* (the greatest good, highest value, or ultimate end of meaning of life). They are:

1. wisdom (philosophy to fill the mind), cf. 1:12–18;
2. pleasure (hedonism to fill the body), cf. 2:1–11;
3. wealth and power (materialism to fill the wallet), cf. 5:8—6:6; 2:8;
4. duty and altruism (ethics to fill the conscience), cf. 4:9–11;
5. conventional religion (religion to fill the spirit), cf. 5:1–7; 7:16b.

Qoheleth tried all five ways and found them lacking in meaning and unable to produce happiness. His approach is not argumentative, but experimental. He lives five lives and shares the result of experience. All five candidates for life's *summum bonum*, all endeavors in which humans place hope and to which they give allegiance, prove futile. The reason for their futility, according to Kreeft, is that they are infected by the five "vanities," each of which can kill meaning. The five vanities are:

1. human endeavors as vain and indifferent (9:1–2, 11);
2. death as the certain and final end of life (3:19–21);
3. time as a boring repetitive cycle (3:1–15);
4. evil as a perennial and unsolvable problem (8:14; 3:16; 4:1);
5. God as an unknowable mystery (8:17; 11:5).

Since most humans disagree with Qoheleth's supposition that "all is vanity," they use three approaches to circumvent his conclusion—psychology, philosophy, and conventional religion—but according to Qoheleth, all are invalid. Kreeft disagrees, finding benefit in all three, but he relies on a fourth—revelation—to provide final answers. Considering Ecclesiastes to be divinely revealed, Kreeft argues that God is using a kind of "Socratic method" here, raising questions and providing challenges that believers must answer with the help of scripture. The Bible, he suggests, is a diptych, a two-paneled picture. Ecclesiastes represents the first panel, the question. The rest of the Bible is the second panel, the answer. Kreeft uses an image from the historian Arnold Toynbee, that history is "challenge and response." Ecclesiastes is the challenge; the remainder of scripture is the response. Kreeft concludes, "Ecclesiastes is the question to which Christ is the answer."[13]

Essay 2: Qoheleth's Enduring Message

Having examined the book of Ecclesiastes contextually, literarily, and thematically, we assess its message. Some interpreters view the book as a critique of Israel's conventional approach to wisdom. Life is essentially unfair; virtue does not bring reward, and evil often goes unpunished. Others approach Qoheleth as a sage who esteems wisdom, utilizing paradox to reflect on the nature of human freedom and on the necessity of emotional and intellectual choice in the face of uncertainty.

Considering Qoheleth to be a philosopher, Peter Kreeft labels Ecclesiastes the greatest of all books of philosophy. Kreeft does not base his assessment on the book's logical argumentation, since the author frequently rambles, changes his mind, and even allows his moods to rule his thinking. He does not consider Ecclesiastes great on account of its thesis, for how can a book about meaninglessness be meaningful? Rather, Ecclesiastes is great because it is profoundly honest. Vanity and meaninglessness cannot detect themselves; it takes wisdom to know vanity, and profundity to know meaninglessness. Ecclesiastes is also great because it poses life's most important ethical question, the question of the *summum bonum*. As a philosopher, Kreeft argues that the question of the *summum bonum* is raised only by existentialist philosophers today, and the answer they give sounds much like Qoheleth's motto: life is meaningless, vain, and absurd. When we explore Qoheleth's axiom, we must be aware that he is not speaking from a "faith perspective" (such as Job's conclusion in 42:5–6), but rather is addressing "the surface of life" (perhaps this phrase captures best the meaning of Qoheleth's "under the sun"). Ecclesiastes is brutally honest, "the truest picture of the surface that has ever been written."[14] An answer is meaningless without its question, and perhaps the purpose of Ecclesiastes in the Bible is to raise life's existential questions.

---

13. Kreeft, *Three Philosophies*, 56. Kreeft's discussion on the five toils and the five vanities is taken from pages 35–53. His view of scripture, naïve by modern standards, nevertheless bears consideration.

14. Ibid., 19.

Kreeft views Qoheleth as more a philosopher than a theologian, claiming that God is only an object in Ecclesiastes, never the subject.[15] While Kreeft's position is debatable (particularly his definition of "philosophy" as humans searching for God and his understanding of "theology" as verbal revelation), Kreeft proceeds to a stunning observation: Ecclesiastes is revelation precisely in being the absence of divine revelation, revelation by darkness rather than by light. Kreeft quotes Kierkegaard "If I could prescribe just one remedy for all the ills of the modern world, I would prescribe silence."[16] Ecclesiastes creates silence, and out of that darkness God reveals what life is like when God does not reveal to us life's meaning. For Kreeft, Ecclesiastes frames the Bible as death frames life.

Roland Murphy asks the same question as does Kreeft, but comes up with a different answer. He notes that it is always risky to use the categories of philosophy and theology because of the varying implied presuppositions. For example, is philosophy limited to the rational, while theology to the suprarational? Presuppositions determine the answer, but ultimately the characterization of philosopher or theologian tells one little about Qoheleth or his book.[17] Rather than declaring Qoheleth a philosopher or a theologian, it is better to declare him a theist. The evidence of theism is found not only in the fact that he mentions God some forty times in his book, but also in the use of the phrase "all is in/from the hands of God," spread evenly across his book (2:24; 3:10, 13; 5:18, 19; 6:1, 2; 7:15; 9:1, 7, 9; 11:9). Qoheleth's metaphysics postulates the existence of God, coupled with God's creative power and limitless sovereignty. Ancient peoples, particularly Jewish sages, would have found it inconceivable to deny God's existence. For Qoheleth, the existence of the world is tantamount to the existence of God. For Murphy, it is Qoheleth's theism that makes his experience with the dark side of life so troubling.

A third perspective, Rabbi Harold Kushner's, recognizes that Qoheleth's conclusion leads readers to determine that life has no meaning. But humans find this conclusion to be counter-intuitive, and so, ultimately, does Qoheleth. Something deep within us overrules our mind's logical conclusion, dismisses the evidence, and insists that in spite of all, human life has meaning. That intuition, Kushner says, is in Ecclesiastes, and is

---

15. Biblical scholars have been intrigued by the presence of Ecclesiastes in the Hebrew canon, since the book lacks divine speech, meaning that God is never quoted as speaking directly.

16. Kreeft, *Three Philosophies*, 31.

17. Murphy, *Tree of Life*, 51.

what distinguishes humans from animals. Kushner finds the answer to Qoheleth's frustration in 9:7–10. Qoheleth's enduring message is this: learn to savor the moment, even if it does not last. In fact, learn to savor it because it does not last. Life is a series of moments (3:1–8); to live each one is to succeed. Kushner's advice, extrapolated from Qoheleth's message, is practical: pursue happiness as the goal of life. Find pleasure in the moment; don't be afraid to make mistakes; take fewer things seriously; travel lighter; accept pain as part of your life; and don't be afraid to die. When we are happy, when we love and are loved, when we are generous or thoughtful, we feel human. And that feeling is more pervasive than logic or philosophy. According to Kushner, such an approach to life—living each moment with enjoyment—is Qoheleth's answer to the question, "What makes life matter?"[18] Kushner agrees with Qoheleth's answer, but he takes the message one step further, recognizing that Qoheleth is no mere hedonist, for he well knows the limitations of that view.

The solution to Qoheleth's *mashal*—as it is for many theists—is not merely to make God an answer to a question. For to do so, to rely on philosophical assumption, is to trivialize religion. The existence of God is not the issue; nor is it enough. What is important is the difference God makes in our lives. Appealing to the points the editorial remarks in 12:13 about fearing God and keeping God's commandments, Kushner argues that by imposing on us a sense of moral obligation, God lifts human life above the level of mere existence. Rather than assume a carpe diem philosophy, which some view as Qoheleth's message, Kushner affirms that life's meaning is not found in eating, sleeping, and reproducing, but in doing God's will, essentially summarized in the injunctions to be kind, thoughtful, and generous. This is what makes us human, what gives us dignity and purpose, and what makes life worth living. For Kushner, only God provides hope. Intellectual faith affirms that God made humans in such a way that only a life of goodness, compassion, and integrity leaves us spiritually healthy and optimistic. That's why Jews read Ecclesiastes during Sukkot, a festival of thanksgiving and hope, a celebration of life.

Qoheleth, like Kushner, finds joy to be God's categorical imperative for humans, not in an anemic or mystical sense, but rather as a tangible, full-blooded experience that expresses itself in the play of the body and the activity of the mind, in the contemplation of nature and the pleasures of love. Qoheleth insists that this pursuit of happiness is a gift from the

---

18. Kushner, *When All You've Ever Wanted*, 140–80.

Creator, and therefore is an inescapable sacred duty and an inalienable right. Read retrospectively, it is possible to see every line in Ecclesiastes as imbued with a clear, brave, and joyous acceptance of life, despite its inevitable limitations and uncertainties.

Judaism and Christianity are not fatalistic. Fatalism denies God's sovereignty and human free will, together with the deep sense of responsibility and satisfaction that come with the free choices we humans make. There are many things humans can't control, but we can control our attitudes, actions, and responses. And we can remain open to new insights and possibilities.

Earlier in the chapter we examined three phases in Qoheleth's spiritual odyssey (his zest for life, justice, and for truth). These three great ideas illumined his way in the world. The love of life was rich with promise of happiness, but the yearning for justice and truth brought him only sorrow and disillusion. The illusion of human justice and the unattainability of truth left Qoheleth frustrated. As an old man he returned to his first love, but the whole-hearted, instinctive joy and optimism of youth were gone. His love of life became his "better *bonum*," the irreducible minimum of his life's philosophy. He sets up the attainment of happiness as the goal of human striving, not merely because he loves life, but because he cannot have justice and truth. Joy is the only purpose he can find in a monotonous and meaningless world, in which all human values (toils) are vain. As an old man, before it is too late, he takes pen in hand to record the result of reflection, truth as he sees it, about the precious blessing called life. And so he writes 9:7–10.

Having begun with Kreeft's observations on Ecclesiastes, we conclude with his intriguing concept that ultimately there are only three philosophies of life, each one represented by a book of the Bible: (1) Life as vanity—Ecclesiastes; (2) Life as suffering—Job; (3) Life as love—Song of Songs. These books epitomize as well the three "theological virtues": faith, hope, and love (1 Cor. 13:13). The lesson Ecclesiastes teaches is the emptiness of life without faith. Qoheleth has intellectual faith; he believes God exists. But that is not enough. Job's lesson is hope, for Job has nothing but hope. When all else is taken away, hope enables him to endure. Song of Songs is about love, the greatest virtue of all. Love is the ultimate meaning of life, the alternative to vanity and the final answer to Qoheleth's quest. More than a virtue, more even than a quest, love is life's greatest journey, the sole purpose of life.

Questions to Ponder

1. What, for you, is the theme or message of the book of Ecclesiastes?
2. In your estimation, what is Qoheleth's candidate for life's "*summum bonum*"? Explain your answer.
3. Do you find the message of the book of Ecclesiastes to be essentially (a) optimistic, (b) pessimistic, (c) upbeat, (d) cynical, (e) uplifting, (f) depressing, or (g) _____?
4. As you think about the meaning of life, is Ecclesiastes helpful? Why or why not?
5. After reading the book of Ecclesiastes, which passage or passages were the most memorable or meaningful? Why?
6. After reading the book of Ecclesiastes, which passage or passages were the most puzzling or confusing? Why?
7. In your estimation, is Qoheleth (the author of Ecclesiastes) a theist, an agnostic, an atheist, or a believing skeptic? Explain your answer.
8. Is Qoheleth's approach in the book of Ecclesiastes more that of a philosopher or a theologian? Support your answer.
9. In your estimation, should Ecclesiastes be included in the Bible? Why or why not?

CHAPTER 3

The Book of Job: A Quest for God's Presence

Overview: The book of Job is the story of a legendary righteous man whose fortunes do not conform to the longstanding doctrine of retribution. In this well-known story, Job struggles to understand why he suffers loss, illness, and despair. This account is used to probe one of the most compelling themes of the biblical wisdom tradition: what is the cause of suffering? Should suffering be viewed as punishment for wrongdoing (as implied in Genesis 3 and in the Christian doctrine of "original sin"), as a test designed to shape our character, or as something arbitrary and capricious, unrelated to ethical living? The book of Job, like the rest of the Bible, is an inquiry into the nature of God, human beings, and the created world.

Assigned Reading: Job 1–14; 19:25–27; 28; 29–31; 38:1—42:6; 42:7–17

Central Theme: Trust God at all times, particularly during life's trials.

Outline to Job
I. Prologue (simple prose) 1:1—2:13
II. Job's Lament (poetry) 3:1–26
III. Dialogue with Friends (poetry) 4:1—27:23
    A. First Cycle of Speeches 4:1—14:22
    B. Second Cycle of Speeches 15:1—21:34
    C. Third Cycle of Speeches 22:1—27:33

IV. Poem about Wisdom (poetry) 28:1–28

V. Job's Soliloquy (poetry) 29:1—31:40

VI. Speeches of Elihu (poetry) 32:1—37:24

VII. Speeches of God with Job's Reply (poetry) 38:1—42:6

VIII. Epilogue (simple prose) 42:7–17

Contextual Analysis

The book of Job is a work of sheer genius, one of the greatest books ever written. Widely considered the greatest monument of biblical wisdom literature, it is arguably the literary masterpiece of the Bible. The book of Job speaks to some of the most profound questions of society, its meaning timeless. Martin Luther, the Protestant reformer, found the book to be "magnificent and sublime as no other book of the Bible." Alfred Lord Tennyson called it "the greatest poem of ancient and modern times," and Thomas Carlyle declared it to be "the most wonderful poem of any age and language. . . . There is nothing written in the Bible or out of it of equal literary merit." The author has been described as "the most learned ancient before Plato" and as "the Shakespeare of the Old Testament."

The book of Job is an immensely learned and cosmopolitan work. Its erudition is evident in the language, which is full of rare vocabulary and archaic verbal forms. Most of the book is poetry, written in an extremely sophisticated Hebrew, with a higher proportion of unique words (*hapax legomena*, "things said once" in a book or text) than any other book of the Hebrew Bible. The complex and beautiful poetry contains numerous mythological allusions, some of which appear to be based on Egyptian and Mesopotamian traditions. The author's command of cultural and literary forms is also evident in his treatment of genres and stylistic features drawn from Israelite tradition. The speeches of Job and his friends are largely shaped as disputations that make use of a rich variety of rhetorical devices one finds not only in wisdom literature but also in prophetic and legal argumentation. The author displays a similar command of the genres of Israelite piety, in particular the hymn, the psalm of praise, and the complaint. Forensic vocabulary, categories, and practices are similarly drawn upon for the development of metaphor through which to explore Job's relationship with God. "The overall impression is of an author who has a remarkable command of the religious literature and traditions of Israel and its neighbors."[1]

The book has inspired countless theologians and philosophers as well as numerous artists. The twelfth-century rabbi Maimonides, mindful of the suffering of the Jewish people of his time as well as reflecting on the experience of human suffering across the ages, took Job's friends as symbolizing a distinct understanding of God and of divine providence. For example, Eliphaz is said to represent the theological perspective that righteousness is ultimately rewarded by God, if one remains patient. Bildad is said to represent God's endorsement of religious perspectives that are compatible with reason and theistic philosophy.

Job's dramatic quality influenced creative artists such as William Blake, Ralph Vaughan Williams, and Archibald MacLeish, who used media such as engravings, ballet music, and drama to further their perceptions of Job's message. MacLeish's play *J. B.*, set in a modern circus, won the Pulitzer Prize for 1959. Unlike Maimonides, MacLeish used a modern setting to portray Job's friends as representing what for many of his contemporaries were mutually incompatible approaches to suffering: religion (Zophar); science, particularly psychology (Eliphaz); and history (Bildad). In MacLeish's version, the three are incompatible and J. B. is forced to reject them all. In so doing, MacLeish promotes a humanist understanding of life, where Man, not God, is the answer to life's problems and dilemmas.

In 1940, before he entered seminary to study for the priesthood, Karol Wojtyla (later Pope John Paul II) was deeply interested in drama and wrote a play called *Job*. Written in the style of Greek tragedy, Wojtyla connected the suffering of Job with the suffering of Christ but also with the Polish people, who at that time suffered invasion by the Russians and the Nazis.

Modern readers should be aware that Job's location in the Jewish canon differs from its place in the Christian Bible. In the Jewish Bible, Job is numbered among the Writings, the third part of the canon, appearing after the Psalms and either before or after Proverbs. In Roman Catholic and Orthodox Bibles, Job generally appears after Esther and 1 and 2 Maccabees, whereas in Protestant and ecumenical Bibles Job follows Esther and precedes the Psalms. Early Christians were familiar with the

---

1. Newsom, "Job," 326.

Septuagint (Greek translation) version of Job, which tones down much of the blunt language and harsh edge of the original Hebrew.

Author and Setting

It is impossible to determine with certainty Job's author, place of origin, or date of composition. As with the authors of most biblical books, the author of Job is anonymous and unknown. On the basis of linguistic criteria and historical allusions, there is hardly a period of biblical literature to which the book does not have affinities. The poetic dialogues contain linguistic forms that one would expect to find in archaic Hebrew, from approximately the tenth century BC. However, these speeches have been written in a deliberately archaizing style, thereby invalidating the argument for such an early date. The prose tale (1:1—2:13 and 42:7–17) also contains narrative and stylistic details that suggest great antiquity, yet here too one notes an artistic imitation of archaic style. Because of the abundance of allusions to the exilic and postexilic portions of the book of Isaiah and the use of the Hebrew *ha-satan* (the Adversary), in a manner similar to that in which the term is employed in the postexilic Zechariah 3, the book of Job as a whole is best taken as a composition of the early postexilic period, from the mid-sixth century (550) to no later than the mid-fourth century (350) BC, which corresponds to the Persian period of rule. Readers should be aware that the book exhibits at least two different styles of writing (poetry and prose) and that it may have been composed in stages. Certain passages, such as the Elihu speeches, seem to have been added later. Recent scholarship has tended to date them in the third century BC.

The setting evokes the patriarchal period, when great biblical heroes like Abraham were the nomadic herders of large flocks of cattle, sheep, and goats. Sacrifices were offered up in a family setting without elaborate temples or officiating priests. The location is Uz (1:1), a poetic name for Edom. The Transjordan, of which Edom is the southernmost part, is often referred to in the Bible and other ancient Near Eastern texts as Kedem, translated in 1:3 as "the east," and Kadmonites (see Gen. 15:19) were known for their wisdom (1 Kgs. 4:30). It is not surprising, therefore, that an author would choose to set the traditional story of Job in Edom, a region within Kedem, the legendary home of wisdom. This setting supports the book of Job, whose characters are non-Israelite. Elihu is the only character who bears a Hebrew name, and his sudden intrusion in the book, the nature of his speeches, and his absence from the conclusion of the story (see 42:9) place him in the role of an outsider.

Ultimately, considerations such as the date or authorship of Job are not critical for our interpretation of the work. Like wisdom literature in general, Job deals with a human situation that cannot be confined to any particular time. Even the Edomite locale of the story is incidental, for the writer deals with human existence, regardless of nationality. In the final analysis, the historical question is the religious question: What is the meaning of *my* life? Bernhard Anderson's depiction of the author's intent is instructive: "The poet, looking into the depths of one person's existence, has exposed the human question."[2]

According to this existential interpretation, who, then, is Job? If we approach the book of Job as fiction, Job and his friends are characters in a story, not actors in history. As a character, Job is a hero of wisdom who, like Qoheleth, insists upon the truth and refuses to settle for less. What he learns in the end is that what he knows is only a fraction of what can be known. In a prototypical way, Job represents the struggling believer, the person of faith who experiences the incongruities of life without giving up on himself or on God. However, to limit Job's significance to the faithful individual is to view Job primarily through a modern Western lens, for Job's story is the story of suffering people everywhere, Jew and Gentile alike; whether ancient Jews during the Babylonian Exile or modern Jews during the Holocaust, who lost everything, including their community life and possibly even their God; whether Armenians, Palestinians, Sudanese, Syrians, or others victimized by bigotry, genocide, sexual trafficking, and other depravities. The message of the book of Job is that God never abandons human victims, whatever their race, creed, or land of origin. The restored Job is the restored Israel, surely, but also the restored Palestinian. Can we see Job as a symbol of hope for the suffering victims of all nations, including the hungry, the homeless, the politically and economically oppressed, even the enemy?

For Anderson, Job doesn't represent one group of people or one solitary individual's experience, but rather is a timeless drama about the meaning of life. Job, the drama's lead character, is every person, in every time. Perhaps that is the most helpful setting of all, the reason for the author's genius and the book's perennial relevance.

2. Anderson, *Old Testament*, 544.

Literary Analysis

Style

Literary analysis of Job remains tenuous, for scholars cannot agree on the role of the prose tale that envelopes the poetic section. The poetic speeches take the form of a symposium, a dramatic dialogue or debate between a suffering individual and some friends, whose words alternate with Job's responses, culminating with speeches from God. If one takes the book as it stands, the most appropriate literary category would seem to be debate or dispute, particularly as this genre occurs in Mesopotamian wisdom. The author of Job seems to have been acquainted with the Babylonian wisdom text *Dialogue about Human Misery*, also known as the Babylonian Theodicy. Written around 1000 BC, the text was apparently quite popular even in the Hellenistic period. The Babylonian Theodicy consists of a dialogue between a sufferer and his friend as an acrostic poem, with a strict alternation of stanzas between the two characters. The formal design is quite similar to that of Job, although in Job the role of the friend is divided among other characters. The genre of debate or dispute follows a particular pattern, consisting of a mythological introduction and conclusion, a dispute proper, and a theophany in which God resolves the debate.

Disregarding the prose framework, two other solutions commend themselves: dialogue and lament. The first seems appropriate to the poetic section, in which Job's speeches are matched by comparable ones, forming a dialogue concerning human response to suffering and the character of God. The dialogue opens with Job's curse (3:1–26) and closes with his submission (42:1–6), making the book a paradigm of an answered lament, which implies that it was intended to serve as a model to teach people how to respond during suffering. Resemblances appear between Job 3 and Jeremiah 20:7–18 as well as between Job and psalms of lament such as Psalm 13.

Despite these elements from various literary strands, the dominant genre is wisdom. The theophany (Job 38–41) preserves examples of nature wisdom, while the entire book owes its inspiration and much of its language to the wisdom tradition. The presence of the unusual poem on wisdom's inaccessibility (Job 28) certainly evokes the spirit of the sapiential tradition, where true wisdom, like God, defies human reason. Through the character of Job, the poet finds his or her mouthpiece, a heroic voice to render advice as a sage on various philosophical and theological topics.

One additional genre vies for attention in the study of Job, the philosophical diatribe. A genre from the classical Greek and Roman literary tradition found in the New Testament book of Acts and in Paul's letter to Romans, this type of classical writing presents a particular viewpoint as if it is being argued in a speech. In some diatribes a second voice is introduced to present an opposing view to that of the main speaker. The sense of immediacy and passion in the book of Job are reflective of this genre.

Structure

The major structural divisions of the book are themselves quite straightforward. The book consists of eight parts (reducible to five); six internal sections of poetry (reducible to three) framed by an older folk tale in prose (see the outline at the head of the chapter).

The relationship between prose and poetic sections raises an immediate problem. Both sections are incomplete in themselves, and together they encompass severe theological and stylistic differences. The epilogue seems to present as many new problems as solutions to the book's questions and issues. For example, missing in the summation are the *satan*, Job's wife, and Elihu. Furthermore, the friends, who in the poetic section espouse traditional views of religion, such as the doctrine of retribution, are found to be in error and must be forgiven by Job (42:7–9).

In addition, the speeches themselves seem to contain compositions added at different times, and a pattern present at the beginning seems to be abandoned by chapter 22. At first, the dialogue follows a cyclical pattern. After an introductory lament by Job (3:2–26), Eliphaz speaks, Job replies, Bildad speaks, Job replies, Zophar speaks, Job replies, and the cycle begins again. Two full cycles (4:1–14:22 and 15:1–21:34) are given. The third cycle (22:1–31:40) is fragmented; the first two friends speak as before, but Bildad's speech is unusually short, Zophar's is missing altogether, and Job's replies are inordinately long, often containing material that seems to contradict his basic point of view, as if they belonged in part to that of the other friends. Some scholars see the dislocation as deliberate, others reconstruct the speeches. Such reconstruction explains why in some translations the verses are sometimes out of numerical order. The sudden intrusion into the debate of the poem of wisdom in chapter 28 seems puzzling, particularly with its unusual topics about mining and metallurgy. Chapters 29–31 (Job's soliloquy) break the cyclical pattern with unusually long speeches by Job.

At 32:2 a new character, Elihu, appears without prior mention, delivers four uninterrupted speeches (32:6—37:24), and then disappears without further mention. At 38:1 God appears, delivering two lengthy speeches, with minor responses by Job. God's speeches are replies not to Elihu but to Job, who has not spoken since 31:40. Furthermore, the issues God raises do not address earlier issues about Job's suffering or about retribution and the need for divine justice. Many scholars view all or parts of the divine speeches as having been added or modified later.

These textual peculiarities have led scholars to propose various theories for the book's composition. Many of these theories suppose that the book grew by stages, the various parts attributable to different authors working at different times. The many versions of this hypothesis usually include the following phases:

Stage 1: The oldest form of the book would have been the prose tale, originally told orally, about Job the pious. This stage is represented by the prologue and epilogue. The middle part of this version of the story is lost, but it would have included a brief dialogue between Job and his friends, in which they spoke disparagingly of God while Job remained steadfast in faith.

Stage 2: An Israelite author who considered the old story inadequate used the framework for a retelling of the story, in which Job does not remain the patiently enduring character of the traditional tale, but challenges God's treatment of him. The poet substituted a new poetic dialogue between Job and his friends (3:1—31:47) and added a long speech by God as the climax (38:1—42:6). The author concluded with the prose ending of the old story. The poem on wisdom in chapter 28 may have been composed by this author, who used it as a transition between Job's dialogue with his friends and with God, or it may have been added later.

Stage 3: Another author, writing later, considered the new version of Job unsatisfactory because he did not find the divine speeches to be an entirely adequate answer to Job, and created a new character, Elihu, inserting his long speech into the book in order to provide what seemed to him a decisive refutation of Job's argument.

Stage 4: Sometime later, copyists who disagreed with Job's blasphemous tone rearranged the third cycle of speeches, putting some of Bildad's and Zophar's speeches into Job's mouth.[3]

The hypothesis of growth by stages is weakest in the supposed rearrangement of the third cycle of speeches, but quite persuasive is the claim that the Elihu speeches are a secondary intrusion. The removal of his speeches would create no disruption in the book, for Elihu is not mentioned outside of chapters 32–37. As further evidence, Elihu's speeches stand apart as a long monologue, unlike the speeches of Job's three friends. Elihu's discourse also explicitly cites other characters' words, a feature which suggests that the author of this section used a copy of Job to compose Elihu's speech. Since Elihu is the only character who bears a Hebrew name, it is possible that Elihu is actually the name of the person who added this material, quite literally writing himself into the book.

The supposition of an oral story, with a different "missing middle" section that was displaced by the poetic dialogues, is attested by Bishop of Mopsuestia (c. 350–428 AD), who was familiar with an oral version of the story of the pious Job that did not contain the angry speeches of the canonical book and that was popular among Jews and Christians. The author of the Epistle of James may be alluding to this familiar oral tale rather than to the canonical book when he says, "You have *heard* of the patience of Job" (Jas. 5:11), rather than "you have *read* of the patience of Job."

Critics who argue that the book of Job developed according to stages rarely address the question of how one should read the book as it currently appears. According to Newsom, modern scholars are increasingly reacting against the tendency to treat the book as an assortment of parts rather than a single whole. Despite the compositional history, what would it mean if we read the book as if it were the product of a single author? As noted above, the content of the book of Job, its characters and its message, has worked its way into the popular imagination. The same can be said for the perplexing structure of the book; it too hooks the reader. Far from being an embarrassment, recognizing that the book is at odds with itself may be essential to understanding its meaning and purpose. "Dialogue is at the heart of the book of Job. The clash of divergent perspectives is represented in the three cycles of disputation between Job

---

3. The discussion on the structure and compositional history of the book of Job is adapted from Newsom, "Job," 321–25.

and his friends."[4] The textual problems at the end of the third cycle of speeches, where Zohar is given no voice, may be intentional. By leaving the debate unresolved, the author may have wanted to demonstrate that his sympathies were not with the friends, since they are not given the final say (see 42:7–9). Even Job's final speech stands over against God's answer from the whirlwind. "By means of the cleverness of editor or author, the whole book is structured as a dialogue of two very different prose and poetic voices, two very different ways of telling the same story that cannot be harmonized into a single perspective."[5] Moreover, the presence of the prose conclusion heightens dissonance and irony.

Like the pieces of a jigsaw puzzle that have been stepped on and slightly misshapen, the literary components of Job do not fit together easily. The storyline deals with the unresolved tensions and issues of life, particularly the problem of human suffering and the apparent capriciousness or inconsistency of divine justice. The story's plot and resolution demand great imagination from the reader. The author of Job, like other wisdom writers, employs literary puzzle (*mashal*) as a way to address the enigmas of life. Despite the impression of misfitting, there is in the book a sense of artistry that would be severely disturbed if its structure were redesigned. The ambiguities and uncertainties of Job's suffering are designed to entangle the reader, making room for personal involvement and enhancing the intrigue. The enigmas created by the structural gaps appear not haphazard but deliberate. As we saw in our study of Ecclesiastes, the structure of Job is part of its message.

Textual Analysis

Prologue (1:1—2:13) and Epilogue (42:7–17)

The prose story in Job resembles a folk tale. It has the "once upon a time" beginning, using various formulas and refrains. The setting is outside Israel and none of the characters are Israelites. The story has a legendary quality, and even Job is a legendary folk hero (Ezek. 14:14). The epilogue was probably part of the original tale, though the two pieces lack a connecting piece, which seems to have been deleted to make room for the poetic addition. The drama is set in five scenes, in an alternating pattern

---

4. Ibid., 323.
5. Ibid., 324.

between heaven and earth (earth-heaven-earth-heaven-earth) that creates a tight symmetry. There are also numerous parallels between chapters 1 and 2: the first chapter represents Job's first test (including the loss of family and belongings); the second represents Job's next test (his body). The principal characters include a narrator, who occasionally interjects his point of view. In addition, the reader is understood to be a character as well, for the reader knows all along that the sufferings of Job are a test by God, something Job never learns. Nevertheless, the narrative presents a consistent picture of Job: he is patient and good, a pious man who never curses God.

The characters in the story raise powerful questions, for Job remains faithful throughout his ordeal, while God seems capricious. The narrative makes us question God's goodness and even God's omniscience. Does God know in advance how things will turn out? Will God be faithful to Job in his suffering? Will God be faithful to us in our suffering? The story introduces a character called the *satan*, a member of the heavenly council. Earlier in the Bible the Hebrew word "*satan*" is used to represent human adversaries (1 Kgs. 11:14, 23, 25). Here he appears as a supernatural being, not in an evil role, for his power is subject to God's will, but as an adversary. This character disappears after chapter 2, for the purpose of the book is not to teach that human suffering or evil are caused by Satan, but rather that they are in the hands of God. In the book of Job, the cause of suffering and evil are left unanswered.

Job's wife makes a cameo appearance; only two verses make reference to her, and she is given a one-liner, "Curse God, and die" (2:9). Job's friends (or counselors) appear in the prologue as comforters. They sit *shiva* with Job for seven days and remain silent, their silence being their most helpful response to Job throughout the book (in 42:7–9, Job is said to intercede for *them*!). From the author's perspective, innocent suffering is certainly possible. Job is singled out for suffering because of his virtue, not because of his sin. In the prologue, the author's picture of how one should respond to adversity is clear: submission is the model. Like Job, one should take what comes.

Job's Lament (3:1–26)

The poetic section of Job, which begins with chapter 3, presents a very different picture from the prose tale. Here we find a deep lament, one that continues in the three cycles of dialogue that follow. In her classic work, *Living with Death and Dying*, published in 1981, Elisabeth Kübler-Ross describes the stages in the grieving process. These stages involve shock (particularly applicable to Job's response in chapter 3, when he curses the day of his birth), refusal, anger, discouragement and depression, followed by a bargaining stage (often characterized by acceptance or submission), and then, after a long process, the sick or grieving person arrives at a form of acceptance. The stages of this process, though perhaps not identical in order to that described by Kübler-Ross, can be identified in the poetic section of Job (3:1—42:6). The key to liberating growth is that it takes time, and that it involves a process, precisely what transpires in the book's poetic section.[6]

Dialogue with Friends (4:1—31:40)

For the sake of brevity, we will treat this entire unit as consisting of three cycles of speeches between Job and his friends, with the insertion of a poem on wisdom (chapter 28) as an interlude. The friends speak in a particular order: Eliphaz, Bildad, and then Zophar, with responses by Job. The first cycle of speeches appears in chapters 4–14; the second in 15–21; and the third in 22–31, though the text is fragmented here, ending with Job's soliloquy or final defense in 29–31.

While this poetic section is termed a dialogue, there is little listening. The three counselors mostly speak past Job, defending traditional orthodoxy, and Job mostly addresses God and his own innocence. The later cycles appear less interesting and vital. Readers in search of a plot or a clear line of argumentation often lose interest, for there is a much repetition and many different points of view, though most of them sound disturbingly similar. While the repetitive nature of the cycles seems excessive and boring to modern readers, such an approach appealed to the ancients, who loved rhetorical fullness.

Disparity marks the starting points: Job's friends assume Job to be at fault, whereas Job assumes God at fault; according to Job's friends, God rewards virtue and punishes vice, whereas Job's experience suggests that God punishes virtue and rewards vice. The two sides produce authoritative warrants for their claims, together appealing to at least eight different

---

6. In *Creative Suffering*, Paul Tournier finds wide application for the grieving stages, applying them to many situations we find hard to accept.

forms of authority to justify their positions, including (a) universally accepted truth; (b) personal experience (central for Job); (c) tradition (central for Job's friends); (d) divine revelation (Job has to wait until chapter 38 for his theophany); (e) wisdom provided by age; (f) nature wisdom; (g) global wisdom; and (h) dreams and visions (see especially Elihu's argument in 33:15). In the divine speeches, God avoids such warrants, for as the final arbiter, God does not appeal to other authorities.

The arguments of the counselors may be summarized as follows (note that I focus on the first cycle):

1. Eliphaz (Job 4–5). This character appears as the wisest and most dignified of the three friends, at his best in chapters 4–5. He attempts to provide comfort by suggesting that Job was once a counselor himself (4:1–5). He reminds Job of the doctrine of retribution, emphasizing that it truly works (4:6–11). He relates a strange religious experience he once had and how he became convinced that all humans are sinners (4:12–21). In chapter 5 he advises Job to trust God, for God can use suffering for human good. This chapter provides a full and fair presentation of conventional theology.

2. Bildad (Job 8). This character appears as a traditionalist, restating accepted virtues. The tone of the discussion worsens as Bildad responds to Job's words (in chapters 6–7) with bluntness and sarcasm, lacking in compassion. Bildad is quick to come to God's defense and is more direct and forceful than Eliphaz in his application of the doctrine of retribution.

3. Zophar (Job 11). The youngest of the three, Zophar possesses the brashness and dogmatism associated with youth. Having listened to the conversation of the others, he decides they have not been forceful enough. Using the approach that the best defense is a good offence, he goes straight for the jugular, challenging Job's hostility toward God, his lack of trust in God's justice, and his exaggerated claims of innocence. His evaluation is forthright: "Know then that God exacts of you less than your guilt deserves" (11:6). In other words, "Job, you are a sinner; just shut up and admit it. And, by the way, God is taking it easy on you."

The problem with the friends is not that their arguments lack meaning, for they represent traditional wisdom, but that their advice relies on pat answers and clichés, orthodox formulas that lack true sympathy or compassion for their suffering friend. Sometimes "good answers" may be "bad," particularly when insights are not applied judiciously.

Job's approach is a bit more difficult to summarize, since it reflects the mood swings of a sufferer. As we noted earlier, his response starts with a lament (Job 3:1–26), one of the deepest in all literature. In 3:3 Job curses the day of his birth, uttering a death wish that comes from the sense of emptiness in his life, caused in part by estrangement from a meaningful relationship with God. Meaninglessness can be a suffering worse than physical pain. In chapter 6 Job becomes defiant. His counselors have raised the issue of his guilt and are planning his "indictment." In chapter 7 Job addresses God, using legal terms and even blaming God (cf. 13:3). Job moves quickly from perceiving God as amoral to accusing him of immorality (9:24) and of being the enemy. He demands a trial and asks for an advocate (9:33–35; cf.16:18–21; 19:25–27). The shift from sufferer to finding fault with God reveals the depth of Job's agony, but also points him in the right direction. In chapter 23 Job becomes hopeful of a direct meeting with God (23:3–7).

Throughout Job's grief process, we note some change in his understanding of death. In the first cycle, Job does not expect anything beyond this life (see 3; 7:7–10; 10:21–22; 14:12). By 14:14 he begins to show a deep longing for something more than the finality of death. His argument, like that of Qoheleth, seems to go like this: If this life is all there is, then innocent suffering is not only terrible, it is meaningless. Job is becoming aware that God's justice is not always going to work out in this life. In 14:7–9, 14–17 Job comes close to admitting that a dead person can live again, but then he comes to his senses (14:10–13, 18–22); such hope remains illusory, too good to be true.

The second cycle contains the famous passage: "I know that my Redeemer lives, and that at the last he will stand upon the earth" (19:25), which concludes with the idea that after Job dies, "in my flesh I shall see God" (19:26). This passage, unfortunately, is notoriously difficult to translate. The concept of "Redeemer" refers to the *goel*, a person in Israelite society who acts on behalf of a relative, often as avenger when a family member has been murdered. The text in 19:26a can either read "in my flesh" or its opposite, "without my flesh." Job's hope here seems to be no more than "If only it were true!" The second half of 19:26, translated in the NRSV as "My heart faints within me," should be taken as the moment when Job's momentary vision vanishes, propelling him back into his tragic reality.[7]

A couple of issues arise before we examine the poem of wisdom (Job 28) and Job's soliloquy (Job 29–31). The first concerns the value

---

7. Gordis, *God and Man*, 263.

of "laments." Traditional wisdom often urges humans to stifle lament, encouraging sufferers not to complain or simply to praise God in all situations. That approach contradicts scripture, which includes numerous laments, especially among the Psalms. Laments can be therapeutic, particularly when they are candid. Even words of blasphemy, uttered as "cries for help," have merit. They seemingly bother us more than they do God. God may be pained by our inability to trust, but God always prefers lament to evasion or disbelief. Laments keep the conversation with God and others open, and it is in that spirit that they are spiritually beneficial.

Up to this point in the poetic section of the book, we have witnessed the silence of God, a condition that most humans find normative. One possibility to consider, however, is that perhaps God is speaking all of the time, and we have not cultivated the apparatus or the discipline to hear. As we shall see, the silence does not last forever. In the meantime, silence can be terrible, lonely, and frightening, which we discern to be Job's situation.

Poem about Wisdom (28:1–28)

This poem is a self-contained literary unit, complete with a refrain (28:12 and 20). The scholarly consensus is that this poem is a later addition, though it makes good sense in its current context, where it provides a helpful interlude to the breakdown of the cyclical pattern in chapters 24–27 and to the monotony of the argumentation. The poem also points to the climax of the book, where God's speech uses similar language and imagery. Robert Gordis views this poem as an earlier treatment of the basic theme that preoccupied the author of Job throughout his life, namely, the mystery of the universe and of human suffering. A later scribe probably inserted the poem at the end of the third cycle because the original text had been disarranged and a portion of the text had been lost.

Gordis detects two types of wisdom here, *hahokmah* (with the definite article), "wisdom par excellence," used in the refrain as reference to transcendent wisdom, and *hokmah*, wisdom as revealed to humans, mundane and practical, equated with organized religion and morality. The poem points out the limits of human understanding and affirms that God is the author of wisdom. The final verse, with its reference to "the fear of the Lord . . . is wisdom" (28:28), is an anomaly in Job, for it seems to contradict the earlier emphasis in the chapter on God as the sole knower of wisdom. This verse appears to be an editorial interpolation of conventional wisdom, similar to the ethical ideal inserted in Ecclesiastes 12:13. Readers may be interested to learn that only in 28:28 is deity called "Lord" (Adonai). In the prose tale, the name Yahweh is preferred, whereas elsewhere in the poetic section of Job, Shaddai (God Almighty) is preferred and Yahweh is never used.

Job's Soliloquy (29:1—31:40)

This passage anticipates the conclusion of the book, each chapter preparing for its climax. Chapter 29 describes the good old days, when Job was happy. Remembering the past can be therapeutic, preparing us for new things in the present and providing hope for the future. But remembering, if it becomes nostalgic, over-sentimental clinging to a past that is gone, can be counter-productive and unhealthy. Chapter 30, a sad song with much unhealthy lament, sketches Job's miserable present condition. Despite abundant God-talk (30:20–23), the tone is negative and accusatory. The future looks so bleak that Job can see only death ahead (30:19, 31). In chapter 31 Job continues to prepare for his trial, uttering a series of oaths to clear himself from guilt. Described as the "code of the Jewish gentleman," this chapter lists fourteen offenses against which Job has guarded himself. He is ready to present his case: "O that I had one to hear me! Here is my signature! Let Shaddai answer me!" (31:35).

Speeches of Elihu (32:1—37:24)

Most scholars treat this section as a later editorial insertion, for the arguments against its inclusion are persuasive. For example, the material interrupts the book's overall argument. Chapter 31 ended with the call for a response by God, and chapter 38 appears to be the next step in the drama. Additional speeches appear unwarranted and excessive. In addition, this section breaks the pattern of cycles, since there is no response from Job. Furthermore, the speeches are by Elihu, previously unknown nor mentioned. Finally, the style and language are different from elsewhere.

Because these chapters are included in the final text, we need to ask how they might contribute to the book's overall effect. It can be argued that the words of Elihu prepare Job psychologically for the divine speeches to come, moving Job from his rut as complainer and prepare him to listen, thereby opening him to new possibilities. They also prepare Job spiritually, by adding that God can speak through visions and dreams (33:15) as well as through sickness (33:19; cf. 36:15). Moreover, Elihu doesn't seek to find fault with Job; he alone of the counselors calls Job by name. In 37:14-20 Elihu asks Job to consider the wondrous works of God, thereby anticipating God's ensuing speech.

Chapters 33-36 are not as disconnected from Job's earlier arguments and concerns as some might suggest, for in this section Elihu cites Job's three major contentions: that he is innocent (33:8-9); that God's action toward him is arbitrary and unjust (33:10-11); and that God has ignored his suffering by refusing to answer him (33:10-11). Having mirrored Job's complaints, Elihu refutes them in reverse order, using a chiastic structure. To Job's contention that God is silent, Elihu responds that God speaks through visions and dreams (33:15). If this mode of communication proves ineffective, God may use pain and illness and even an angelic voice (33:19-23); once restored, the sufferer understands that discipline saves him from perdition (33:24-28). To Job's contention that he is innocent, Elihu's response is that God plays no favorites. God is Creator of all and is just in destroying wickedness (34:12). Humans should not second-guess God, for they live in a theocentric universe, not in an anthropocentric one (Job 35).

Most of chapter 36 is recapitulation. Elihu concludes his discourse with praise of God's power (36:22—37:24), thereby anticipating the divine speeches that follow. Elihu employs many rhetorical questions, as God will do in chapters 38-39. The passage begins with reference to the cycle of rain, which is both beneficent and dangerous (36:22-33). Chapter 37 continues the imagery of storms in nature, deriving lessons from them. God uses the forces of nature to chastise or to bless. The storm passes, and the chapter concludes by affirming that the wise and righteous will pass through the storms and adversities of life and into the light of God's favor. Elihu's speeches, however, seem to be ineffective. They are no more persuasive than are those of his predecessors.

Speeches of God with Job's Reply (38:1—42:6)

This section consists of two speeches by God and two short responses by Job (40:4-5; 42:1-6). Unlike Job's earlier speeches, in which he asked "why" questions, God's answers address "who" questions. To the modern reader the divine speeches might appear randomly organized, but in fact they are carefully designed responses to two Jobian charges: that God governs the world unwisely and unjustly. The first speech (38:1—40:5) addresses "design" in nature. God treats Job as a rival, asking him questions only a deity could answer. Can Job play God, bring a universe into being, sustain it, and control it? While some things in nature might appear bizarre or useless, such as the ostrich, proverbial for its stupidity, the passage is a reminder that God creates according to inscrutable purposes. Wild beasts, we are told, are intended for God's pleasure and use, not for mankind's. The second speech (40:6—41:26) defends God's justice. The subject is surprising, for it almost wholly describes two massive beasts: Behemoth (40:15-24) and Leviathan (40:25—41:26). While the beasts have mythological connotation, they actually portray the hippopotamus and the crocodile, viewed by humans as frightening and physically repulsive. This speech answers Job's charge of unjust governance by showing that God controls cosmic evil, represented by Behemoth and Leviathan. The bottom line comes through clearly: God's ways are not accessible to humans; in his encounter with God, Job is simply out of his league. Job's response in 42:3 indicates that he understands. In the long run, anthropocentric perspectives are simply inadequate.

There is bad news here but also good news. The good news is that God finally appears to Job. The silence is broken, and Job's hope is fulfilled. The bad news is that the conversation will be on God's terms, not on Job's. God sets the agenda, which does not include answers to Job's questions. Job never learns why he suffers. He remains in the dark regarding the *satan*'s wager or the role of his testing. Like most people who suffer, Job does not receive adequate answers for his tragic circumstances. As throughout the book, this section provides two ultimate realities that humans must accept: the sovereignty of God, including God's awesome power and absolute freedom, and the ambiguity and mystery that underlies life. In the Bible, God is never in the dock, answering charges or accusations; rather, humans are in the dock, questioned by God. For the author of Job, humanity's ultimate questions about life and its meaning are simply silenced by God's presence. From this point on, the book presents us with a transformed perspective, in which realities are reversed. God sets the agenda—a biblical "given"—which offers Job release from concentration on self. More importantly, God takes Job seriously enough to speak, and in so doing, addresses Job's most bitter complaint (the silence of God) and his greatest distress (his isolation from God).

These chapters are among the greatest nature poetry in world literature. Their purpose, however, is not the glorification of nature, but the vindication of nature's God. According to Gordis, humans do find an answer here to their questions, but it is a Hebraic answer, not a Greek one. The answer is not rational but intuitive and subtle, couched in allusions and implications: "just as there is order and harmony in the natural world, though imperfectly grasped by humans, so there is order and meaning in the moral sphere, though often incomprehensible to mankind."[8]

Thematic Commentary

Thematic Overview

The book of Job, through its intriguing plot, provides theological commentary on various interrelated themes. The author uses the problem of suffering and its corollary, divine justice, as an occasion for pondering additional and even deeper questions, including the doctrine of retribution (reward and punishment), the problem of evil (vindicating the integrity of God), the discontinuity of tradition and experience, the motivation for human behavior (whether by promise of blessing or fear of punishment), and the mystery of God.[9]

1. *Reward and Punishment.* The theory of retribution undergirds most of the wisdom literature, especially conventional Jewish wisdom such as found in the book of Proverbs. The need for retribution is obvious: some answer is better than no answer. In the midst of the uncertainties of life, a partial explanation provides at least some meaning. Furthermore, this doctrine protects God's image as both powerful and good. Humans have trouble living in a world without some final authority or moral arbiter. They worry that if they relax this belief, all ethical motivation may be lost. In addition, retribution is the basis of any notion of justice. Goodness should be rewarded and evil punished. Job's dilemma comes from knowing that he has done nothing to deserve his misfortune. Still, a strict understanding of retribution offers no other explanation for his troubles, so Job blames God. Being a man of faith, he believes that God is the architect of the order in the universe. Ultimately, God decides who

---

8. Ibid., 133.
9. What follows in this segment is adapted from Bergant, "Wisdom Books: Job," 238–42. Additional thematic analysis appears in essay 3, at the conclusion of the chapter.

will be rewarded and who will be punished. God usually accomplishes this through the laws established at creation. When they seem to fail, God can and should intervene to enforce justice. From Job's point of view, God has failed to do this in his case. The book of Job raises serious questions about divine justice and makes us ask whether God is indifferent to Job's faithfulness. The author clearly does not equate human suffering with guilt or wrongdoing. To do so rigidly leads to falsely impugning the character of the sufferer or the character of God.

2. *The problem of evil.* In a universe created and ruled by an all-good and all-powerful God, evil is surely *the* problem of problems.[10] Once we are convinced that some suffering is undeserved, we are faced with the troubling question: Why does God allow injustice to occur? Theodicy (from the Greek for "justifying God") is the name we give to explain the problem of evil, while maintaining belief in a benevolent Creator. If Job did not believe that God is a moral God, the question of evil would take a different turn. If God is not just, then Job's suffering would be equally unbearable, but it would not be as puzzling. Many modern thinkers, including theists as well as agnostics and atheists, question or reject God's sovereignty, but such questioning does not square with the views of Israel's sages. None of the characters in the book of Job doubt God's control. In fact, if Job could relinquish belief in an almighty creator, his torment might even be lessened. Theodicy is not an issue for Job's friends, since Job's misery is not a puzzle for them. Job is intent on defending his own integrity rather than God's, and so theodicy is not his concern either. However, theodicy is of major importance to the author of the book, who depicts God as all-powerful, provident, and omnibenevolent. At the end of the book, the problem of evil may be left unanswered, but the integrity of God is no longer questioned.

---

10. In the vocabulary of the Hebrew scriptures, suffering and evil are identified. In fact, that vocabulary lacked a specific word to indicate "suffering." Thus all suffering was defined as evil. This background is helpful in understanding the warning in Genesis 2:9 about the consequences of eating of the tree "of the knowledge of good and evil," as well as in understanding the statement in Isaiah 45:7, which attributes evil (the word translated as "woe" is the same found in Genesis 2:9 for "evil") to God. The reference to evil in Isaiah is not to cosmic evil in general but rather to the evil of the destruction of the Temple in Jerusalem by the Babylonians in the sixth century BC and the ensuing Exile. In Jewish tradition, omnipotent God is constrained from destroying evil for by doing so God could well destroy good. While an omnipotent deity could violate universal laws, to do so might unravel the cosmos.

3. *Tradition and experience.* A fundamental principle underlies wisdom thought and plays an important role in the book of Job: the relationship between faith/tradition and experience in the formation of new theological understanding. We have all been taught the importance of conforming to the teachings of tradition, whether familial, cultural, or religious. Together, like Qohelth's threefold cord (4:12), such tradition is not easily broken. In Job's day, suffering and poverty were viewed as karmic, as resulting from human sin. In traditional societies, "life commandments" (values taught by parents and revered as the wisdom of the ages) are hard to overturn (see Bildad's appeal to tradition in Job 8:8–10).

A new and sometimes conflicting attitude is seen today, in which contemporary values are said to trump tradition. Rather than pitting them against one another, it is healthier to affirm a dynamic relationship between them, whereby each influences and refashions the other (that is one of the meanings of the expression "iron sharpens iron" in Proverbs 27:17). In the book of Job, neither Job nor his friends take note of this dynamic. Others evaluate Job's life according to tradition, as he himself does in the final summary of his cause (chapter 31), in which he insists that he has complied with the prescriptions of Israel's legal tradition.

With regard to traditional doctrines such as belief in retribution, we can examine three negative effects on Job's friends: (a) they deny experience in order to protect doctrine; (b) they assume Job to be wrong, and in assigning blame are unhelpful as friends or as counselors; and (c) by remaining on the theoretical level, they remain closed to the truth and hardened to Job's pain. Their assessment by Job is telling: they are "miserable comforters" (16:2), their words "windy" (16:3), vacuous, and untrue. The effects of belief in retribution are even more devastating on Job: (a) condemned by others, he feels alone; (b) God, the arbiter of justice in the universe, becomes the enemy; and (c) intellectual answers are unhelpful. As long as sufferers seek intellectual answers, they will experience frustration and disappointment. In many cases, sufferers are driven to blame themselves, while friends and family members become codependents, blaming themselves as well. Job does not take this path. He believes in his cause, defending it to the end.

Job is not willing to question his personal integrity, but he is also not ready to challenge tradition. Job's experience of innocent suffering calls for a new and more critical look at the tradition. It is strange that neither Job nor his friends challenge this unbending interpretation of tradition, "because it is precisely the ability to be faithful yet flexible in new situations that constitutes wisdom. Perhaps the author of the book wanted to demonstrate what could happen when theology is rigidly applied."[11]

4. *The Motivation for Human Behavior.* In a very real sense, the drama of the book of Job stems from the *satan*'s challenge found in 1:9: "Does Job fear God for nothing?" As adversary, the *satan* implies that Job's behavior is motivated by promises of blessing. It is easy for Job to be loyal to God when things are going well. Take away his prosperity and happiness and he will actually curse God. God takes the dare, and Job is assaulted by a series of devastating losses. However, throughout his agony he never curses God or strays from his attachment to God. The content of Job's laments and pleading show that Job does not look for recompense; he wants vindication. He is not concerned about possessions; he insists only that his integrity be acknowledged. When he finally understands the lesson God set out to teach him, he is silent and seems content with his new insight. It is apparent that the depth of Job's piety is based on his relationship with God, not on promise of reward or fear of punishment. The fact that at this time Israelites did not have a clear idea of reward or punishment in an afterlife makes Job's disinterested piety even more admirable. From the author's perspective, Job is "the real deal!" He is truly a person of integrity and faith.

5. *The Mystery of God.* Up to this point, most of the themes we have considered focus on Job. The book's portrayal of God is fairly traditional; Job's companions describe God as a prosecuting judge, whereas Job characterizes God as powerful yet oppressive and unconcerned. In the divine speeches, God is portrayed as transcendent and imminent, as powerful yet more like an awe-inspiring teacher than a divine judge, as one who leads Job into new horizons of understanding (42:3). Ultimately, the reader is left with the incomprehensibility of much of life, but also with hope in this transcendent God, before whose glory and majesty all humans stand in awe and in silence.

Lessons at the End of the Book

The following points adequately summarize the message of the book of Job:

1. God is present in human suffering, perhaps more so than in all other circumstances;

---

11. Bergant, "Wisdom Books: Job," 242.

2. There are no final answers; faith and trust in God are adequate;

3. Job was right about the doctrine of retribution; it is inadequate to explain all suffering;

4. Job was right in emphasizing that all humans die. However, the book opens the door to the question of resurrection and life beyond death. The Septuagint adds a note at the end indicating that Job will be among those whom the Lord will raise from the dead;

5. The Jewish community (as eventually the Christian community) viewed the conclusion of the book (the divine speeches and Job's response) as good news rather than bad, affirming that God is a friend to humanity and not an enemy, present and gracious in all human suffering;

6. The ending of the book is both realistic and unrealistic. Life does not have a happy ending (we all die), meaning we shouldn't accept the "doubly blessed" conclusion as the norm. The book's enduring message is not Job's restoration, but rather the coming of God to Job in his suffering. Nevertheless, restoration is important because it affirms that suffering is not the final word; hope is. Hope in a God who is "for us," not "against us" (Rom. 8:31–39);

7. The epilogue endorses Job's honest struggle for a faith that seeks understanding. Madeleine L'Engle states it well: "I seek for God that He might find me, because I have learned, empirically, that this is how it works. I seek. He finds";[12]

8. God's final word to Job (42:7–8) is to intercede for his friends (even when they become enemies), which includes everyone.

Throughout the book, Job's friends give orthodox answers, but sometimes orthodoxy is not enough: "I had heard of you by the hearing of the ear," Job remarks at the end (42:5a). Job's friends spoke about God—but that was not enough. Head knowledge, sometimes referred to as "dead orthodoxy," is insufficient. Job must speak *with* God: "now my eye sees you" (42:5b), and in so doing, he is said to repent: "therefore I despise myself, and repent in dust and ashes" (42:6) Thus ends the book's poetic section. The notion of Job's repentance makes sense in the context of conventional wisdom (voiced by Job's friends and in the prose tale's

---

12. L'Engle, *Irrational Season*, 171.

"Hollywood ending"), but appears incongruous with the poet's own unconventional perspective.

Two things need to be said about 42:6: (1) this verse is essential for understanding the book's meaning, and (2) the verse is difficult to translate, like many others in the poetic section of Job. The English translation, as in crucial passages such as Job 19:25–26,[13] represents an educated guess. Some translations vary the meaning of the first part of the verse, such as the New Jerusalem Bible's (NJB) rendering: "I retract all I have said," or the New American Bible's (NAB) "Therefore I disown what I have said," providing a radically different understanding from the New Revised Standard Version's (NRSV) "therefore I despise myself," though the meaning of the second half of the verse remains the same: Job repents. The Jewish Publication Society's Tanakh Translation, found in the Jewish Study Bible, renders the verse: "Therefore, I recant and relent, being but dust and ashes." The first part of the verse is similar to the New Jerusalem Bible's translation, but the second part differs from others. The notes in the Jewish Study Bible are important: "As Job's final comment, this verse would seem to be key to understanding the book as a whole. The Hebrew of the text, unlike the rest of Job, is not difficult, but is very ambiguous."[14]

The ambiguity is caused, in part, by the verbs translated as "despise/recant," or "relent/repent." Neither verb has a direct object, meaning we are not told from what Job recants/despises or relents/repents. Does he recant/despise himself (as in the NRSV), or his mortality (as in the Tanakh)? Is he recanting the presumptuous words he has uttered (NJB; NAB), or is he rejecting his angry complaints? Has he decided to retract his lawsuit against God and put off his "dust and ashes," the traditional costume of a lamenter or complainant? This possibility may be closest to the intention of the passage, as translated by Richard Clifford: "Therefore I retract and give up my dust and ashes."[15] The Hebrew verb *niham* in 42:6b with the preposition means "to relent" or "to change one's mind." Why would Job do that? Because he has "seen God," thereby accomplishing his goal. One further possibility should be considered: "Therefore I despise and repent of dust and ashes." If "dust and ashes" stands for

---

13. This passage, often taken as early biblical support for belief in bodily resurrection and in God as Savior, lacks reference to God, speaking only of a blood avenger (a *goel*); the doctrine of the general resurrection of the dead, particularly as understood by Christians, is clearly not intended.

14. Gruber, "Job," 1561.

15. Clifford, *Wisdom Literature*, 95.

the religious ritual surrounding repentance, representing the concept of guilt and innocence as the central issue of life, then Job rejects it all. Job's friends urged him to repent, and so he does, but not as they thought. According to this interpretation, Job repents of repentance, taking religious action (42:5) to renounce religion.[16]

Essay 3: The Mystery of Suffering

The satisfactory interpretation of a book requires that its literary components fit together harmoniously. In the case of Job, the juxtaposition of elements raises more questions than answers. For example, why does Job repent? Why does God restore him? Why do God's words ignore Job's suffering? Is the wisdom teaching that God rewards the good and punishes the wicked upheld or overturned? Does the book have a primary purpose? The probing of such questions yields possibilities, but not clear answers. For Job, the most important question is why he suffers, and by extension, why innocent people suffer. Fellow sufferers often find that to be the main subject of the book as well. In the study of Job, two concerns predominate: why innocent people suffer, and the nature of the divine-human relationship.

To the first question, three answers seem to be given. The first attempt to explain suffering appears in the prologue: (a) *innocent suffering arises from arbitrary divine decisions*. Job is but a pawn in a heavenly challenge, and humans are unwitting victims. Job's friends propose a different interpretation: (b) *suffering is due to sin*; hence Job's suffering is deserved. Job's own experience, and the reader's knowledge of the situation, invalidates this conclusion. (c) *The Creator of all things must be the cause and source of suffering*. According to Job, humans suffer because God is capricious and unreliable. In the divine speeches, God merely ignores Job's questions, changing the subject from Job's pain to the creation of the cosmos.

In the past, the customary way of understanding suffering was as punishment for sin, an approach seemingly validated by Job's "repentance" in chapter 42. Recent biblical and theological study has led to more viable explanations, including viewing suffering as:

1. *A test of one's character and integrity*. The prologue itself tells us that God allowed Job's misfortunes to befall him so that Job's integrity

---

16. Good, "Job," 431.

might be tested (2:3). Elsewhere in the Bible God is said to test individuals, such as when Abraham was told to sacrifice his son Isaac (Gen. 22:1). While experiences certainly test our character, we must add that in Job's case he never regarded his misfortune as a test.

2. *A source of moral discipline.* In the book of Job, Elihu claims that pain and sickness sometimes act as warning against sin and as a defense against pride and complacency (33:15–33).

3. *Vicarious suffering.* This view is depicted in the Suffering Servant poems in the book of Isaiah, particularly in 52:13—53:12, interpreted by Jews as reference to Jewish Diaspora experience and by Christians as a reference to Christ's atoning sacrifice on the cross. Such suffering is said to be an instrument whereby God's will is accomplished, bringing blessing to the world.

4. *A place of encounter with God.* As in Job's case, God can be experienced either as absent or as particularly close and available in suffering and pain.

5. *An impersonal result of universal sin.* In the Bible, this is how death seems to be understood, as a sort of karmic effect of cosmic rebellion and human wrongdoing (Rom. 6:23). The Christian doctrine of "original sin," which views Adam's sin as having infected all humans, is sometimes introduced as a variant of this explanation.

6. *A Mystery.* Innocent suffering is simply beyond human comprehension. Ultimately no one can give Job an adequate explanation for his suffering. Only God knows, though people of faith expect that one day all will become clear.

While the book of Job offers various explanations of suffering, none seem satisfactory, for the issue of suffering, fundamental and critical to the human condition, has a preliminary role in Job, functioning as a set-up to the author's (and by implication to Israel's and to Christianity's) primary concern, the divine-human relationship: "The real subject of the Book of Job and the crux of the human problem for Israel is not human suffering, but human relationship with God in the midst of suffering."[17]

Paralleling the book's three explanations of human suffering are four characterizations of the divine-human relationship:

1. *Interested piety.* This view, articulated in the prologue by the *satan*, claims that God and humans relate to one another for purely mercenary reasons. God buys the friendship of Job by giving him gifts, while

---

17. O'Connor, *Wisdom Literature*, 104.

Job is loyal to God for benefits received. If gifts are withdrawn, humans reject God. The book of Job discredits this interpretation. The *satan* does not reappear after the prologue because he is proved wrong. Job remains loyal to God.

2. *Human obedience is primary.* This view of the relationship is promoted by Job's friends, for whom there can be no human-divine relationship apart from the moral correctness of human behavior. In this relationship, there is no friendship, only rules to follow. By eliminating freedom, mystery, and grace from the interaction between God and humans, this view is as inadequate as the *satan*'s. Magnifying Job's suffering, this approach deafens his friends to the depth of his anguish.

3. *God is capricious and unreliable.* This view, promoted by Job, is caused by the collapse of his friends' theology. Unable to interpret his pain, which seems utterly senseless, Job assumes that God is the culprit, the friend-turned enemy. Ironically, divine-human friendship seems impossible to Job because God is unfaithful.

4. *Human beings come under God's care.* When God appears out of the whirlwind, God speaks to Job and Job responds. According to the divine speeches, the God-human relationship is one of freedom, mutuality, and surprising grace. Encounters with deity lead to transformation. When God and humans finally meet at the end of the story and speak to one another "face to face," the drama is over, and the book's conflicts are resolved. The epilogue points to a new start for Job, his family, and his friends. Despite the predictable ending, we should not view the epilogue as providing simple restitution. Restitution keeps the cycle going, but doesn't produce change. Personal transformation produces hope, blessing the future.

The divine speeches contain the key to understanding the nature of Job's personal transformation. While these speeches do not explicitly engage Job's particular arguments, they implicitly call into question their fundamental assumptions. As the juxtaposition of Job's soliloquy (Job 29–31) and the divine speeches (Job 38–41) show, Job's theological categories had been derived from the traditional social and moral assumptions of his faith community. From these assumptions Job had extrapolated his expectations concerning God and the world. God's speeches, by beginning with the general structure of the cosmos, expose the limits of Job's anthropocentric categories. Similarly, Job's legal model for understanding divine-human relationships is also implicitly challenged. According to Job's paradigm, the fundamental categories are "right and wrong."

Through images of the sea, wild animals, and the legendary beasts of chaos, God confronts Job with categories that go beyond his legal parameters. The evocative but elusive language of the divine provides resources for the reconstruction of theological language of a very different sort than that employed by Job and his friends.

Job's brief and enigmatic words in 42:1–6 do not make clear exactly how his understanding has changed, but we surmise that the divine speeches have provided him with a transformed vision of God and thus a very different basis for reverence (42:5). If the author had made Job's interpretation of the divine speeches more explicit, then the reader would have been left with little to do beyond approving or disapproving of Job's response. By making Job's response elusive, the author forces readers "to grapple more directly with the meaning of the divine speeches and so enter into the work of theological reconstruction that they invite."[18]

Having the scope of Job now before us, the book appears to have been directing readers from less to more adequate perspectives. The naïve prose tale presents a moral perspective that is made to appear inadequate by the more sophisticated dialogues. Within the dialogues, the friends' moral perspectives are shown to be inadequate by the compelling power of Job's words. The inadequacy of Job's perspective, however, is disclosed by the extraordinary divine words from the whirlwind. Surely one should adopt and endorse the perspective articulated by God. Yet the book gives the final word to the prose tale. Moreover, the transition to the prose conclusion creates ironies that undermine the conviction that endorses the divine speeches. By having God declare that Job has spoken rightly (42:7), and by having events turn out just as the friends had predicted (see, for example, 4:6; 5:8–27; 8:6–7; 11:5–6a, 15–19), the book affirms perspectives that had appeared to be superseded and rejected.

As Carol Newsom indicates, "what gets challenged in this process is the very notion that discerning truth is a matter of choosing one perspective and rejecting all others, that the truth about a complex question can be contained in a single perspective."[19] Individual perspectives in the book of Job, taken alone, contain valid insights. Yet each one seems oblivious to the other. It may be that the truth about complex questions can be spoken only by a plurality of voices that can never be merged into one, because they speak from different experiences and different

---

18. Newsom, "Job," 337.
19. Ibid., 338.

perspectives. The truth emerging from dialogue is not to be found either in the triumph of one voice over the others or in an emerging consensus, but in the intersection of the various voices in their mutual interrogation. Such a perspective does not mean that one never gets beyond talk. On the contrary, every person must choose how to live and what to affirm. "The book of Job models a kind of theological inquiry in which multiple perspectives are not merely helpful but essential. By closing in a manner that frustrates closure, the book signals that the conversation it has begun about the nature of the divine-human relations is not finished but requires to be continued by new communities of voices."[20]

The question of human suffering, like its corollaries, the presence of evil and the mystery of God, has been argued and addressed since time immemorial, without resolution. More lectures, articles, sermons, and books have been devoted to these topics than any others combined, with no diminution in sight, for these questions cannot be answered conclusively. Whenever I ponder these topics, I am reminded of the axiom: "Life is an adventure to be lived, not a problem to be solved." Stated spiritually, the motto asserts: "Life is a mystery to be affirmed by faith, not a problem to be solved by reason." These words, like markers on a compass or routes on a map, always lead us home.

When it comes to suffering and pain, most important is not what happens to us but how we respond. Though not always welcome, pain has proven to be a great mentor, valuable for its transformative potential. Below is my list of reasons to be grateful for pain, whether physical, emotional, and spiritual:

1. Pain creates perspective;
2. Pain builds character;
3. Pain produces compassion;
4. Pain instills hope;
5. Pain enhances listening skills;
6. Pain increases self-awareness;
7. Pain brings me closer to God;
8. Pain makes me appreciate better times;
9. Pain makes me feel alive;

20. Ibid.

10. Pain lets me know things could be worse.

Questions to Ponder

1. What, for you, is the theme or message of the book of Job?
2. In your estimation, does the fact that the prologue (chapters 1–2) and epilogue (42:7–17) of the book of Job are written in prose and the rest in poetry affect the message and interpretation of the book?
3. How important is "the *satan*" to the author's (and to your) understanding of the nature of evil?
4. Is the story of Job based on a real situation or is this work primarily a literary fiction?
5. In your estimation, does the book of Job provide a satisfactory explanation to the problem of human suffering, particularly to the question of innocent suffering? Explain your answer.
6. Briefly summarize Job's point of view in his lament in chapter 3.
7. Briefly summarize Job's argument (including his concerns and questions) in his response to the three companions in the cycle of speeches.
8. Explain the presence and role of the poem of chapter 28 in the flow of the book's argument.
9. What new ideas—if any—do the Elihu speeches add to the book's overall argument?
10. In your estimation, do the divine speeches in chapters 38–41 provide a satisfactory answer to the questions raised by Job in his earlier speeches? Why or why not?
11. In your own words, explain your understanding of the meaning of Job 42:5–6.
12. According to your reading of the book of Job, what is the nature of the relationship between God and humans?

CHAPTER 4

The Song of Songs (The Song of Solomon)

Overview: The Song of Songs (also known as the Song of Solomon or Canticles) is a collection of love poetry, a celebration of the love between a man and a woman. On the surface, these short poems recount a human love story, beginning with a woman (later identified as a bride) as she invites the embrace of her lover (subsequently identified as the king, presumably Solomon). In these poems male and female speakers voice freely their affection and desire for one another in passionate, but never lurid, expressions of love. Although one of the shortest books in the Bible, this anthology is deeply revered in both the Jewish and Christian traditions. For Jewish interpreters, the Song was taken as an allegory of God's relationship with his "bride," Israel. Christian commentators saw in the imagery a symbol of Christ's love for the church. As with Job, it may be helpful to think about Song of Songs as drama, as Israel (or the church) yearning deeply for the Lord. This work echoes the view of human sexuality that Genesis presents as the way God intended it to be (Gen. 1:27–28; 2:24–25). In this sense, the Song's portrayal is in keeping with the way of life promoted by Israel's sages.

Assigned Reading: Read Song of Songs 1–8

Central Theme: The ultimate purpose of life is love.

Outline to Song of Songs
  I. The Rustic Maiden 1:1—2:7

II. Courtship in Spring 2:8—3:5

III. A Wedding Song 3:6—5:1

IV. Love's Trial and Triumph 5:2—6:3

V. Betrothal in the Garden 6:4—8:4

VI. The Seal of Love 8:5–14

Contextual Analysis

As we have seen, an objective of Jewish wisdom literature is to provide context for dealing with the problem of human suffering. In Proverbs, the solution is the doctrine of retribution; in Ecclesiastes, no answer is given because no satisfactory answer seems possible; for Job, the answer is to place one's hope and trust in God; for Song of Songs, the answer is love.

The title "Song of Songs," like "king of kings," is a superlative construction, meaning "the most sublime of songs." However, the phrase may be taken more literally still as "a song of (many) songs," suggesting a collection or anthology of songs. The Song of Songs, then, is a collection of lyric poems that celebrates human love. Nowhere else in the Bible do we have such a sustained description of the love between male and female, with such graphic suggestiveness and sensual imagery. The book is completely taken with that one theme. Surprisingly, no morals are drawn, nor is there any mention of God.

Nevertheless, this book has been a favorite of Jewish and Christian theologians, saints, and mystics. Its most famous interpreters include Pope Gregory the Great, who wrote a famous commentary; Bernard of Clairvaux, the twelfth-century monk who preached eighty-six sermons on the book over a period of eighteen years, having only reached the beginning of chapter 3 when he died in 1153; the theologian Thomas Aquinas, who was writing a commentary on the book at the time of his death; and the sixteenth-century Spanish monk St. John of the Cross.

The author of these poems remains anonymous. Since the poems are told primarily from a woman's perspective, some scholars have suggested that the author may have been a woman, though this notion is not widely accepted. More plausible is the possibility of multiple authors, including a redactor. Though the book is ascribed to King Solomon (1:1; cf. 1:5; 4:7; 8:11–12), perhaps due to his many wives, like other attributions in Jewish wisdom literature, Solomonic authorship is contrived. Though some of these poems may go back to folk and earlier literary traditions, linguistic evidence suggests a relatively late date, sometime between the fourth and second century BC. This material has many parallels with Egyptian and Mesopotamian love poetry, some dating to the thirteenth century BC.

Setting

Since the poems lack historical context, their setting has been the subject of much research and debate. Three major theories predominate: (1) The Song is the script of a drama about a love affair. Two versions of this theory were once quite popular, (a) the two-character version (Solomon and the Shulammite of 6:13), in which the king falls in love with a beautiful country girl, and (b) the three-character version, in which Solomon vies with a youthful shepherd for the love of the maiden. Solomon is unable to court her and in the end he allows her to return home to her true love. Scholars now view the main male character to be a shepherd lover, and the Song's references to a king, including to Solomon, as feature of a literary creation known as the "king fiction." This feature allows the author to idealize the shepherd lover as royal.

(2) The Song evolved from a Mesopotamian liturgy that described the marriage of a god and goddess. This theory is based on perceived similarities between the Song and ancient Mesopotamian sacred marriage texts, such as pagan rituals of the Tammuz/Adonis cult (cf. Ezek. 8:14 and possibly Isa. 17:10–11). These texts speak of the god of fertility—a dying and rising god—and the goddess who laments his death until he returns, at which times a sacred marriage is performed. This ritual would have entered Israel's cultic liturgy through the annual New Year's festival as poetic material that was modified to suit Israel's monotheistic perspectives. Like the dramatic theory, this one has become less popular in recent years, though it remains possible that some of the images of the poem originated in liturgical or mythological traditions. (3) The third theory maintains that the text is a collection of poems about human love, some of which may have originally been used in wedding celebrations, a practice that continues in Judaism today.

Genre

The Song of Songs is an anthology of lyric love songs, ranging in length from a few brief stanzas to lengthier poems, such as found in chapters 4–7, which praise the physical features of the two young lovers. Such poems belong to a similar genre of Arabic love poetry called *wasf* ("description"). The vivid imagery is never coarse or vulgar and is said to have its apogee in 8:6–7. Several types of lyrics appear in these poems, including (a) "love monologues," where a lover speaks to or about a beloved, (b) "love dialogues," in which two lovers converse, and (c) "a monologue," where a lover addresses a variety of audiences other than the beloved.

The Song exhibits characteristic features of Hebrew poetry, including parallelism, repetitive structural patterns, assonance, the use of chiastic structures, and synergism. The latter is a progression or building quality throughout the text whereby the more one lover gives, the more the other responds with increasing love (cf. 1:15–16). The diverse features, designed to create momentum and overcome boredom or triviality, are somewhat muted by the uniformity of language, representing a late stage of biblical Hebrew and applied by the final editor.

The text as we have it contains a certain amount of dialogue and a number of short poems that were connected to provide a consistent story. As we saw with Job, it may be helpful to think of the Song as a drama, not a formal drama in the modern sense, with stage directions and characters identified, but as a unified story with a dramatic quality.

Canonical Status

Modern readers, once exposed to the setting and genre of the Song, wonder how love lyrics composed for public performance found their way into the biblical canon. It is quite possible that the ascription to Solomon, found in the editorial introduction (1:1), was a factor, for it gave the collection credibility, linking it with other wisdom traditions. The placing of the Song in the Five Scrolls (Megillot) of scripture indicates that the material was used during Jewish religious holidays and recited at banquets and weddings. The Song is read on the last day of the celebration of Passover, perhaps because the announcement of the end of winter (2:11) made the poems suitable for use during a spring festival. In addition, reference to the horses and chariots of Pharaoh (1:9) is a clear allusion to the Exodus, the event commemorated at Passover.

The decisive event seems to have taken place near the close of the first century AD, when the book received staunch support from Rabbi Akiva, a famous Jewish mystic, who memorably argued for its inclusion among the books that were to be considered canonical: "All the world is not worthy as the day on which the Song of Songs was given to Israel, for all the Writings are holy, but the Song of Songs is the Holy of Holies." By this time, the allegorical view of the book had gained widespread currency among the rabbis and doubtless among the Jewish populace as well. The Song came to be interpreted as an allegory of God's love for Israel, building on marital images found in Hosea 1–3, Jeremiah 2:2, and Isaiah 50:4–7. The use of marriage as a symbol, characteristic of the Song, is found extensively also in the New Testament (Matt. 9:15; 25:1–13; John 3:29; 2 Cor. 11:2; Eph. 5:23–32; Rev. 19:7–10; 21:9). In Christian tradition, the Song has been interpreted in terms of the union between Christ and the church or with the individual believer.

As a whole, the Song echoes the view of human sexuality that Genesis presents as the way God intended it (Gen. 1:27–28; 2:24–25), for under the rubric of creation theology, sexuality is a gift of God and marital love an appropriate metaphor for the divine-human relation.

Literary Analysis

Structure

The structure of the Song, as with its compositional history, remains under debate. Is the book a single poem with a relatively small number of parts, or a collection of poems? If the former, is the unity sequential (a drama) or schematic (an artistic arrangement)? On these questions there is little consensus, and the proposals legion. Finding a uniform structure and consistent pattern to the book's content is not possible. Those who perceive any literary coherence to the poetry usually argue on the basis of their own aesthetic insights and not from any accepted criteria. The position we will take is to divide the work into six dramatic units, as indicated by the outline at the head of this chapter.

While we lack the clues needed to understand some of the individual lines, the main story is relatively clear. It begins with a young woman who has committed some indiscretion, and her brothers have punished her. They make her do manual labor in the vineyards, where the sun has darkened her pale complexion, making her more beautiful. The maiden and her lover anticipate being together (1:1—2:7). The next scene tells of a courtship taking place outdoors in the spring. The scene ends with a strange episode, possibly a dream, in which the maiden searches the streets madly for her lover, unexpectedly finding him (2:8—3:5). Next we have a strange procession, perhaps a wedding procession or a procession on the way to an espousal ceremony. In the process, we read a lovely poem from the man, singing his lover's praises, followed by a brief dialogue (3:6—5:1).

Another strange scene follows. A male chorus (acting as city watchmen), thinking the lady is a tramp or prostitute, give her a beating. The maiden appears to be talking to a second chorus (the women of Jerusalem), and she sings a song comparing her betrothed to a heroic statue. The chorus asks the beloved's whereabouts and she answers (5:2—6:3). This is followed by their reunion, in an enclosed garden. The reunion may represent their marriage or betrothal, in which they speak their mutual commitment. The scene includes poems about the maiden's beauty (6:4—8:4). The closing scene represents the climax of the story, where the maiden asks her beau to place her as a seal upon his heart (8:5-14).

Two interpretations of the Song existed in the first century AD: the literal and the allegorical. The Jewish rabbis suppressed the literal, allowing the allegorical interpretation to dominate for centuries. As with Ecclesiastes, on a subconscious level there was always a genuine affection for this book, and it was this appreciation that overrode objections to the text. As a biblical book, the song gives poetic expression to a fundamental emphasis in Judaism, that there is no dichotomy between body and spirit because both are recognized as gifts of God and as twin aspects of the unending miracle called life. Ultimately love is recognized as both physical and spiritual, and these components should remain united. Like marriage, what God has joined, let no one divide.

The Medieval Quadriga

During the medieval period, the greatest amount of Christian writing was commentary on the Bible, for the Bible was viewed as a map of divine reality, as the means whereby ultimate reality was revealed to humanity. Presupposing that divine revelation was cryptic rather than clear, hidden behind the words and metaphors of scripture, medieval exegetes devised a hermeneutical method known as the "medieval quadriga."

This standard method of biblical interpretation was based on a fourfold sense of interpreting scripture: (a) literal (reading a text naturally, at face value), (b) allegorical (reading a text in search of theological truth), (c) tropological (reading a text morally, as guidance for Christian conduct), and (d) anagogical (reading a text eschatologically, as futuristic hope). While Augustine was one of the earliest biblical expositors to suggest a fourfold approach to scripture, it was the fifth-century monk John Cassian who set forth the medieval quadriga that became the standard for medieval Latin exegesis.

Origen of Alexandria (185–254), generally considered the father of the Christian allegorical method of interpreting scripture, was a man of prodigious intellect. He wrote the first systematic theological treatise (*De principiis*), in addition to many homilies and commentaries on the Bible. His approach to scripture influenced many patristic thinkers, including Jerome, who translated the Bible into Latin (known as the Vulgate), and Ambrose, the most important expositor of the mystical sense of scripture in the early Latin Church and the teacher of Augustine, the most formidable Christian theologian of the early medieval period.

Origen wrote the first important Christian commentary on the Song of Songs. Influenced by Jewish scholars, he modified their approach to address Christian needs. For Origen, the Song of Songs could be read simultaneously on two levels, as the love between Christ and the church and as the love between Christ and the individual soul. For example, he took the words "your anointing oils are fragrant, your name is perfume poured out" (1:3) as a reference to Christ, the anointed one (messiah); the words "my nard gave forth its fragrance" (1:12) as a reference to the woman who anointed the feet of Jesus in John 12:3; and the words "his left hand is under my head, his right hand embraces me" (2:6) as a reference to the right and left hand of wisdom (Prov. 3:16). Origen's approach can be criticized as woefully subjective, but in his mind all scripture could and should be cross-referenced allegorically.

Honorius Augustodunensis, a twelfth-century monk, wrote a landmark commentary on the Song that represents an extreme form of allegorical exegesis. His approach views the Song as a reference to the love between Christ and the Virgin Mary, seen as a type or personification of the church. He approaches the book as a reference to a wedding that can be interpreted according to the four senses of scripture: (a) literal (as reference to Solomon and the daughter of the Pharaoh, or as a reference to Joseph and Mary's betrothal); (b) allegorical (as reference to the incarnation or to the marriage of Christ and the Church); (c) tropological (as reference to the love of the soul and Christ through desire and through spiritual ascent); and (d) anagogical (as reference to the resurrection of Christ and the final church of heavenly glory).

Honorius superimposed an imaginative understanding of the text by dividing the Song into four parts, based on the four corners of the earth and the four Gospels. He also equated the four corners of the earth with four ages and four brides. These brides represented four historical ages (patriarchs, prophets, apostles, and the age of the antichrist). The scheme of four brides also suggested a division of the text into four sections (1:1—2:17; 3:1—6:10; 6:11—7:10; and 7:11—8:14). Honorius divided his commentary into four books, each dealing with the story of one of the brides. While the four senses of scripture were seen to operate in every verse of the Song of Songs, the interpretation was primarily in the allegorical mode, a replica of the love between Christ and the Church.

In medieval Europe, Bernard of Clairvaux traveled widely representing popes and monarchs. Called "the conscience of Europe," he influenced bishops and church councils, becoming involved in every theological and ecclesiastic issue of his day. He also produced eighty-six sermons, using the Song to speak about the life of the soul (understood as the quest for union with God) and as a commentary on many current events of his time. In his sermons he alternates between the allegorical and the tropological, addressing the monks of his Cistercian monastery, which he founded in 1115 in Clairvaux, France. He uses the Song as a guide to the ultimate goal of Cistercian spiritual discipline, union with God. For example, the Latin version of Song 1:2 reads: "let him kiss me with the kiss of his kisses." Bernard finds in this reference a description of the three stages of mystical ascent: "kiss of the foot" (represents the beginning stage of penitential devotion); "kiss of the hand" (represents the practice of the holy life); and "kiss of the mouth" (represents the ultimate gift of spiritual grace). In 1:7 Bernard finds a warning about the dangers of heretics (the Latin version reads: "lest I begin to wander after the flocks of you companions," whereas the NRSV reads: "why should I be like one who is veiled beside the flocks of your companions?"). Earlier in the verse, in the passage that reads: "where you pasture your flock, where you make it lie down at noon," Bernard allegorizes the text once again, finding a reference to spiritual noon, viewed as the full presence of God, and to the Eucharist, God's spiritual food that sustains the "flock" (the brethren).

Though much of this appears far-fetched to readers who interpret literature more literally, Christian medieval exegetes were building on the vast allegorical base that for centuries dominated the Jewish rabbinical interpretation of the Song, who expounded the Song as a description of Israel's ongoing history of redemption by God. In addition, a particularly interesting interpretation advocated by medieval and later commentators was the view that the bride represented wisdom. While there has been within Judaism a constant tradition of theological interpretation of the Song, there has also been a tradition of secular, humanistic interpretation. Words and images from the Song have figured prominently in Jewish marriage, art, music, and liturgy. The Song was also a popular biblical text for the early Zionist movement. Its lush descriptions of the natural world and the flora and fauna of the land of Israel gave voice to the early Zionist love for the land.

Thematic Analysis

Discussion of the Song's all-encompassing theme, love, is addressed below, in essay 4.

Essay 4: The Pursuit of Love

The fundamental question for Jewish wisdom literature, particularly the four books we have examined thus far, is: "What is the meaning of life?" In Proverbs, the answer is "Fear God and keep the commandments." That book presents two ways, virtue and vice, and exhorts us to seek Lady Wisdom as our companion, to choose her way, which is the way of life. For Ecclesiastes, there is no existential meaning to life; life is meaningless, empty, and vain. Qoheleth urges his pupils to choose temporary happiness, even though it is elusive: Enjoy your childhood, because adult life is disappointing. Nevertheless, the book ends with the editorial admonition: Fear God and keep the commandments. For the author of Job, life is suffering. Meaning comes with hope in God, through encounter with the divine. The Song of Songs views all of life as a love song: "Every subatomic particle, from the Big Bang to the senility of the sun, is a note in life's incredibly complex symphony. Every event . . . is a theme in the surpassingly perfect melody of this song."[1]

---

1. Kreeft, *Three Philosophies*, 105.

The Song of Songs, symbolically interpreted, describes the ultimate purpose of life as the meeting (marriage) between ourselves and God. "This is the highest and holiest and happiest hope of the human heart, the thing we were all born hungering, hunting, longing. This is the last chapter of life's story, the point and purpose of it all.... The point of the real story of life is love. The whole Bible is a love story because God is love.... Thus Song of Songs is the definitive answer to the question of Ecclesiastes and to the quest of Job."[2]

In *Three Philosophies of Life*, Peter Kreeft examines twenty-six characteristics of love, human and divine, that Song of Songs implies. I select fourteen as thematic summary:

1. Love is a Song: God is love, and music is the language of love;

2. Love is the Greatest Song: the story of God's love for humanity;

3. Love is Dialogue: whereas theism exemplifies dialogue between the Creator and the creature, atheism signifies no dialogue and pantheism only divine monologue;

4. Love is Synergistic: in the Song, each participant responds with increased love for the beloved;

5. Love is Alive and Grows: the Song contains imagery of growing things, such as a garden (4:12, 16), a vineyard (7:12; 8:11–12), and a well of living water (4:15);

6. Love is Active: in the Song, both woman and man participate actively in love, each uniquely;

7. Suffering Goes with Love: love suffers because it exposes one's vulnerability (1:6; 2:5); in the Song, the maiden's suffering increases her love;

8. Love Moves Mountains: the beloved comes "leaping upon the mountains, bounding over the hills" (Song 2:8; cf. Matt. 17:20);

9. Love is a Surprise: note the Song's imagery of a gazelle, bounding and unpredictable (2:8–10);

10. Love is Self-Giving: those who love give themselves away, receiving the gift of the receiver in exchange (2:16; 7:10);

---

2. Ibid., 99–100.

11. Love is Natural: nature imagery is everywhere in love poetry because love is everywhere in nature (4:1–5); love is the theme of nature's song;

12. Love is Ready: "I slept, but my heart was awake" (5:2);

13. Love is Sexist: the mystics say that to God all souls are feminine—not female, but feminine. The groom symbolizes God; the bride symbolizes the soul. In mystical language, God impregnates the soul. It is God who creates new life in us, not we ourselves. God is the giver and the gift, we are the vessel;

14. Love Can Do Anything: love can fulfill Qoheleth's emptiness and Job's hope ("the greatest is love"; 1 Cor. 13:13).

Questions to Ponder

1. What, for you, is the theme or message of the Song of Songs?

2. What contribution does the Song of Songs make to our understanding of wisdom?

3. Should love poems containing graphic sexual imagery be in the Bible?

4. Compare the view of sexuality in the Song of Songs to attitudes prevalent in American popular culture. Which do you find most beneficial? Why?

5. If Song of Songs makes no explicit mention of God, why is this book in the Bible?

6. For allegory to succeed, the literal storyline should work well. Do you find that the storyline in the Song of Songs is internally consistent and tells a significant story?

7. What, according to the "medieval quadriga," are the four levels of interpreting scripture? Which best describes your approach to scripture? Explain your answer.

8. In essay 4, which of the characteristics of love do you find most intriguing? Why?

PART III

Wisdom in a Hellenistic World
QUESTS FOR IDENTITY

Chapter 5

The Book of Sirach (Ecclesiasticus)

Overview: The book of Sirach, also known as Ben Sira (or Ben Sirach) and in some Bibles as Ecclesiasticus, is the longest of the Jewish books of wisdom. Its perspective and style clearly resemble that of the book of Proverbs. It contains poetic essays collected in the early second-century BC (c. 180) by a sage who during his lifetime compiled a considerable body of wisdom teaching. He demonstrates mastery of the entire tradition, ranging from proper household management to the origin of evil, which he synthesizes persuasively. Avoiding the dissenting approaches and the paradoxical writing styles of Job and Qoheleth, Ben Sira weaves the old proverbial sayings into moral essays, fashioning new wineskins for older wine. Ultimately wisdom is identified with Torah. While the basic goal and prize of traditional wisdom is life, particularly long life well-lived, in Sirach the basic goal involves having and preserving an honorable name.

Assigned Reading: Read the prologue and then Sirach 1; 24; and 44–51.

Central Theme: Life's forward momentum requires a solid foundation.

Outline to Sirach
  I. Foreword (by Ben Sira's grandson)
  II. Part I 1:1—4:10
  III. Part II 4:11—6:17

IV. Part III 6:18—14:19

V. Part IV 14:20—23:27

VI. Part V 24:1—33:18

VII. Part VI 33:19—38:23

VIII. Part VII 38:24—43:33

IX. Part VIII 44:1—50:24

X. Conclusion 50:25—51:30

Contextual Analysis

Sirach goes by three different names, depending on the linguistic tradition. Written originally in Hebrew, as the grandson states in the foreword, the original title was "The Wisdom of Jesus son of Eleazar Ben Sira." The title Sirach derives from superscriptions to Greek manuscripts. The name Ecclesiasticus derives from the Vulgate (Latin) version and means "belonging to the church." This is the only wisdom book in the Bible that identifies its author (50:27), as well as the only biblical book that refers to the date of the translation, which occurred immediately following the death of the Egyptian (Ptolemaic) ruler Euergetes II.

The original Hebrew of the book was not maintained and became lost for centuries, though it was apparently known to Jerome (347–420), who used it in translating the Bible into Latin. Portions were recovered from the geniza of a Cairo synagogue between 1896 and 1900. Additional fragments have been recovered since, accounting for about 68 percent of the Hebrew text. The Hebrew text was unknown to Jews and Christians during the early church and medieval periods. The lack of a Hebrew version, coupled with disapproval by Pharisees of Ben Sira's theology (particularly his denial of life after death or of resurrection) and his support for a Temple-centered approach to Judaism (controlled by Sadducees and other members of the aristocratic priestly party), led to the book's exclusion from the Jewish canon. Nevertheless, Sirach was often quoted, even as sacred scripture, by later rabbis. The early church considered Sirach canonical, as evidenced by many citations by church fathers. The book was appended to some Greek and Latin manuscripts of the Bible, in part because the early church fathers made extensive use of Sirach to instruct converts and the faithful. Various books of the New Testament, particularly the Epistle of James, contain allusions to Sirach.

True to its church title, Ecclesiasticus played a double role in the early church: as a handbook of practical ethics and in lectionary readings. The book contains numerous essays on topics related to morality and decision-making, including choosing a mate, the family, friendship, education, poverty and wealth, the law, religious worship, and social customs.[1]

Ben Sira's grandson states in the foreword to his Greek translation that he arrived in Egypt in 132 BC. The grandson made the Greek translation in the following years and published it after the death of Euergetes in 117 BC. Going back two generations from 132 we arrive at a date close to 180 for the composition of the Hebrew original. In 50:1-21 we find praise for Simon II, high priest in Jerusalem from 219 to 196 BC. Ben Sira writes in such a way as to suggest that Simeon had been dead for some time. Because the book shows no signs of the policy of forcible Hellenization enacted by the Seleucid king Antiochus IV Epiphanes (175-164 BC), or of the social chaos that erupted during the Maccabean revolt in 167, scholars generally date Sirach in the period between 195 and 180 BC.

There is little doubt that the entire book was composed by one author. A native of Jerusalem, he devoted his life to the study of scripture and became a highly respected scribe and teacher, directing an academy for young Jewish men (51:23-30). In his extensive travels (34:12-13) he came in contact with other cultures and wisdom traditions and acquired "much cleverness" (34:11); and he did not hesitate to utilize his learning as long as he could make it conform to his Jewish heritage and tradition (39:1-11).

The book must be understood against the backdrop of Hellenism and the ongoing crisis Hellenism caused for the Jewish religion and for Jewish identity. Sirach did not intend to write a systematic polemic against Hellenism, but rather to demonstrate that the Jewish way of life was superior to the Greek way of life, thereby creating a buffer for Jews who might be attracted to compromise with or capitulate to the enticements of Hellenistic culture. Hence Sirach, with its essay-like instruction, "opens a window into a community struggling with its identity as it finds itself at the crossroads of traditional religion and contemporary culture.[2]

---

1. An inventory of topics appears in Clifford, *Wisdom Literature*, 118-20, and Murphy, *Tree of Life*, 73.

2. Bergant, "Reading Guide: Sirach," 279.

The book of Sirach, together with Daniel and Wisdom, provide alternate ways of responding to this challenge.

Ben Sira's approach, unlike Daniel's call for resistance or Wisdom's appeal for reinterpretation, is to honor the essential aspects of his heritage—Torah, Temple, and traditional beliefs and values—while honoring the universality of wisdom. A traditionalist more than a conservative, Ben Sira is an inventive thinker who employs old traditions in highly original ways. Rather than belittling Hellenism, he treats it with great respect, accepting some of its values, appreciating its devotion to learning and the questions it raises about life's meaning. But he does not support Hellenistic answers or conclusions, which he finds overly humanistic and individualistic. Traces of Stoicism, with its emphasis on the principle of rationality in the universe, have been found in Sirach, in his ideal of human dignity (41:14—42:8), of the unity of the world (43:27) and of the human race (36:1-4, 22). Echoes of Epicureanism, which believed a life of reason led to moderation, have also been detected in Sirach (14:11-16; 30:21-25; 31:27-29). However we assess Ben Sira, whether as conservative, traditionalist, or polemicist, he always returns to answers drawn from the Jewish scriptures. His grand poetic vision is grounded in the assertion that only in relationship with the God of Israel can one gain wisdom.

The struggle against Hellenism would reach crisis proportions in the next generation, as evidenced by such works as Daniel, 1 and 2 Maccabees, and a century later, by Wisdom of Solomon. Sirach's teachings reflect a calmer, less intense period. They demonstrate a readiness to borrow Greek expressions, ideas, and concerns, as long as they are subjected to thorough Hebraizing. Whatever approach he uses or whatever philosophical concepts, literary styles, or terminology he borrows—whether concepts such as free will (15:11, 14-17), genres such as the encomium (44:1—51:10), customs such as the symposium (31:12—32:24), or ideals from Stoicism, Epicureanism, or the larger Hellenistic environment—Ben Sira places these methodologies and ideals at the service of monotheism; God alone is their source (43:28). While many of the points and questions he raises have Hellenistic context, his answers and conclusions are rooted in traditional Jewish thought, particularly in the Jewish wisdom tradition. While his hearers may be partly attracted and impressed by Hellenism, Ben Sira's aim is to build bridges between their mindset and his more Torah-centric, Temple-centric stance.

Nevertheless, Ben Sira breaks with traditional Jewish wisdom in at least three significant ways: (1) his work is sprinkled with references and allusion to biblical persons and events (particularly chapters 44–50), unlike the authors of Proverbs, Job, and Ecclesiastes, who scrupulously avoid allusions to Israel's sacred history; (2) he is the first sage to identify wisdom with Torah (15:1; 19:20; 24:1–34, especially verse 23); and (3) in connecting wisdom with Torah, Ben Sira links wisdom with Temple worship, cultic requirements, and the service of the priests (35:1–13). In chapter 50, where Simon the high priest is praised for his leadership, Ben Sira placed great hopes on the priesthood. These hopes, however, would be dashed shortly thereafter when Jason, the son of Simeon, supported Antiochus IV Epiphanes's policy of forced Hellenization, having replaced his own brother, Onias III, as high priest, a prize he secured through bribes and promises to hasten Hellenization in Jerusalem. The high priesthood eventually went to Menelaus, who offered an even larger bribe to Antiochus. In 167, the Seleucid king went so far as to forbid Jewish festivals and sacrifices, including the practice of circumcision and observance of dietary laws. Ben Sira says nothing about these disturbing events, presumably because he died before they took place. In the future the hopes of Judaism would move from a Temple-centered religion to a Torah-centered religion.

Literary Analysis

Style

Sirach is a collection of proverbs, organized in a novel way to resemble short essays (Murphy calls them mini-treatises and Crenshaw dubs them "didactic essays") on a variety of topics. This collection and its themes resemble the wisdom poems in Proverbs 1–9. An obvious example is chapter 24, a personification of wisdom modeled on Proverbs 8. Sirach takes Proverbs' motto, "fear of the Lord," and develops this theme in a creative and expansive way in 1:11–30, as an acrostic poem of twenty-two lines based on the Hebrew alphabet (this approach was also used by the authors of Proverbs, as in 2:1–22 and 31:10–31). Sirach also imitates the ending of Proverbs with a closing acrostic poem (51:13–30).

Like Proverbs, Sirach's aphorisms, maxims, and clever statements have to do with practical daily existence. The subjects range widely, extending from inner feelings, like a sense of shame, to external behavior, such as slander, from religious acts of charity to conduct at banquets, from proper attitudes toward money to the disgrace of being reduced to begging. The teachings also take up existential issues such as sickness and death, wrestling with the ethical question of whether one should consult physicians, a profession perceived as interfering with divine punishment for sin. Like previous sages, Ben Sira takes no refuge in belief in the afterlife, a disbelief that allows divine justice—or more correctly its absence—to weigh heavily on him, as it did on the author of the book of Job. In Sirach, rarely does a proverb exist without interpretation. Like Proverbs, Sirach occasionally sets one saying against another to provide contrasting descriptions, as in the contrast of poverty and wealth (11:11–13; 13:3; 20:5–6).

In addition to proverbial material, Sirach also contains wisdom hymns (or poems with wisdom themes, as in 16:24—18:14; 39:12–35; 42:15—43:33; 51:1–11); a collection of beatitudes (25:7–10, which culminates with the proverbial "fear of the Lord"); petitionary prayers (22:27—23:6; 36:1–22); and an encomium, an "epic" poem in praise of ancestors (44:1—50:24).

Structure

Efforts to detect a structure in Sirach have been unsuccessful. Ben Sira seems to have had no clear plan for arranging his various subjects. Clifford lists sixty-three units, revolving around eight parts and a conclusion. While there is no explicit arrangement in the book, one can divide the material both thematically and according to literary form. Chapters 1–43 are primarily concerned with moral instruction, a characteristic that Sirach has in common with the rest of the wisdom literature. This segment can be subdivided into two sections, each introduced by a poem praising wisdom (1:1–29 introduces chapters 2–23 while 24:1–29 introduces chapters 25–43). The entire first section ends with a poem extolling God's activity in nature (42:15—43:35). The ensuing section (chapters 44–49) is an encomium, a poem honoring ancestors. As we have seen, 50:1–24 honors the high priest Simon II. The epilogue (50:25–29), a brief statement denouncing traditional enemies, is followed by two appendices, a psalm of thanksgiving (51:1–12) and a personal testimony in acrostic format (51:13–30).

The book appears to be a compilation of class notes accumulated by Ben Sira over many years of teaching. Some topics are discussed more than once, in different parts of the book. Given the repetitive nature of Hebraic instruction, this approach comes as no surprise. Scholars generally interpret chapter 51 as an addition or appendix to the work, though even this assessment lacks consensus. The first of several authorial self-references, 24:30–34 implies that Ben Sira understood his teaching as inspired utterances that began small but grew unexpectedly, like a canal expanding into a huge stream. His own learning, directed initially toward personal enjoyment ("I will water my garden and drench my flower-beds," 24:31), soon lost its private character and became available to everyone (24:34).

Textual Analysis

In deference to Sirach's length and to its circular rather than its linear approach, we will limit textual comments to three great wisdom poems, which serve as the book's infrastructure, supporting the beginning (chapter 1), the middle (chapter 24), and the end (chapter 51). Approaching Sirach through its presentation of Lady Wisdom, primarily in these core passages, means we will postpone the practical application of Sirach's message until the thematic segment of the chapter.

Chapter 1: This passage consists of two poems about wisdom: (a) wisdom's relation with God (1:1–10) and (b) wisdom's relation with humans (1:11–30). The latter poem, an acrostic, functions as a frame with the closing poem (51:13–30), also written acrostically. In the opening poem, wisdom alternates with God as the subject. The alternation of poetic subjects in this poem creates the impression of a mysterious intertwining of roles and relationships between the two figures. The role of wisdom in these verses is to provide humans a pathway to God. Three points become clear: (1) wisdom is a quality of God (1:1); (2) wisdom is the order within the world (1:2–3); and (3) wisdom is a divine gift (1:4–9). The logic of Hebrew thought is clear here, as one point builds upon the other. The world is theocentric, for reality is oriented toward the divine. Wisdom is the teacher, informing humans of their place in the universe. Humans are made for God's sake, not for their own, and in worship they discover their purpose. The purpose for human life is to revere God. That is the theme of the second poem, into which the opening poem blends.

To revere God, to "fear the Lord," is to be a worshiper of Yahweh. Worship is the outward expression of wisdom. For Sirach, wisdom and "fear of the Lord" are practically synonymous (1:14).

Ben Sira's point in the opening poem is that God alone knows and understands wisdom. While humans find wisdom remote and inaccessible, she is intimately related to God. Therefore, to acquire wisdom, humans must first befriend her Creator. In Sirach's metaphorical language, wisdom is the desirable one, but she can be pursued only through her intermediary, who is God. This is unexpected, for we would imagine the reverse. Consequently, if humans wish to acquire wisdom, they must first befriend God, who sends her to those connected to him.

The poem establishes a twofold claim about wisdom: (a) that the source of wisdom is the God of the Jews, and (b) that wisdom is not the sole possession of the Jews or of any isolated community. "She has a mission to all people, to everyone who loves God. In language rife with a history of accumulated meaning, Sirach asserts that every human yearning, every inclination of the mind and the spirit, every desire of the heart bound up in the notion of wisdom in Judaism and Hellenism, is realized in communion with this God."[3]

In Sirach's second poem (1:11–30), wisdom is not distant from humanity. Identified with the "fear of the Lord," wisdom is an expression of the human response to God. Wisdom and fear of God are intertwined as mysteriously and inextricably in this poem as are God and wisdom in the first poem. To the question, "How can I be wise?" Sirach's answer is: "Fear Yahweh!" The phrase "fear of the Lord" begins and ends the poem and is repeated twelve times, significant in that this is the number of the tribes of Israel as well as the months of the year. For Ben Sira, "fear of the Lord" is not simply the way to wisdom, it *is* wisdom. By equating wisdom and the fear of the Lord, the sage affirms that wisdom expresses humanity's free response to the transcendent God. Furthermore, by equating Lady Wisdom with the Fear of Yahweh, Ben Sira makes explicit what is implied about her in Proverbs. Wisdom mediates in two directions: she communicates with God on behalf of humans while communicating with humans on behalf of God. Therefore, from both divine and human perspectives, wisdom "not only enables relationship between the two; mysteriously, she is that relationship."[4]

---

3. O'Connor, *Wisdom Literature*, 139.
4. Ibid., 140–41.

In this poem, the mood is similar to that of Job 28, where wisdom is also identified with the Fear of Yahweh (28:28), though Sirach moves beyond Job. While wisdom is beyond reach, for Ben Sira wisdom is now accessible. Sirach's second poem takes the concept of the fear of the Lord and develops it in a series of powerful metaphors: fear of the Lord is the "beginning" (1:14), "fullness" (1:16), "crown" (1:18), and "root" (1:20) of wisdom. "Crown" and "root," as merisms (pairs that express totality), divide wisdom into two constituent parts. In sum, revering God is the fundamental attitude one needs in order to live wisely and thus enjoy life's benefits. The poem mentions attitudes characteristic of the wise person: self-control, correct speech, sincerity, and humility. Also mentioned are obstacles to wisdom: impatience and hypocrisy. In 1:26, a new and significant addition is made: "If you desire wisdom, keep the commandments." The connection of wisdom with Torah is developed more fully in chapter 24 (see 24:23).

Chapter 24: As Ben Sira began the first half of his book with poems on wisdom, he begins the second half with a poem, his most famous (24:1–29). Previously, the focus of Sirach was on the relation of wisdom to humans, but here wisdom is personified. The poem in chapter 24 is inspired by Lady Wisdom's in Proverbs 8. The correspondence is clear: both passages consist of the same number of lines (thirty-five), and Sirach 24:9 explicitly cites Proverbs 8:22. An additional reference to Proverbs appears in Sirach 24:19–21, Lady Wisdom's banquet (see Proverb 9:1–6). Like Proverbs 31, Sirach 24:3–22 form a twenty-two-verse alphabetic acrostic.

The setting for chapter 24 appears to be a liturgy celebrated in the Temple, as suggested by 24:2, which speaks of "the assembly of the Most High," and references in 24:10 to "the holy tent" and to "Zion." The poem, which tells the origin and history of wisdom, is structured in seven parts: (1) wisdom identifies herself (24:1–2) (2) wisdom's origin (24:3); (3) wisdom's search for rest and inheritance (24:4–7); (4) God's command to settle (24:8–9); (5) wisdom's settlement and subsequent growth (24:10–17); (6) wisdom's invitation to her banquet (24:18–21); and (7) wisdom's identification with Israel's Torah (24:22–29). The passage ends with the vocation of Ben Sira as disciple and as teacher of wisdom (24:30–34).

Three points deserve special mention. First, verse 3 is unique in mentioning that wisdom came forth from the mouth of the Most High. For Ben Sira, wisdom is a literary representation of the word of God; she is God's word (see Gen. 1:1; John 1:1). Second, wisdom is universal (24:6), although she is explicitly active in Israel's history and dwells in the Temple (24:8–12). Third, wisdom is identified with Torah (24:23), though not so fully that they do not have their distinct identities. This identification may have been influenced by Psalm 19, which links creation with Torah, and by Deuteronomy 4:6–9, where observance of Torah is seen to impart wisdom to the nations. It is clear that wisdom now includes far more than the wisdom of the sages, though Ben Sira cannot resist speaking of his book and his teaching as an ever-rising river, which, like prophecy, are extensions of Torah (24:30–34).[5]

Chapter 24 is the integrating center of the book, both physically and theologically, and in connecting wisdom with Torah, marks a major expansion of wisdom thinking. Here wisdom speaks directly to the audience for the first and only time in the book. In all her other appearances, Ben Sira speaks about her in the third person. She is born from God, not as a subordinate creature, but as God's Word. She is regarded as God's self-expression, as God's revelation. Her location is in the court of heaven, though this is not her permanent abode. She is like God in that she participates in the event of creation (24:3), yet she is also like Israel wandering in the wilderness looking for a promised land to inhabit, a place of rest (24:7). Her mission, we learn, is among the special people of Israel and her abode is in God's holy Temple in Jerusalem. To an age that sought wisdom in nature and in human experience, Sirach makes clear that wisdom is to be found in the Temple, through worship of the true God. There she takes root and flourishes. The language of 24:12–17 evokes the Garden of Eden, artistically depicted in the architecture and furniture of the Temple as well as in the mystical image of the "tree of life" (Gen. 2:9), echoed in the first psalm, noted for its Torah and wisdom imagery (Ps. 1:2–3). The language in 24:15 is also reminiscent of Exodus 30:22–23, which speaks of the place of anointing oil in Temple worship.

In imagery similar to Proverbs 9:1–5, wisdom invites everyone who desires her to come to her banquet (24:19–23). However (in language that anticipates the institution of the Eucharistic meal celebrated by Christians), Sirach describes a startling change in the menu: wisdom herself is the meal; *she* is food and drink (24:21). Like the Christian Eucharist, the more one eats and drinks, the more one seeks wisdom and the less one sins (24:21–22). This brings us to the culminating concept in the passage, Sirach's most radical and original innovation: the identification

---

5. By identifying wisdom with Torah, yet not precluding distinct identities, Ben Sira's imagery prefigures the Christian understanding of Jesus as Word and incarnation of God and yet as human and distinct from God.

of wisdom with Torah. To commune with wisdom is to study and obey Torah, that is, to become an observant Jew. Those who obey the Torah of Israel are said to live in union with Lady Wisdom, participating in her festive banquet. Sirach's emphasis has been described as "Torah piety," a way to pursue God that permeates Psalm 1, 19, and 119. This emphasis should not be construed as legalistic, but rather as a lifestyle in conformity with divine will: "Your word is a lamp to my feet and a light to my path" (Ps. 119:105).

Scholars note a paradox in chapter 24, one found throughout Sirach, that while wisdom is described as a cosmic entity wholly inaccessible to humans, yet human effort is required (24:22). The two aspects are brought together ingeniously by identifying the primordial wisdom with the Mosaic Torah. The identification of heavenly wisdom with a written document means that wisdom is now available to all who seek her. Elsewhere Ben Sira claims that those who master Torah will achieve wisdom as well (15:1). Emphasis on disciplined learning is also evident in 6:18-23 and 8:8-9. This focus on the sage's intellectual sphere differs from earlier assessment, where reflection on nature and human experience seemed to suffice.[6] For Ben Sira and other Jewish sages living in a Hellenistic environment, communion with God becomes possible through Torah. Life is secured through divine Torah, not through Hellenistic humanism. Like the fear of the Lord, obedience to Torah joins one to wisdom and brings one to God.

Chapter 51:13-30. In the final poem of Sirach's book, Lady Wisdom appears again, this time as the object of Sirach's attention. The poem is constructed as an autobiographical testimony of the author's quest for wisdom. While the poem's origins are disputed, it summarizes Ben Sira's instructions and inspires students to follow his example. Like the hymn to Lady Wisdom in Proverbs 31:10-31, this too is arranged acrostically.

In the confessional style of the poem, the author speaks as an older person reflecting on a lifetime relationship with wisdom. No matter how arduous the road, he never abandoned his pursuit of this woman: "My soul grappled with wisdom, and in my conduct I was strict" (51:19). According to the sage, the wooing of wisdom and union with her involves a tension between human dedication and divine gift. This paradox is also evident in the New Testament understanding of the Kingdom of God, which according to Luke's Gospel is both a task ("strive for [God's]

---

6. Crenshaw, *Old Testament Wisdom*, 155.

kingdom"; 12:31) and a gift ("it is your Father's good pleasure to give you the kingdom"; 12:32). With the gift of wisdom comes enlightenment, manifest in eloquent praise: "The Lord gave me my tongue as a reward, and I will praise him with it" (51:22).

For Ben Sira, the work of the scribe (one who studies Torah) is the most exalted of human occupations (39:1–11), likened to prophetic ministry (39:1; cf. 24:33). Based on his relationship with wisdom, Ben Sira now has the authority to invite others to seek her. Like the sages before him, he claims to be the model, able to guide others along the same path. Modeling himself after wisdom, he issues his own invitation, not to a banquet but to another source of nourishment, to a life of study and meditation (51:23–26). "Put your neck under her yoke," he declares (51:26), thereby indicating submission to the study of Torah. The author concludes by alluding to two themes he regularly associates with wisdom: Fear of the Lord (worship) and Torah (disciplined living): "Never be ashamed to praise [God]. Do your work in good time, and in his own time God will give you your reward" (51:30).

Thematic Analysis

As we have noted, Sirach is a vast collection of essays, ethical teachings, and reflections about dozens of topics related to wisdom and Judaism. Three themes, however, predominate—wisdom, Torah, and fear of the Lord—and the author brings them together in 19:20: "The whole of wisdom is fear of the Lord, and in all wisdom there is the fulfillment of the law." Often these ideas blend into one another so thoroughly that one can barely distinguish them. By so doing, Sirach examines wisdom from many perspectives, creating a new synthesis of wisdom thought.

1. The concept of *wisdom* is found frequently in Sirach, as shown by its presence in the key passages of the book. In addition, each of the eight parts of the book is prefaced by a poem on wisdom. Chapter 24, the central poem on wisdom, personifies wisdom and identifies her with the word of the Lord and hence with Torah (24:3, 23).

2. *Fear of the Lord*, which speaks of reverence for Yahweh, is related both to moral and to cultic life (worship). The concept, so all-encompassing, can practically be equated with organized religion and spirituality. Ben Sira highlights this virtue beyond others, to a point that many

interpreters see it as his dominant virtue. In the book, fear of the Lord is not, however, subordinate to wisdom, for the moral life begins and ends in fear of the Lord.

3. In Jewish practice, *Torah* has multiple applications. Ben Sira uses the term in two ways, (a) as a general reference to the commandments and (b) as a way of speaking of the entirety of revelation in the Bible.[7]

Other important topics and themes include prayer (Ben Sira speaks of prayer more than do other sages); the history of Israel (Ben Sira is the first to have created a bond between wisdom and Israel's historical traditions. This is manifest particularly in the list of Israel's heroes in chapters 44–50); and living in right relationships with others.

Wisdom, fear of the Lord, and Torah were relational terms in Israel. Sirach borrows much of his teaching on human relations from Proverbs. One's respect for the dignity of others, he advises, should extend to even the most ordinary courtesies (21:22–24), including table manners (31:12—32:2). Because of his appreciation of the bonds among all people, Ben Sirach underscores responsibility to the poor and afflicted in society. The Hellenist culture of his time neglected social responsibility, placing economic gain at or near the top of personal values. Help the poor, he urges in 29:10. Such behavior not only benefits the poor, it also enables one to live according to Torah, and to practice Torah is to live in the presence of God. However, Sirach demands more than charity; one should become actively engaged with the sufferings of others (4:8–10). With uncompromising insistence Ben Sira teaches that those with resources have obligations for those in need (4:1–6). In a similar vein, Ben Sira also departs from proverbial wisdom in his attitude toward wealth. While maintaining that wealth can be a relative good, wealth is not the great good we find in Proverbs (29:33). Be content with the basics in life, Sirach urges (29:23).

Nevertheless, Ben Sira does not exclude regard for oneself from the network of relationships toward which one is responsible. In the spirit of the Great Commandment (Lev. 19:18; Deut. 6:5; cf. Matt. 22:37–40), he admonishes true self-love to be the basis for loving others and for praising God (37:13). The subject of friendship, described as a gift of God (6:14–17), ranks high in Sirach's list of priorities, to the extent that the quality of friendship with others is said to express the quality of one's friendship with God (6:16–17). Perhaps this is because human friendship,

---

7. This topic is discussed further in essay 8, "Wisdom and Torah."

like friendship with God, requires honesty with oneself and others. But Ben Sira is a realist, urging discernment in choosing friends (6:6–12).

In the end, Ben Sira desires for his readers what Hellenists desired, to reach full humanity and achieve individual potential. They differed, however, on the means to that end. Whereas Hellenists were humanists who emphasized human effort, Ben Sira argues that wisdom (his *summum bonum*), which results from communion with God, is attained through proper worship (fear of the Lord) and disciplined living (Torah).

Essay 5: Scripture as Canonical and Deuterocanonical

A strong connection exists between "scripture" and "tradition," terms of special significance for scholars and others who think historically. It is helpful to start with a definition of scripture. By scripture we mean a book or a collection of books preserved by religious communities as authoritative sources of teaching or worship. The main point to remember about scriptures is that they are historical objects crafted in human cultures. The texts are preserved by human memory and recorded in human languages, even if they are believed to have come to humans by revelation. Scriptures enjoy special prestige as "holy" or "sacred" texts only because human communities have at some point agreed to treat them in certain ways. Any text regarded as scripture came to be so because a community, formally or informally, so decided. The process that led to authoritative designation is called "canonical," meaning "rule of authority." This decision to accept a text as canonical is often a source of conflict, as different segments of a larger community might dispute whether a particular writing is truly authoritative for all members. Thus it often happens that a text considered as scripture in one community is simply a book in another.

The decision to regard a text as scripture often brings into play the term "tradition." Most simply, tradition means "that which has been handed down from the past." Tradition sustains a book in the life of a religious community long enough for it to acquire the status of scripture. Relatively few examples of writings penned by a known author have attained scriptural authority in that person's own lifetime. Once a traditional literary work becomes scripture, it is usually preserved in a fixed text not to be modified or emended. Scripture and tradition, to summarize, are intertwined realities. Scripture is the collective term for literary traditions that enjoy the veneration of a specific community. A "canon," or closed collection of scripture, is thereby a tradition, passed on as a unique and unchangeable record of communal memory, belief, and discipline.

During the period between 200 BC and AD 100, various types of religious literature not found in the Jewish canon or in the New Testament emerged. Collectively, these works are sometimes labeled Intertestamental Literature because, for the most part, they came into existence between the times in which the Old and New Testaments were written. The expression "Old Testament," widely used for the Hebrew Bible, is a Christian designation. For the Jewish community, there is only one "Testament" or "Covenant," namely, the Hebrew Bible. Today the Jewish people refer to their scriptures as Tanakh, an acronym made up of the initial consonants of the three major divisions of the Hebrew Bible: Torah (Law), Nebiim (Prophets), and Ketubim (Writings). In this essay we will examine the Jewish Intertestamental Literature and note some of the ways in which deuterocanonical wisdom books reflect the literature of the Tanakh and foreshadow the New Testament.

The Hebrew Bible is fundamentally the same as the Christian Old Testament, although the arrangement differs. To understand the Hebrew Bible, we can imagine three concentric circles: "The inner circle, the Torah, presents the basic story of the people and includes laws to guide them in living. The next circle, the Prophets, is a critical commentary on the life of the people to whom the Torah is given. The outer circle, the Writings, is a diverse and open-ended collection that broadens out from Israel's worship and festal celebration to wisdom reflection."[8] While the Christian Old Testament begins with the five books of Torah, it then departs from the Hebrew Bible in order and, in certain cases, in content. These differences are largely accounted for by the fact that many early Christians were Greek-speaking, meaning that they read or heard the Hebrew Bible read in Greek, particularly in the translation called the Septuagint, begun in the third century BC in Alexandria Egypt. This translation places the prophetic writings last, while the Hebrew Bible concludes with the Writings (ending with 1 and 2 Chronicles). Moreover, the Septuagint includes works not part of the Hebrew Bible, though these works were originally highly regarded in Jewish circles, for they were written by Jews for Hellenized Jewish audiences.

---

8. Anderson, *Old Testament*, 3.

The use of the Septuagint in Christian worship led to disagreement over the number of books in the Christian Old Testament. The translators of the Septuagint added books such as Sirach (Ecclesiasticus), the book of Wisdom (Wisdom of Solomon), First and Second Esdras, First and Second Maccabees, Tobit, Judith, Baruch, Susannah, and several additions to existing biblical books. These made their way into most Greek and Latin copies of the Christian Old Testament but not into the Hebrew canon, meaning that they came to be considered scripture by Eastern Orthodox Christians and Roman Catholics but not by Jews, although there is evidence that these books were regarded as canonical by numerous Hellenistic Jewish communities during the late Intertestamental period and beyond, even though they were not part of the official Hebrew canon. During the Reformation, Protestants followed the Hebrew canon, restricting their Old Testament canon to the Tanakh.

Protestants relegated the extra books in the Septuagint to the "Apocrypha" (a name meaning "hidden" or "secret writings"), with an explanatory note that they deserve to be read but are not equal to other scriptures. In the sixteenth century the designation "deuterocanonical" was adopted to reaffirm that though not part of the "first canon" (the Tanakh), these writings should be regarded as having authority. In Catholic usage protocanonical refers to the books whose place in the canon was never challenged, and deuterocanonical refers to those recognized only after a period of debate (although individuals familiar with the history of the canonical process in Judaism as well as in Christianity are aware that many if not most of the protocanonical books, both in the Old and New Testaments, also were challenged at some point). Scholars now prefer "deuterocanonical" as more descriptive and neutral than "Apocrypha," a pejorative term. Despite the problem of fixing the outer boundary of the Old Testament, one should not overestimate these differences. It is clear that Jews, Orthodox Christians, Protestants, and Catholics share substantially the same body of sacred literature.

The preface to Sirach, written by Ben Sira's grandson and dated 117 BC, refers to the Law, the Prophets, and "the other books that followed them," suggesting that in his day the first two divisions of the Hebrew Bible existed as distinct entities and that a third group was acknowledged, though not yet fixed. Ben Sira's praise of ancestral heroes (Sir. 44–50) supports this evidence; he knows the chief characters in Genesis through Deuteronomy and mentions Isaiah, Jeremiah, Ezekiel, and the Twelve, as well as prominent persons from historical writings such as

Joshua, Judges, Samuel, and Kings. Among the Writings he mentions the books of Job and Nehemiah, but he was probably familiar with Psalms and other books as well.

Sirach and the book of Wisdom, like Proverbs, Job, and Ecclesiastes in the Tanakh, are examples of wisdom literature. Sirach, like Ecclesiastes, is an old sage's collected wisdom, its style and view of life similar to those found in Proverbs. Its famous catalogue of heroes may have inspired a similar passage in the New Testament book of Hebrews (11:1—12:2). The author of the Epistle of James appears to have been influenced by Sirach as well. The book of Wisdom is written to demonstrate the superiority of the ethical and religious wisdom of the Tanakh to the wisdom of the Greeks. In fact, the work is a creative synthesis of ideas drawn from canonical wisdom writings and Greek concepts such as immortality of the soul. Although there are in the New Testament no direct citations of the book of Wisdom, the theme of a personified, preexistent wisdom may have been part of the background for the imagery of the preexistent Logos in the prologue to the Gospel of John. In addition, the imagery of the "whole armor" of God (Wis. 5:17–20) appears in Romans 13:12; 2 Corinthians 6:7; and Ephesians 6:14–17.

During the Intertestamental period additional Jewish religious writings were recorded, though not regarded as canonical by Jews or Christians today. Scholars collect and publish some of these under the title Pseudepigrapha because, as the name suggests, many are falsely attributed to famous persons such as Enoch, Noah, Moses, or Isaiah, who did not actually write them. Another set of writings, called the Dead Sea Scrolls, were found during the 1940s and 1950s in caves on the western shore of the Dead Sea. These scrolls include canonical and deuterocanonical works as well as additional non-canonical sectarian writings from this period. The scrolls were most likely the library of an Essene community that awaited the final battle between "the sons of light" (the Essenes) and "the sons of darkness," the latter an appellation for remaining humanity, including Jews whom they considered apostate because they did not support the Essene cause. The influence of these sectarian scrolls on Christianity and the New Testament is a source of ongoing scholarly inquiry.

Throughout most of this period traditions of Pharisaic Judaism circulated orally and were first published in written form around AD 200, resulting in the Mishnah and later in the Talmud, the great depository of rabbinic lore. Rabbinic traditions came to be divided into two categories of authority, *halakah* ("the way") and *haggadah* ("narration"). *Halakah* lays down obligatory principles on how people should order their lives and *haggadah* is edifying lore. A number of literary forms found in rabbinic literature were utilized by New Testament authors, including the parables of Jesus, similar in style to rabbinic parables. Paul, himself a rabbi, frequently draws on rabbinic literary forms and devices in his letters. His retelling of the story of Abraham in Romans 4 is an example of *haggadic* biblical interpretation.

Questions to Ponder

1. What, for you, is the theme or message of the book of Sirach?
2. What contribution does Sirach make to your understanding of wisdom?
3. What correlation do you find between wisdom and "fear of the Lord"? How are they similar and how dissimilar?
4. According to Sirach, where is wisdom to be found? Compare this perspective with the portrayal of wisdom in the book of Proverbs and in Job 28.
5. In what significant ways did Sirach break with traditional Jewish wisdom?
6. Should Sirach be in the Jewish canon? Explain your answer.
7. Should Sirach be in the Christian canon? Explain your answer.
8. Name three themes or distinctive points of emphasis found in Sirach 24.
9. Read Hebrews 11:1–40 in the New Testament and compare it with Sirach's catalogue of heroes (44:1—50:24). Could the author of the letter to the Hebrews have been influenced by this passage from Sirach? Support your answer.

CHAPTER 6

The Book of Daniel

Overview: The book of Daniel presents to readers a number of difficulties that render it a challenging yet fascinating text. Although placed among the Prophets in Christian Bibles, its inclusion among the Writings in the Hebrew canon indicates that Daniel was recognized as a different type of literature, completed after the prophetic canon was closed. In Daniel we find an approach to wisdom that uses story and narrative, but the specific wisdom element comes through dreams and visions. The book can be divided into equal halves of different genres and origins. The first half is a collection of stories about a Jew named Daniel and his companions, courtiers taken into exile to Babylon. These tales are instructive, modeling exemplary behavior in situations of crisis. The second half is a collection of four apocalyptic visions, with interpretations by angels, received and recorded by Daniel. The visions are graphic symbols of the unfolding of history from the time of Daniel until the end, when an everlasting kingdom will be established. The background of the events described in these visions is the second century BC, when the Seleucid king Antiochus IV Epiphanes attempted to proscribe Judaism through a policy of forced Hellenization. The book sets forth the theology of the Maccabean revolt.

Assigned Reading: Read Daniel 1–12

Central Theme: God's protective presence surrounds those who remain faithful under duress.

Outline to Daniel

    I. The Court Tales 1:1—6:28

    II. The Four Youth at the Babylonian Court 1:1–21

    III. Nebuchadnezzar's Dream 2:1–49

    IV. The Fiery Furnace 3:1–30

    V. Nebuchadnezzar's Second Dream and Subsequent Madness 4:1–37

    VI. Belshazzar's Feast 5:1–31

    VII. Daniel in the Lion's Den 6:1–28

    VIII. The Apocalyptic Visions 7:1—12:13

    IX. First Vision: The Four Beasts and the Son of Man 7:1–28

    X. Second Vision: The Ram and the Goat 8:1–27

    XI. Daniel's Prayer and the Third Vision: The Seventy Weeks 9:1–27

    XII. Fourth Vision: A Visionary Review of History and the End of Time 10:1—12:13

Contextual Analysis

Christian Bibles place Daniel after Ezekiel and before Hosea, the first of the twelve Minor Prophets, suggesting to Christian readers that Daniel should be considered a prophet and his book a prophecy. Jewish Bibles place the book among the Writings, together with the other books of wisdom literature. In this chapter we will follow the Jewish perspective, treating the book of Daniel in historical context.

    The Bible considers Daniel as primarily a sage, a view supported by the book of Daniel's first six chapters, which clearly have their roots in Israel's wisdom tradition. In this section, Daniel and his three Jewish companions are depicted as wise men, dream interpreters, and ideal courtiers who remain faithful to Yahweh while finding success in the courts of Babylon and Persia (see 1:17). As a sage, Daniel is given the ability to interpret dreams, and, though he is not a prophet by vocation, like prophets he receives divinely inspired visions. A connection between wisdom and prophecy is found in Job 33:14–18, where Elihu tells Job that God speaks to humans through visions and dreams. This point is corroborated in the book of Genesis, where Joseph is both recipient of inspired dreams (37:1–11) and interpreter of dreams (40:1—41:36). Other passages of the Bible, however, warn Israel against false prophecies, particularly based on dreams (Deut. 13:1-5; Jer. 23:1-40; 27:9-18; 29:21-32; cf. Sirach 34:6). The first half of Daniel clearly has an apologetic bent. The book's foreign setting and Daniel's faithfulness to Yahweh show the superiority of Israel's wisdom to that of the surrounding nations, while emphasizing God's providential care for Israel in times of duress.

Authorship and Setting

Daniel is one of the few books in the Hebrew Bible that can be reliably dated. The book is said to set forth the theology of the Maccabean revolution and to represent the manifesto of the Hasidim. The book's final form, especially the second half, can be dated to the period 167-164, when the Seleucid tyrant Antiochus IV Epiphanes ruled the Jewish homeland. While the author of the book of Daniel remains unknown, he belonged to the resistance movement called the Hasidim ("faithful ones"), a group of nonconformists who resisted the Seleucid policy of Hellenization, a coercive policy that forced Jews to compromise or abandon key distinctives such as monotheism, the Sabbath, circumcision, purity codes, kosher food laws, and the sacrificial system.

The book of Daniel consists of two evenly divided halves. The first six chapters contain six accounts of Jewish heroes exiled to the Babylonian court in the sixth century BC. The function of these chapters is to provide role models for members of the Hasidim. The last six chapters of the book contain four of Daniel's visions, functioning to provide assurance to the Hasidim that the future is in God's hands and that all will end well for God's faithful remnant.

The two halves of the book appear to have originated separately. Chapters 1-6 probably circulated orally during Israel's Restoration Period (500-200 BC), being attached to chapters 7-12 around 164 BC, the final year of the Maccabean Revolt. Chapters 7-12 would have been written then and were never oral. Evidence for this dating is extensive, particularly since the final vision concerning the death of Antiochus is misleading and stops short of the rededication of the Temple in 164 BC.

Like the book of Ezra, part of Daniel is written in Hebrew and part in Aramaic. Beginning in Hebrew, the book shifts to Aramaic in the middle of a conversation between the Babylonian king Nebuchadnezzar and his dream interpreters (2:4b) and continues to the end of chapter 7; then from chapter 8 to the end of the book the language reverts to Hebrew. The most common explanation is that Daniel was originally written in Aramaic, the international language of the ancient Near East beginning with the Persian period in the sixth century BC and extending to the Roman Period in the Common Era. Portions of the book, particularly the introduction and most of the second half, were translated into Hebrew to make the book more acceptable to devout Jews. The linguistic peculiarities, particularly the incongruity between the Aramaic sections and the two-part structure of the book, point to the book as drawn from different sources, some of which may have been preserved in Aramaic.

The traditional view of authorship, which dates the entire book to the sixth century (c. 530 BC), considers the second half of the book as predictive prophecy and therefore as written by Daniel himself from Babylon. This view is now considered to be flawed, for it cannot be supported textually or historically. The primary problem is that when the author talks about the sixth century (presumably his own time period), his information is vague and inaccurate. When he talks about the second century BC, especially about the events in Judah from 167–164, the evidence is detailed and generally precise.

In placing the narrative at the time of the Babylonian Exile (597–539 BC), the author makes historical blunders. The book begins with the glaring historical error that Nebuchadnezzar besieged Jerusalem in the third year of King Jehoiakim (606 BC). That event occurred in the first year of his son Jehoiachin (597 BC), who was borne away to captivity (see 2 Kgs. 24). The author did not correctly understand the history of the Persian empire, as shown by his confusion about the sequence of kings (see Dan. 5:11, 31; 9:1) and by the telescoping of historical periods (11:2). The author imagines that Belshazzar was the son of Nebuchadnezzar (5:11), though he was the son of Nabonidus, who was not related by lineage to Nebuchadnezzar. This means that the author was ignorant of the lineage of a ruler in whose court he is said to be chief magician. The author claims that Belshazzar was slain by Darius the Mede (5:30), but it was Cyrus the Persian who conquered Babylon in 539; Darius succeeded Cyrus's son Cambyses in 521. Paradoxically, though the author is intimately acquainted with the career of Antiochus Epiphanes, he is incorrect about the details of Antiochus's death (11:45). Antiochus does not die, as Daniel says, between Jerusalem and the Mediterranean Sea, but in Persia in 164. And the eschatological end does not arrive with the death of Antiochus, as Daniel imagined (11:40).

The reason for these blunders is clear: the author lived and wrote in the final years of the reign of Antiochus, who died shortly after the book was written. In addition, the author was a sage, not a prophet, for it is evident that he was unable to predict the future. Despite these blunders, the book of Daniel was accepted into the Hebrew canon because of its emphasis on the resurrection of the dead (see 12:1–2) and because its apocalyptic language and imagery were capable of reinterpretation, as evidenced by later Jewish and Christian writings, who interpret Daniel's fourth beast as Rome rather than Seleucia (cf. 2 Esd. 3–14; Mark 13; and the book of Revelation).

Literary Analysis

Genre

The book of Daniel belongs to a literary genre called apocalyptic, a type of literature written during times of persecution or distress. Such writings revolve around two mysteries, two basic problems faced by people everywhere, secular and religious alike: the problem of evil and the nature of hope. Apocalyptic authors are concerned with cosmic justice, seen as an extension of the doctrine of retribution, which promises punishment for enemies and reward for the faithful. The authors of apocalypses believe they are living in the end time, so their writings focus on the end of history, viewed generally as a Golden Age resulting from divine action. Because apocalypses present heightened views of evil, divine intervention is necessary; only God can defeat evil, and only a remnant is perceived as faithful. Apocalyptic literature is written from an insider perspective, by authors who convey their divinely revealed message in code, utilizing numbers and images in highly symbolic ways. As insiders, the members of the target audience know not to interpret the symbolism literally.

The prophetic writings, with their themes of evil and hope, were composed between the eighth and the fifth centuries BC. The apocalyptic tradition emerged in Jewish circles during the centuries that followed. For two centuries before and after Christ, the Mediterranean world witnessed a time of apocalyptic fervor, during which time there appeared a considerable number of Jewish and Christian apocalypses. Though Jewish apocalyptic literature is said to begin with the book of Daniel, apocalyptic tendencies can be seen earlier, in passages such as Isaiah 24–27, Ezekiel 38–39, and Zechariah 9–14, where there are frequent references to the approaching "Day of the Lord." Important Jewish apocalyptic writings outside the Old Testament include the book of Enoch, the Apocalypse of Baruch, the Fourth Book of Ezra, the Ascension of Isaiah, the Apocalypse of Zephaniah, and parts of the Sibylline Oracles. The first-century Jewish community that wrote the Dead Sea Scrolls also wrote and preserved apocalypses.

One feature in particular distinguishes the apocalyptic tradition from the older prophetic tradition: a sharp dualistic contrast between the powers of good and of evil, between those who side with goodness and those who side with wickedness. Apocalyptic thinking divides history into two ages, the present, in which evil is operative, and the coming age, when goodness will prevail. According to the apocalyptic mindset, evil is so great that humans cannot eliminate it; only God can do so. Divine intervention (often called the "Day of the Lord"), said to be imminent, will result in the judgment of the world, including the vindication of the righteous and the setting right of all things. While the prophetic tradition spoke of good and evil largely in human terms, the apocalyptic tradition tended to view evil cosmically, as a demonic force operative in the world.

Modern people tend to view evil psychologically, as forces within themselves, or sociologically, as destructive patterns that can influence entire groups. But for those who view the world apocalyptically, evil is cosmic, and humans cannot remain neutral; one sides with either good or evil. According to this perspective, evil cannot be defeated gradually or progressively in history but only in the future and only by God. During the apocalyptic period, the classic scenario expected God to act decisively to end present evil by defeating its powers, thereby inaugurating a new era, accompanied by the resurrection of the dead. The emergence of many Jewish sects during this period, including Christianity, is directly attributable to the apocalyptic mindset.

Structure and Exegesis

As we have seen, the book of Daniel contains two evenly divided halves: the public and the private history. Chapters 1–6 tell how Daniel and his friends were brought to Babylon and trained for royal service. Their attitude and behavior serve as models of heroic virtue. Chapters 7–12 consist of four visions that Daniel receives about God's plan for history and for Israel.

The Aramaic section (chapters 2–7) contains three corresponding themes: (a) chapters 2 (Nebuchadnezzar's dream) and 7 (Daniel's first vision) are related, as are (b) chapters 3 (the three companions in the fiery furnace) and 6 (Daniel in the lion's den), and (c) chapters 4 (the humiliation and breakdown of Nebuchadnezzar) and 5 (the humiliation and stripping of power from Belshazzar, seen as Nebuchadnezzar's son). The middle chapters function as the hidden core of the passage, disclosing the author's central message that God will be present with Israel, protecting and caring for Jews in their war against Seleucid oppression.

Daniel 2 tells of Nebuchadnezzar's troubling dream, which his interpreters were unable to decipher. Daniel receives a revelation, which enables him to disclose the dream and its meaning. The dream was of a statue made of four different materials, a head of gold, torso and arms of silver, abdomen and thighs of bronze, and legs of iron with feet of iron and clay. A stone that smashed the statue was transformed into a great mountain. The four materials, Daniel explains, are four kingdoms, each weaker than the previous. The stone is a new Kingdom established by God and therefore one that will endure forever.

Daniel 7 is a vision of four beasts, described as four successive empires: the Babylonian (a lion with eagle's wings), the Median (a bear with three ribs in its mouth), the Persian (a leopard with four wings and four heads), and the Hellenistic or Seleucid empire (the ten horns refer to Seleucid kings and the little horn "speaking arrogantly" is Antiochus Epiphanes). The "Ancient One," presiding over the heavenly council at the last judgment, sentences the fourth kingdom to destruction; the other three, whose rule had not been so evil, are deprived of their dominion and permitted to survive for a time (7:9–12). Then, with the clouds of heaven, in contrast to the beasts' origin from the depths of the "great sea" (that is, the watery chaos, the mythical source of powers hostile to God's creation; cf. Rev. 13:1; 21:1), comes "one like a human being" (7:13), that is, a figure that is human but clearly more than human.[1] The angel interprets this heavenly figure to symbolize Israel ("the holy ones of the Most High"; 7:25, 27).[2] Instead of a temporal kingdom, they will receive an

---

1. This designation, commonly titled "Son of Man," figures prominently in the New Testament (see Mark 8:38; 13:26). There the figure is understood as a reference to Jesus in his saving role or in his eschatological role as coming Judge.

2. This figure can also be identified as the angel Michael, who elsewhere in the book of Daniel is a leader, together with Gabriel, of divine forces against Persia and Greece, and who is also the protector of the Jewish people.

everlasting and universal dominion that is inaugurated after "a time, two times, and half a time" (7:25; see 12:7; cf. Rev. 12:14) of the little horn, a cryptic reference to the three and a half years when Antiochus Epiphanes persecuted the Jews (167–164 BC).[3]

Chapter 7 is the book's foremost chapter, the fulcrum on which the rest pivots. Notice the change at this point from the third-person narration of external history (chapters 1–6) to the first-person account of Daniel's inner life as visionary. In this chapter the faithfulness of the heroes of the book's first half is connected with the destiny of the faithful saints in God's coming Kingdom on earth, elevated to eternal reward. At this point particularly, readers must keep the temporal focus in mind; the author and the original audience (the Hasidim) are not concerned with the distant future, but rather with events facing them in the present.

The same theme is developed in the second vision (8:1–27), interpreted by Gabriel, patron angel of the Jewish people (compare Michael in Dan. 12:1). A ram with two horns (understood as the Medes and the Persians)[4] charges to the west, north, and south. He holds undisputed sway until a male goat comes from the west with a single horn (the Greek empire, ruled by Alexander the Great). Ultimately, the goat's horn is broken (the death of Alexander) and four horns emerge (the partition of Alexander's empire into four kingdoms). From one of these horns (the Seleucid kingdom) comes another, a little one (Antiochus Epiphanes), whose power extends southward and eastward, particularly over Judah, the Jewish homeland. In his pride, this horn exalts himself against God by plundering and desecrating the Temple in Jerusalem, casting truth to the ground and interrupting daily sacrifice. The expression "the transgression that makes desolate" (8:13; cf. 9:27; 11:31; 12:11) is a reference to the profanation of the Temple by the erection of an altar to Zeus on the altar of burnt offering. A celestial voice announces that the daily sacrifice will resume after 2,300 evenings and mornings, almost as long as the length of time in 7:25 and 12:7, namely three and a half years, which corresponds roughly to the period of the desecration of the sanctuary (see 1 Macc. 1:54—4:52). Of course, the hoped-for end of evil in history

---

3. This phrase represents a word of assurance that "in a short time" the kingdom will be taken from the tyrant Antiochus and given to the saints (either the Hasidim specifically or righteous Jews) to rule forever.

4. The author mistakenly understands the Medes to follow the Babylonians and to rule jointly or simultaneously with the Persians.

did not occur, but shortly thereafter the Jews began a period of home rule that lasted until 63 BC.

Chapter 9 combines Daniel's prayer for the Jewish people with a reinterpretation of Jeremiah's prophecy of a seventy-year exile (9:2; Jer. 25:11–12; 29:10). The author wishes to reassure Jews that their religious persecution by Antiochus Epiphanes will soon end. A historical problem arises in 9:1 (see also 5:31), since Darius the Mede is not a historical figure. The reference here is to Cyrus the Great of Persia, and Darius is simply modeled after Cyrus. As Daniel is pondering Jeremiah's prophecy that seventy years must pass before the end of the desolation of Jerusalem, he prays to God for light on this mystery. While Daniel is praying, the angel Gabriel comes to interpret the seventy years (9:20–27). In the prophecy of Jeremiah, seventy apparently referred to the full span of a human life, but here Gabriel provides a mysterious timetable, referring to "seventy weeks of years" (lit. "seventy sevens"). According to Daniel, as Jeremiah's period of "seventy years" ended with Cyrus, a messianic figure ("an anointed prince"; 7:25), so his period of seventy weeks of years will end with the coming of a messiah ("an anointed one"; 7:26).[5] The cryptic timetable presented in Daniel 9:24–27 has fascinated scholars and lay persons alike. Its decipherment need not now concern us, except to say that Daniel imagined that the end of this period of seventy weeks of years would culminate in the death of Antiochus, the end of Seleucid persecution, and the vindication of the Hasidim and all Jews who remained faithful to God in times of persecution and cultural compromise.

The author's backward glance from the Maccabean period explains why historical knowledge about the period before the rise of Alexander the Great is blurred, and why historical information becomes more exact as one approaches the time of writing. An example is the final vision (Dan. 10–12), which repeats the history from Cyrus to the defeat of Antiochus, viewing history as a great drama of good versus evil played out according to a heavenly script (the divine book of destiny; 10:21). Though the vision is dated in the third year of Cyrus of Persia (10:1), the author sketches the Persian period in just one verse (11:2), enough space, however, to make a major historical blunder, for ten Persian kings (not the stated three) succeeded Cyrus. The author knows of Alexander's triumph over Persia

---

5. Christians find here a prediction of Jesus, and some dispensational Christians understand Daniel's last week of years as a reference to the Great Tribulation, the seven-year period yet ahead, during which time the antichrist will rule on earth. Of course, none of this is envisioned by the author of Daniel.

(11:3) and that the lack of an heir meant his empire was divided (11:4). From this point on, the author's historical memory improves, providing a surprisingly detailed account of the immediate Seleucid predecessors of Antiochus Epiphanes, including during the period of the Ptolemies (11:5–9) and the reign of Antiochus III (11:10–19), concluding with the reign of Antiochus IV (11:20–35) and a portrait of the tyrant (11:36–39).

Although Daniel's historical summary is cast in the form of a vision of coming events, written down in God's "book of truth" (10:21), very little is prediction. Rather, the material is postdictive, that is, written after the events had occurred. The only event of pure prediction is the prophecy concerning the death of Antiochus IV (11:40–45), an event that had not yet transpired in the author's time. As it turned out, in his one prediction, the author was wrong. We can assume that he was living between 11:39 and 40, and that the Temple was cleansed shortly thereafter, in 164.

The book ends strangely. To the questions, "How long shall it be until the end of these wonders?" (12:6) and "What shall be the outcome of these things?" (12:8), the traditional enigmatic answers are given: the time of the end is imminent, and the outcome is to remain "sealed until the time of the end" (12:9). Verses 11 and 12 appear to be glosses, either by the author or a later editor. These verses lengthen the time before the culmination to 1290 days and 1335 days respectively, perhaps as anxious adjustments when the expected end didn't materialize.

Thematic Analysis

Central to the book of Daniel are two themes, one traditional and the other novel: God's providential role in history, and hope for the resurrection of the dead.

God's Providential Role in History

The most important point of contact between apocalyptic literature and the wisdom tradition is the idea of predetermined cosmic order. As you will recall, it was the concept of a cyclical pattern inaccessible to human understanding that led to Qoheleth's musing on the vanity of human effort. Apocalypse translates this ordered pattern into God's providential plan for history. The book of Daniel tells the story of the past so that persecuted Jews can see their sufferings in the perspective of God's historical purpose. The author insists that none of these events happened by accident. Even the tyranny of Antiochus is part of God's preordained plan: "He shall prosper until the time of wrath is completed, for what is determined shall be done" (11:36). This emphasis on God's absolute sway in human affairs is "not intended to encourage complacency, any more than the Marxist vision of the inevitable movement of history toward the classless utopia is meant to discourage revolutionary activity. On the contrary, the confidence that history moves inevitably and by prearranged plan toward the Kingdom of God fired the zeal of a small band of Jews, enabling them to act and hope when everything seemed against them" (11:32).[6]

Hope for the Resurrection of the Dead[7]

The apocalyptist's preoccupation with ultimate matters did not stop with history. Affirming that God's power could not be limited even by the existence of death, apocalyptic eschatology was personal as well as cosmic and historical. Humans came to be seen as citizens of an extra-terrestrial dimension. Chapter 12 of Daniel marks the first place in the Bible to refer unambiguously to the resurrection of the dead ("some to everlasting life, and some to shame and everlasting contempt," 12:2), together with the rewards and punishments that await in the life to come. Other biblical texts may be seen to anticipate this belief, including Isaiah 26:19 and 66:24, both apparently related to Ezekiel's symbolic vision of the return of God's people from exilic death in Babylon (Ezek. 37:1–14). Passages in the Psalms, such as in 17:15 and 73:24–26, are vague, with references in 49:8–9 and 15 negated by surrounding verses.

Biblical scholars are adamant that there is no sense of heaven in the Hebrew Bible; hence no description of the afterlife. Indeed, prior to the Maccabean period, counterevidence to bodily resurrection is overwhelming. When speaking of death, the psalmist regularly refers to Sheol, a vague and shadowy afterlife reserved for all humans, not merely the wicked. As described in Psalm 49:17–19, death is bleak: "For when they die, [humans] will carry nothing away.... Though in their lifetime they count themselves happy ... they will go to the company of their ancestors, who will never again see the light. Mortals cannot abide in their

---

6. Anderson, *Old Testament*, 584–85.
7. For additional information on this topic, consult essay 7, "Hope for the Afterlife."

pomp; they are like the animals that perish." To the rhetorical questions raised in Psalm 88 about whether there is life after death, the expected answer is "No" (cf. 89:48; 146:4).

Wisdom writers, like psalmists, traditionally raise the question of the resurrection of the dead, but it isn't until Daniel 12:2 and Wisdom 1:15; 2:23; and 5:15, that the answer is "Yes." Other Jewish authors of this later period, who assume belief in resurrection, disagree as to who will be resurrected, whether all humans or only righteous Jews. There are likewise divergent views about whether the dead would be resurrected to immortality or to populate a newly created world. Additionally, there is difference of opinion as to whether resurrection was spiritual or corporeal. This divergence is evident in the book of Enoch, a collection of apocalyptic writings attributed to that ancient sage. In certain passages, including chapters 1–36; 62:14; and 83–90, the author envisages the resurrection of the body, whereas in chapters 91–94, the resurrection of the soul. The former is the view of 2 Baruch 50:1—51:6, while the declarations of the martyred brothers in 2 Maccabees 7 presuppose a resurrection of the flesh and even a reassemblage of dismembered limbs.

The dawn of the Common Era found Jews divided on the topic. While Sadducees insisted that retribution and divine justice occur in this life, the Pharisees adopted the doctrine of the bodily resurrection of the dead, as did many Christians, influenced by their experience with their risen Lord and by the sermons and letters of the apostle Paul, a former Pharisee influenced, like other Pharisees, by the book of Daniel. As we read in 12:3: "Those who are wise shall shine like the brightness of the sky, and those who lead many to righteousness, like the stars forever and ever"; the simile is doubly appropriate: the righteous, "who sleep in the dust of the earth" (12:2), will return to life to "shine like the brightness of the sky." The apocalyptist has his visionary eye on the realm above the sun where Qoheleth, for whom "there is nothing new under the sun," had failed to look for an answer. The problem of theodicy and the lack of divine retribution, painful questions of Job, are resolved by Daniel through the promise of life beyond death, where the wicked are punished and the righteous enjoy the uninterrupted bliss of the divine presence.[8]

When he spoke of "the wise," the author had in mind the Hasidim and all who resist compromise and persecution; it is they who are promised a glorious and eternal future. Faithfulness to God and the covenant

---

8. Seltzer, *Jewish People*, 162.

seem to be meant in this unique passage. The doctrine of the resurrection originated, then, out of the doctrine of retribution. Though questioned by Job and Qoheleth, belief in resurrection would continue as bedrock for Jewish sages well into the Greco-Roman era, providing a rich quarry for Christianity.

Essay 6: Judaism and Hellenism

The period between 200 BC and AD 100 was one of the most vital and creative periods in the history of Judaism, or of any other religion for that matter. From a historical perspective this period witnessed the flowering of a number of movements within Judaism, one of which became its dominant form in the Common Era (the movement known as Rabbinic Judaism, associated with the Pharisees). Another became a new and influential religion in its own right, the movement known as Christianity, associated with Jesus of Nazareth.

From a literary point of view, this period witnessed the creation of numerous works associated with early Judaism's wisdom tradition, including the books of Sirach, Daniel, and the Wisdom of Solomon. These books are written against the backdrop of Hellenism, a movement and an ideology that goes back to ancient Greek (Hellas). Hellenism, associated with Greek culture and values, was initiated by Alexander the Great (336–323 BC), who invaded the eastern Mediterranean region in hopes of uniting the whole world under Hellenism's cultural tradition. Claiming to be a superior and civilizing influence, Hellenism blended philosophy, religion, and culture to create a civilization that extended from Italy to India and encompassed the Mediterranean world for over half a millennium, well into the Christian era. Hellenism exalted humanity, valued learning, and speculated about ultimate reality. Through Alexander and his successors, the cultures and societies of the ancient East were confronted by Hellenistic values and perspectives. Over time, diverse religious and philosophical systems and values proliferated, promoted by trained sages and enthusiastic converts. These religions and philosophies became all-embracing intellectual-ethical systems, competing for disciples.

Alexander was an advocate for Greek language and Hellenistic culture, as were his successors. When Alexander established Alexandria in Egypt, the most splendid city to bear his name and one destined to eclipse Athens as the intellectual capital of the Greek-speaking world, he invited Jews to settle there under favorable conditions. The Alexandrian community became (with the Babylonian) one of the two most brilliant and prosperous Jewish Diaspora communities. The legacy of Alexandrian Greek-speaking Jews featured both a person and a book: Philo, one of the most creative philosophers and biblical interpreters of antiquity, and the Septuagint translation of the Hebrew scripture.

After Alexander's untimely death, his empire was divided among four feuding generals. The two who loom largest in biblical history were Ptolemy, who established a dynasty in Egypt, and Seleucus, who established one in Babylon and Syria. The land of Israel first fell to Ptolemy (323–198), though eventually the Seleucids gained control (198–142). For the Jews, little seemed to change when the Ptolemies took control. However, when Sirach wrote in the early second century BC, the Seleucids who occupied Canaan and Judea actively sought to Hellenize the Jews, imposing pan-Hellenic values. The book of Sirach ends its famous praise of the heroes of Israel (44:1—50:29) with a reference to the high priest Simon II. According to tradition, Simon had one foot in an old order that was passing away and one in a new, emerging order. He was the last of the great Zadokite high priests and, in the eyes of later rabbis, the patron of an emerging pietism that bore Judaism's ultimate future.

Jewish responses to Hellenism were fourfold: (a) fierce resistance to cultural and religious compromise; (b) legalistic piety and zealous devotion to Torah; (c) isolationism or withdrawal; and (d) attraction and accommodation. By the first century BC, these attitudes resulted in the proliferation of Jewish sects, attitudes embodied to varying degrees by Zealots, Pharisees, Essenes, and Sadducees respectively. During the early second century BC, the influence of Hellenism was most attractive to members of the Jewish elite. This latter group, particularly the young students of the Jewish upper class who attended Ben Sira's school in Jerusalem, was the target audience for his book.

The term "Hellenistic Judaism," a catch-all phrase for a variety of forms of Judaism that developed after the time of Alexander, refers to those Jews who continued to consider themselves Jewish after they had become native Greek speakers and assimilated other aspects of Hellenistic culture. These Jews for the most part lived in centers of the Diaspora like Alexandria (Egypt), although a Greek-speaking synagogue was located in Jerusalem, together with a theater, a stadium, and a gymnasium, all Hellenic institutions. By the start of the second century BC, some prominent Jewish priests were using Greek names. In due course this

Hellenizing tendency threatened traditional Jewish belief and practice, a collision that resulted in tumultuous political developments.

Early in the second century BC, the Seleucids became overlords of Judea. Their loss to Rome at the Battle of Magnesia in 190 meant that they owed the Romans tribute, which they exacted from subject peoples. This may explain an attempt to loot the Temple treasury during the reign of Simon's successor, Onias. With the coming of Antiochus IV Epiphanes to the Seleucid throne in 175 BC, the situation of the Jewish community deteriorated. According to some sources, Antiochus was ambitious and highly eccentric; his throne name, Epiphanes, means "God (Zeus) manifest," an appellation he may have taken literally. Antiochus was approached by Onias's brother, Joshua (who took the Greek name Jason), and bribed into deposing Onias and installing Jason as high priest. The tables were turned on Jason by the unscrupulous Menelaus (another Jew with a Greek name), who offered Antiochus a bigger bribe. This intrigue upset the customary inheritance of the high priesthood through the Zadokite line.

In 167 Antiochus went so far as to proscribe Judaism, forbidding the celebration of festivals and sacrifices, the practice of circumcision, and observance of dietary laws, and mounting a statue of Zeus over the altar in the Temple at Jerusalem. The horrified author of Daniel designates this statue the "abomination" of desolation (8:13; 9:27; 11:31; and 12:11; cf. Mark 13:14–20). A group known as the Hasidim practiced passive resistance, suffering torture and death as a consequence. This resulted in the birth of an active resistance movement, led by a father and three of his sons, called the Maccabees ("hammerers") for their hammer-like guerilla tactics. The book of Daniel was written around 165 BC, shortly before the death of Antiochus. Its ideology, called "the Manifesto of the Hasidim," sets forth the theology of the Maccabean Revolt.

The Maccabean movement, including Daniel's exhortation to resistance, became a powerful option to Jews in their struggles with Hellenism. When Rome terminated the Seleucid empire in 63 BC, the Romans became the masters of Syria, Judea, and the entire eastern Mediterranean world. The Maccabean option eventually inspired the Zealot uprising that began in Judea in AD 66, against the better judgment of many priestly notables and Pharisaic leaders. The fiercely nationalistic Zealots gained major popular support, leading to the destruction of Jerusalem and the Temple in 70. Jewish Christians were forced to flee the devastation, and Judaism would not recoup its loss until 1948, when the traditional Jewish homeland was restored through the establishment of the modern nation of Israel.

Hellenistic Judaism did not survive the classical age. Some of it was assimilated into Christianity, some passed into the pagan world, and some accepted rabbinic norms. The writings of Philo of Alexandria are Hellenistic Judaism's finest surviving intellectual monument. Philo used Greek allegorical interpretation to demonstrate that the Mosaic revelation had anticipated and indeed excelled the truths later discovered by Greek philosophy. The Septuagint, the earliest Bible of Greek-speaking Christians, became Hellenistic Judaism's most influential legacy.

Questions to Ponder

1. What do you regard as the main point of the stories in the first section of Daniel?
2. What do you regard as the main point of the stories in the second half of Daniel?
3. What, for you, is the theme or message of the book of Daniel?
4. What contribution does the book of Daniel make to your understanding of wisdom?
5. In your own words, define "apocalyptic." What similarities and differences do you notice between Daniel's version of the apocalyptic genre and New Testament versions (Mark 13; 2 Thessalonians 2; book of Revelation)?
6. How would you characterize of the figure of Daniel in this book?
7. Explain why portions of Daniel were written in different languages.
8. In your estimation, what contributions does the book of Daniel make to the biblical message?
9. Evaluate dreams and visions as avenues for divine revelation.
10. What event underlies Daniel's "abomination" (desolating sacrilege)? Why did it appall the author?
11. What can we infer from the accounts in the book of Daniel about the problems confronted by the Jewish community living under Seleucid rule in the mid-second century BC? What solution does the author of Daniel recommend regarding the resolution of these problems?

Chapter 7

The Book of Wisdom (Wisdom of Solomon)

Overview: The Wisdom of Solomon, also called the book of Wisdom, seemingly addresses a world different from that of the other wisdom books. The only major early Jewish wisdom book not written originally in Hebrew, Wisdom represents the Jewish community in Egypt, struggling to maintain its identity. The author discusses life lived wisely, in vibrant relationship with God and others. The book combines wisdom and history, helping the community to value its heritage and to regain its lost confidence. Jewish wisdom, says the author, is a manifestation of the divine power that rules the world. The Wisdom of Solomon, like the book of Sirach, reflects the interaction of Judaism and Hellenism during the late Intertestamental period and offers a way of understanding how the old and the new can be integrated in the late first century BC.

Assigned Reading: Read Wisdom 1–19

Central Theme: Life should be lived fully, in vibrant and unending relationship with God.

Outline to Wisdom of Solomon:
  I. The Book of Eschatology (chiastic structure) 1:1—6:21
  II. The Book of Wisdom 6:22—9:18
    A. Description of Wisdom 6:22–25
    B. "Solomon's" Respect for Wisdom (chiastic structure) 7:1—8:21

C. "Solomon's" Prayer for Wisdom 9:1–18

III. The Book of History 10:1—19:22

    A. Wisdom and Prominent Biblical Heroes 10:1–21

    B. Wisdom and the Exodus (seven antitheses) 11:1—19:22

        1. Antithesis 1 (flowing water) 11:6–14

        2. Digression 1 (the nature and purpose of divine mercy) 11:15—12:27

            a. Egyptians 11:15—12:2

            b. Canaanites 12:2–18

            c. Israelites 12:19–22

            d. Egyptians 12:23–27

        3. Digression 2 (critique of idolaters) 13:1—15:19

            a. Worship of Nature 13:1–9

            b. Critique of Idolatry (chiastic structure) 13:10—15:13

            c. Critique of Egyptian Worship 15:4–19

        4. Antithesis 2 (frogs; quail) 16:1–4

        5. Antithesis 3 (locusts and flies; bronze serpent) 16:5–14

        6. Antithesis 4 (hail and storms; manna) 16:15–29

        7. Antithesis 5 (darkness; light) 17:1—18:4

        8. Antithesis 6 (death of firstborn; Israel spared) 18:5–25

        9. Antithesis 7 (drowning in the sea; safe passage) 19:1–12

        10. Summary and Conclusion 19:13–22

Contextual Analysis

Like Sirach, the book of Wisdom enjoys canonical status in Orthodox and Roman Catholic churches. It is absent from the Jewish Bible (in large part because it was composed in Greek and not in Hebrew), while in Protestant denominations it is relegated to the Apocrypha. A number of ancient Christians, including Clement of Alexandria (c. 150–215), regarded the book as scripture. The book is cited among the list of books held to be canonical in the Muratorian Canon (c. 180). Interestingly, in that canon the book of Wisdom is located among the canonical books of the New Testament. This book goes by two different names on account of its presence in the Septuagint, where it is named the Wisdom of Solomon, and in the Vulgate, where it is known as the book of Wisdom. The association with Solomon derives from the middle section of the book, where the unnamed speaker is recognized as Solomon—the king who preferred wisdom to fame and riches. Relying upon the authority of Solomon, the unknown author presents a dramatic exhortation to seek justice, the gift of wisdom that makes it possible to live justly and to receive lasting friendship with God.

The writer was a well-educated Jew living in the Jewish Diaspora of Alexandria, Egypt, where conflicts between Jews and non-Jews were common. Linguistic evidence points to a date near the beginning of the reign of Roman Emperor Augustus, possibly around 20 BC. Scholars often address this unknown author as "Pseudo-Solomon" or simply as "Sage." The style of writing is poetic with a strong emphasis on paradoxical and forceful images rather than on logical arguments. Composed in an elegant, sometimes lyrical, Greek, this book is a highly Hellenized work. It evidences numerous interactions with Greek culture, especially Greek philosophy. The strong attack on Egyptian animal worship in 15:14–19 suggests that the Jews are living in an environment where they were viewed with suspicion and often faced with inducements to abandon their distinctive way of life. The Jewish community in Egypt was sizeable at this time. According to Philo of Alexandria (c. 20 BC–50 AD), the Jewish population in Egypt reached one million, the majority in Alexandria. Many Jews had fled to Egypt during the campaign by Seleucid ruler Antiochus IV Epiphanes (175–164 BC) to forcibly Hellenize them. Prior to the Seleucid takeover of Palestine, the Jews of the region had been under the influence of Ptolemies in Egypt (323–198 BC). Many fled to Egypt during the Seleucid rule (198–142 BC) and in ensuing years.

A cosmopolitan port city at the mouth of the Nile River, Alexandria had been founded by Alexander the Great in 331 BC, and by the first century was one of the largest and grandest cities in the world. It had a famous museum, the greatest library in the world, and a lighthouse that was considered one of the Seven Wonders of the Ancient World. To meet the needs of Greek-speaking Alexandrian Jews, the Septuagint translation of the Hebrew scriptures developed. An ancient document known as the Letter of Aristeas states the legend that at the request of the librarian at Alexandria, the Hebrew Torah was translated by seventy (or seventy-two) scholars, twelve from each tribe.

The Jewish elite in Alexandria thrived in that setting, learning to combine faithfulness to Judaism with love of Greek learning, culture, and philosophy. The remaining Jews, viewed as foreigners and barbarians, were ridiculed, ostracized, and treated with suspicion. There is no evidence of outright persecution, but the Jews, remembering the Seleucids, were always on the defensive.

In the late first century BC, Alexandria was a place of religious and philosophical ferment. New ideas—cultural, religious, and philosophical—clashed in public as advocates of competing ideologies and religions expounded their views and searched for converts. Classical Greek philosophies, such as those of Plato and Aristotle, were challenged and became reinterpreted, with religious speculation rising to fill the void. Various concerns dominated the discussion, prompted by the quest for human ideals (including anthropological debates on the nature of man, free will, and the search for an ethical *summum bonum*) and for a cosmology governed by a rational principle (the Stoics called it "Logos," the rational principle governing the universe). Proposals and propaganda regarding the nature of the universe and of the human condition, including speculation about the immortality of the soul, were rampant. These ranged from Stoicism to Middle Platonism, Epicureanism, and the worship of Isis, the great mother goddess of Egyptian wisdom and patron of culture.

The author of the Wisdom of Solomon is believed to have been a sage in a rabbinical school in Alexandria. His book represents an ingenious and daring integration of Jewish and Hellenistic ideas and literary features that exceeded anything seen to date. It is clear that the Jewish perspective predominates, however, and where Hellenistic ideas such as body-soul dualism and immortality are utilized, they always reinforce Jewish beliefs and practices.

The intended audience for the book of Wisdom seems to have been the younger generation of Jews in Alexandria, attracted to forsake their religious traditions as outdated and primitive in comparison with the novelties, sophistication, and enchantments of Greek culture. The author is eager to demonstrate the superior wisdom of divine revelation. He does so by attacking the foolishness of Epicurean thought and by showing that the Hebrew scriptures include most of the important lessons taught by Greek philosophy, especially Platonic thought. The teachings of the Greek thinker Epicurus, though sometimes understood purely hedonistically, were sophisticated. Epicurus examined the various forms of pleasure and pain, acknowledging that certain types of pain can contribute to long-range pleasure. However, Epicurus and his Roman follower Lucretius ridiculed belief in God. They scorned religious belief as superstitious, made up to counter fear of death. For Epicureans, death results in annihilation of consciousness and being, meaning one has nothing to fear. The author of Wisdom disagrees vehemently.

Some of the younger Jews, falling away from the disciplines of the Jewish wisdom tradition, were attracted by some of Hellenism's stranger beliefs, including belief in astrology, fertility rites, and bizarre rituals of the mystery religions that prospered in Alexandria and across the Roman world. These too are addressed in the book of Wisdom, as they are to a certain degree in the books of Sirach and Daniel; a culture war was needed to preserve traditional Jewish values under sophisticated attack by a clever alien civilization.

Scholars use a variety of terms and expressions to characterize the Sage's approach and methodology. Some call him a "progressive theologian," by contrast to Sirach's more traditional approach, believing that by reinterpreting his own religious heritage, the Sage helped Judaism not only survive in its new context, but also acquire new insights into its own identity. With this assessment, however, we must keep in mind that it was not the author's intent to reconcile Judaism with Hellenism. Instead, "he used the ideas, the language, and the literary style of Greek culture to demonstrate the excellence of the Jewish faith."[1]

The author's central aims, then, were (a) to reclaim Judaism for his followers by showing that biblical morals and the Jewish perspective of life surpassed Hellenistic ideals; (b) to justify God's actions toward the Israelites, especially in the Exodus, when he blessed them while punishing their idolatrous enemies (see Wisdom 11–19); and (c) to display encyclopedic knowledge (much of it scientific) capable of impressing sophisticated readers. Like the author of the book of Job, much of Wisdom's vocabulary appears only once in the book, while 20 percent of the terms are biblical *hapaxes*, appearing nowhere else in the Bible.

---

1. Bergant, "Wisdom Books: Book of Wisdom," 276.

Literary Analysis

Genre and Style

The book of Wisdom does not fit any particular genre. The work is the result of an imaginative Jewish writer who, influenced by Greek literary standards, produced a unique piece of literature. Hellenistic religions featured aretalogies—lists of miracles attributed to a deity—interest in immortality, and claims of great antiquity, all three of which left their mark on Wisdom of Solomon. Ancients loved rhetorical devices, and therefore the Sage incorporated various forms of discourse influenced by Hellenistic rhetoric, including the *diatribe*, a form of argumentative discourse developed in Greek philosophical schools (see 1:1—6:11 and 11:15—16:1), and the *eulogy*, used in the latter part of the book to sustain the contemplation of wisdom's beauty and attractiveness. Some passages also feature a Greek literary convention known as *synkrisis* ("comparison"). This is especially noticeable in the first part of the book, where the lives of the just are contrasted with the lives of the wicked, and in the latter part of the book, where the Egyptians are contrasted with the Israelites. The Sage frequently uses *chiastic structures* (1:1—6:21; 7:1—8:21; 9:1–18; and 13:10—15:13) and a device known as *inclusion* (a repetition of words, usually to mark the beginning and ending of a section), a feature more obvious in the original Greek than in translation.

Despite its Greek literary influences, Wisdom is essentially a Jewish work. Every section of the book makes reference to images, concepts, and stories from the Torah, the Prophets, and the Writings. In the first part of the book, Hebrew poetic parallelism is used to great effect. The final section of the book has been termed a "midrash" on the events of the Exodus from Egypt and the journeys in the wilderness. Midrash is a form of Jewish interpretation designed to help rabbis apply the Bible to new situations. Unlike Philo, the Alexandrian scholar who used allegory to *reconcile* Judaism with Hellenism, the Sage used narrative and legal traditions (*haggadah* and *halakah*) to *accentuate* and interpret Jewish traditions.

Textual Analysis

Scholars point out that the Wisdom of Solomon, like Ecclesiastes, contains an intentional symmetry: the book can be divided into two parts of

251 poetic verses. The break occurs between 11:1 and 11:2. The difficulty with this argument is twofold: (1) the prayer of Solomon seems to end at 9:18; and (2) chapters 10–11 appear to be part of a larger unit explaining the saving acts of wisdom, continuing into chapter 12. Unlike Ecclesiastes, such symmetry is not germane to our discussion, which is guided by a tripartite division.

The Book of Eschatology 1:1—6:21

This segment, united by its chiastic structure, utilizes the Greek literary convention of addressing readers by royal titles such as "rulers of the earth," (1:1) "kings," and "judges" (6:1, 9, 21). Applying Plato's famous image of the "philosopher king," Hellenistic rulers were idealized to represent perfect human beings. Ruling the world, including oneself, was considered the true vocation of humanity. Hence the Sage adopts the role of ruler in chapters 6–9, not, however, as a Greek king, but as King Solomon, the ideal of Israel's wisdom tradition.

The chiastic structure (in this case involving two sets of comparisons, A and A', B and B', with C standing alone at the center), essential to understand the unit and its central message, progresses according to the A, B, C, B', A' plan:

A Exhortation: 1:1–12
B Plan of the Unjust 1:13—2:24
C Destiny of the Just and Unjust 3:1—4:20
B' Judgment of the Unjust 5:1–23
A' Exhortation 6:1–21

Ancient readers would realize that A' (6:1–21) refers back to A (1:1–12), bringing its themes to completion. Structurally, the chiastic device informs readers that 1:13—2:24 form a logical section. As they read 2:23-24, they will hear echoes of 1:13—2:1 and conclude that the section is ending. Noting the contradiction between the opening affirmation (1:13–15) and the speech of the unjust (1:16—2:20), they would understand that the dramatic tension establishes the basic antitheses of chapters 1–6: life and death, the just and the unjust, God and human rulers.

The unit exhorts readers to "love righteousness (justice)" (1:1), a term that extols reliable and just relationships at all levels of life and thereby appeals to the highest virtue within Greek and Hebraic traditions, as later in Pauline Christianity (Rom. 1:17). In Judaism, to live in righteousness meant to be faithful to God and the covenant traditions of Israel, but also to avoid injustice and unrighteousness. While the author points to justice as a way of life, he promptly warns against injustice, which is said to bring death (1:12). Death is presented as a fundamental obstacle to the practice of justice. While the ungodly view death merely from the point of view of human mortality, weakness, and suffering that reduces ethical perspectives to those of pleasure, power, and violence (2:6–20), the author attempts to liberate the reader from the fear of death to the love of justice and wisdom.

By pointing to the rewards of covenant faithfulness and fidelity to wisdom, the author is not simply restating the doctrine of retribution, for he understands that suffering is not always caused by sin, and that virtue does not guarantee length of life. The author not only challenges some traditional views, but also introduces new ideas. Chapter 3 reverses conventional wisdom, such as the notion that childlessness is a mark of divine displeasure and that untimely death is a curse, by emphasizing that "barren women" will have fruit (3:13; cf. 4:1), that the "eunuch" will receive special favor (3:14), and that those who die young will be rewarded (4:7; cf. 4:14). The dichotomy in this unit between the righteous and the unrighteous (1:1–11) is not presented as a dichotomy of retribution, but rather as a dichotomy in thought. The ungodly, oriented only to this life, are said to have a covenant with death (2:1), whereas the righteous, oriented to wisdom, have a covenant with life (1:15; 5:15). The concepts of "death" and "life" here clearly denote more than the end of a person's life. "Death" signifies all the forces of evil at work in society, and those who live only for this life are said to find little reason to live justly. Wisdom, described as a holy and disciplined way of life, represents the opposite of selfish, unjust, temporal living. Wisdom 1:6–8 remind the disheartened Jewish community in Alexandria that despite appearances to the contrary, God does not abandon suffering people or tolerate injustice. In 5:15 the reward of virtue is described as a vibrant relationship with God that is life unending.[2]

In the Sage's theology, God is the author of life, not death. In 1:15, righteousness is called "immortal" (the Greek term here is *athanatos*, lit. "not death"), an unfortunate translation, for it suggests Greek notions

---

2. The concepts of death and life, temporal and everlasting, are addressed more fully in essay 7, "Hope for the Afterlife."

of body-soul dualism.³ For the author, immortality is a gift of God, not an intrinsic human quality. The Sage's concern in this unit is with the final vindication of the faithful, as he makes clear in 5:15, where a great reversal occurs: the persecuted, martyred, and rejected will rule forever. It is they who will achieve what the Hellenists longed for.

In 2:21-24 the author assesses the reasoning of the ungodly. Blinded by their unrighteousness, they are unable to comprehend God's "secret purposes" (2:22; cf. 13:1; 14:22; 16:16). Instead they have been corrupted by the "devil's envy" (2:24), a reference to the temptation story of Genesis 3:1-24.⁴ The righteous, by contrast, are by definition those who possess such knowledge (2:13; cf. 6:22; 10:10). They are destined for "incorruption" (2:23, i.e. immortality), which represents the true purpose of human life.

The concluding passage in unit one (6:17-21) is remarkable for its use of a Greek style of reasoning known as sorites (cf. Rom. 5:3-4; 2 Pet. 1:5-7), a chain argument in which the predicate of one statement becomes the subject of the next (A=B=C=Z=A). Note that the section begins with the word "desire" and returns to "desire" in verse 20.

The Book of Wisdom 6:22—9:18

While the term "wisdom" is mentioned only occasionally in the first unit of the book, wisdom is central to the second unit. Whereas the book begins by exhorting rulers (the audience) to seek wisdom, Wisdom 6:22 introduces the use of the first person, whom we assume to be Solomon, though the author does not use his name. "I will tell you what wisdom is and how she came to be," he promises; 6:22-25 introduces the section, but 6:22 is the key verse. The Sage's purpose in 6:22—9:18 is to reveal Lady Wisdom's true identity so that his readers will find communion with her and have life to the full.

---

3. The Hebraic term "*nephesh*," meaning "life," is often translated by the term "soul" in English Bibles, a practice inherited from the King James translators. Because there is no Hebrew version of the book of Wisdom, we cannot be sure what the author means by "soul" (*psyche*) in passages such as 1:11 or 3:1; here the term can be understood in the Hebraic sense, whereas in passages such as 1:4 the author seems to be using the term in a Greek sense, suggestive of body-soul dualism.

4. The author of Wisdom is the first biblical (or deuterocanonical) writer to identify the serpent of the Genesis account with the devil.

Much of the material in chapters 7–8 is a prayer for wisdom, culminating in the great prayer of "Solomon" in chapter 9. Chapters 7–8 form a single literary unit, as evident by the chiastic structure. The chiasm consists of three sets of comparisons, having as their center 7:22b—8:1, the praise of wisdom. The personification of Lady Wisdom in 7:22—8:1 is one of the most famous and striking passages in the Bible, and one of the most mysterious.

Chapters 7–9 include a great many influences from Hellenistic sources, particularly liturgical texts in praise of Isis, the Egyptian goddess of wisdom. The twenty-one qualities of wisdom listed in 7:22b–23, representing perfection (3 x 7 = 21), resemble aretalogies of Isis, which list her virtues, qualities, and miracle-working abilities. In Hellenistic environments, "performing miracles was what made a god."[5] Another Hellenistic influence appears in 8:7, where mention is made of the four cardinal virtues of Plato, a staple of Greek moral teaching found only here in the biblical and deuterocanonical literature. In mentioning the ways the Sage is indebted to Hellenism, it is important to note how he modifies his Jewish sources. Like the authors of Proverbs 8 and Sirach 24, he affirms wisdom's role in creation (wisdom is "the fashioner of all things," 7:22a), but unlike his predecessors, he develops a new role for wisdom as the savior of God's people throughout history (9:18; cf. 10:1—19:12). Here we find another connection with Isis, for she too is frequently called savior, and numerous dedications recall her saving deeds. In addition, many of the qualities, attributes, or titles wisdom is given in chapters 7–9 had been used of Isis, including emanation from God (7:25), radiance brighter than the sun (7:29), craftswoman (8:6), guide (8:9), throne partner of God (9:4), bride (8:2), giver of immortality (8:13, 17), and teacher of "the structure of the world" (7:17). These and other parallels are so substantial that any listener raised in an environment where the cult of Isis flourished would have thought Isis to be the subject of these descriptions.

In 7:17–21, the list of encyclopedic knowledge that Solomon claims to have received from wisdom—cosmology, time, astronomy, zoology, demonology, psychology, botany, and pharmacy—would have deeply impressed an educated Hellenist. In addition, the statement in 8:1: "She reaches mightily from one end of the earth to the other, and she orders all things well," reflects Stoic cosmology. The Stoics held that God was the immanent principle of energy by which the natural world is created and

---

5. Clifford, *Wisdom Literature*, 136.

sustained. He also created the *logos* (world reason), which manifested itself in the world's beauty and order. In 7:24 wisdom is described as the organizing principle of reality, the world soul that renews all things, and in 9:1–2 she can be spoken of in the same breath with God's *logos*. The Sage is willing to go so far as to say that wisdom is a "breath of the power of God, a pure emanation of the glory of the Almighty; . . . and an image of his goodness. . . . In every generation she passes into holy souls and makes them friends with God" (7:25–27). To find such a series of statements from the pen of a monotheistic Jew is truly remarkable.[6]

However, remaining aware of theological propriety, the Sage refrains from exceeding his bounds, for he never identifies wisdom with God. In Wisdom 9:17–18 we read that wisdom is subordinate to the biblical God. In a new development, here wisdom is identified with God's "holy spirit from on high." While she is sent from heaven, even from God's glorious throne (9:4, 10), and while she is said to "live with God" and be "an associate in his works" (8:3–4), wisdom is never identical with the Almighty, who still dwells in heaven once wisdom has been sent.

From these passages one gets the impression that the author is talking about something greater than one god in a pantheon of deities, and yet less than an exhaustive description of the God of Israel. Because the author certainly did not want to say anything that would compromise his monotheism, this may account for some ambiguities in the text. Some scholars consider this section of the text a polemic against the cult of Isis, particularly in assigning to wisdom Isis's attributes as savior and guide. The author is clearly not promoting polytheism, for that would work at cross purposes with the aim of his book, "which is to encourage Hellenized Jews in the Diaspora to maintain their Jewish faith and identity, while not abandoning dialogue with the larger world."[7]

Solomon's prayer for wisdom in chapter 9 is the climax of this unit. The prayer is structured chiastically and consists of five sets of comparisons, with 9:10a at the center, a prayer for God to send wisdom from the heavenly throne of glory. The prayer is in three sections (1–6; 7–12; and 13–18), each containing a prayer for wisdom (verses 4, 10, and 17). The prayer points backward to earlier chapters, which highlight wisdom's role as Creator (7:22a and 9:2), while adding a new role — wisdom as Savior (9:18). Verses 17–18 represent the climax of chapters 7–9, in which

---

6. This theme is further developed in the Logos Hymn in John 1:1–18.
7. Witherington, *Jesus the Sage*, 109–10.

wisdom is identified with God's Holy Spirit. The entire book contains a tantalizing interplay between wisdom as spirit and wisdom as God's Holy Spirit. Christians note the parallel between 7:27 ("in every generation she passes into holy souls") and references in the book of Acts to baptized believers receiving the regenerating Spirit of God (2:38; 8:15, 19; 19:2).

The Book of History 10:1—19:22

The final point made in unit two, that humans are "saved" by wisdom (9:18), is illustrated in chapter 10 by seven diptychs (the literary term is derived from iconography, where two images are set side by side for the purpose of complementarity or contrast), seven sets of contrasts from the Torah: Adam and Cain; Noah and the flooded earth; Abraham and the nations put to confusion; Lot and his wife; Jacob and Laban; Joseph and Potiphar's wife; and the last, Moses and Pharaoh. The final reference, the Israelites and the Egyptians (10:15—11:4), points to the main theme of the remainder of the book, which is a reinterpretation of the Exodus (chapters 11–19).

The final section of the book develops a second series of diptychs (seven antitheses) that relate the punishment of the plagues to a particular sin of the Egyptians. In addition, two major digressions occur after the first diptych. The second digression uses satire to ridicule idol worshippers (13:10—15:13). Structured chiastically, the passage contains two sets of contrasts, with 14:11–31, a section assuring punishment of idolatry, at the center.

The main point in the Book of History is to demonstrate that wisdom is the central and saving figure of biblical history. The Sage takes the Exodus, considered by Jews to be the greatest event of God in history, and in midrashic style, gives it immediacy to his own community. Like the present community, their ancestors faced death at the hands of wicked idolaters, and like them, this generation will be rescued by wisdom. The Exodus is viewed as seven miracles of God, whereby natural phenomena are used to bless the Israelites (the just) and punish the Egyptians (the unjust). The Sage refers to the past to assure his readers that the same God who "has not neglected to help them at all times and in all places" (19:22) is still with them, to rescue them from persecution and to lead them into communion with everlasting wisdom.

The end result of the Sage's work is "an intriguing marriage of Jewish and Hellenistic ideas, though clearly the former predominate, and the latter (such as body-soul dualism or immortality) are used in the service of those Jewish ideas. The author sees no contradiction in combining or adapting Greek ideals about the afterlife with early Jewish eschatological notions."[8]

The Sage's intellectual and theological creativity goes well beyond anything we have examined to this point. In the Common Era, various Jewish rabbis took a dim view of the writings of Ben Sira and the book of Wisdom, finding in these works excessive compromise with Hellenism. The material studied in this chapter raises the question of how subsequent Jewish sages, including Jesus, Paul, James, and the composers of early Christological hymns, might build on this framework and methodology. The answer is pursued in subsequent chapters.

Thematic Analysis

According to Richard Clifford, the book of Wisdom presents four principal themes: justice and immortality (Wis. 1—6:21); wisdom's governance of the world (Wis.6:22—8:21); the attainment of wisdom (Wis. 9:1–18); and Israel as the chosen people (10:1—19:22).[9] Throughout the discussion, the question arises as to how one attains wisdom. The answer appears in chapter 9: ask for wisdom, for those who request wisdom receive God's Spirit, God's gift of salvation.

The unifying theme of the book of Wisdom is "praise of wisdom." Each major section addresses this theme from its own distinctive point of view. The first part summons Jews to fidelity to God and Israel's religious traditions, which guarantees the rewards of wisdom in this life and in the afterlife. The second part indicates how we might attain God's wisdom, while the third extols the God of Israel, the source of wisdom.

Having completed our study of early Jewish wisdom literature, we can assess the role and value of wisdom by examining her literary profile and pilgrimage. The study of key passages in Proverbs, Job, Sirach, and the book of Wisdom reveal the following picture:[10]

1. Wisdom has her origin in God (Prov. 8:22; Sir. 24:3, 9; Wis. 7:25–26);

---

8. Ibid., 111.
9. Clifford, *Wisdom Literature*, 138.
10. Witherington, *Jesus the Sage*, 114–15.

2. Wisdom preexisted and likely has a role in the work of creation (Prov. 3:19; 8:22–29; 24:3; Sir. 1:4, 9–10; 16:24—17:7; Wis. 7:22; 8:4–6; 9:2, 9);

3. Wisdom pervades creation, accounting for its coherence and endurance (Wis. 1:7; 7:24, 27; 8:1; 11:25);

4. Wisdom is identified with the divine spirit (Wis. 1:7; 9:17; 12:1) and in some sense is immanent in the world (Wis. 7:24; 8:1);

5. Wisdom comes to the human world with a distinctive mission (Prov. 8:4, 31–36; Sir. 24:7, 12, 19–22; Wis. 7:27–28; 8:2–3);

6. Wisdom is especially associated with Israel (Sir. 24:8–12) and with Torah (Sir. 24:23), and was at work in Israel's history (Wis. 10:1–21);

7. While a gift from God (Prov. 2:6; Sir. 1:9–10, 26; 6:37; Wis. 7:7; 9:4), wisdom is associated with disciplined effort to obtain her (Prov. 4:10–27; 6:6; Sir. 4:17; 6:18–36; Wis. 1:5; 7:14).

Essay 7: Hope for the Afterlife

The book of Wisdom witnesses to a trend in late postexilic Jewish thought that anticipated life after death. The author significantly advances the formal treatment in Judaism of the status of individual humans after death, though his view falls short of the notion of a bodily resurrection, espoused at the start of the Common Era by Pharisaic Jews and then by Christians.

 The ancient Israelite view of life after death was complex. In general, there seems to have been popular belief in some sort of survival for the dead, a weak and pale existence in a place called Sheol, where the dead survived as equals. As Creator and sovereign Lord, Yahweh has control over Sheol, as over matters on earth. Reward and punishment take place now, in this world, with long life, a large family, riches and prestige for the just, and misfortune in all of these areas for the wicked. The early Greeks held similar views of the afterlife, envisioning all the dead together in the underworld. By the fifth century BC, Greek writers speak of certain souls surviving elsewhere, in "the upper regions," and slightly later there developed the notion that the spirit or soul (*psyche*) of the person was distinct from the body. In the dualism of the Greek philosopher Plato and his followers, while the physical part of the person ceased to exist at death, the soul lived on. Under the influence of Greek thought, this belief is also found in Jewish writings of the Hellenistic period.

Among Jewish wisdom sages, traditional notions of earthly retribution did not square with the hard facts of experience, so various solutions were proposed to the problem in its national (Deuteronomy and Deutero-Isaiah) and individual aspects (Job, Ecclesiastes). Some psalms express hope for the individual of life with God beyond the grave (Ps. 49:15; 73:23-26; cf. Isa. 26:19). The book of Wisdom synthesizes and builds on these and other texts and presents the most extensive discussion on the subject in the canonical and deuterocanonical Hebrew literature.

The Sage may have been aided in his thinking on future life by Greek concepts such as body-soul dualism and immortality, though his reasoning process remains Jewish, based on Hebraic ethical understanding. The author sustains the idea of the post-death survival of the just with such words as "immortal" (1:15; 3:4; 4:1; 8:17; 15:3) and "incorruptible" (2:23; 6:18-19), but an ethical perspective is used to condition this notion of immortality. The author does not posit an inherent immortality that all humans possess. Rather, immortality depends on the inner life of virtue. Immortality is the divine life toward which human life has been destined from the dawn of time (2:23), but the decisions and actions of humans determine the quality of final life.

A life of justice and virtue leads to immortality (3:4; 6:17-20), while a life of injustice and wickedness leads to death (1:16; 2:24; 5:17-23). Chapter 5 is the counterpoint to chapter 2. In chapter 2 the wicked express their own philosophy, which includes hatred of the just person; in chapter 5 the wicked are filled with remorse and overcome by their folly. In a striking judgment scene, the wicked acknowledge the great reversal: "These are persons whom we once held in derision . . . fools that we were! . . . They have been numbered among the children of God. . . . What has our arrogance profited us?" (5:3-8).

Although the author's presentation of the immortality of the just could be reconciled with the notion of bodily resurrection, there is in Wisdom no mention of such resurrection. Some scholars maintain that silence on this point is out of deference to the Greeks, who regarded physical matter, including the human body, as evil; but such arguments are unconvincing, for it seems that Wisdom does not envision the resurrection of the body. The idea of bodily resurrection developed separately from that of the immortality of the soul, and was not universally held. According to Josephus, the first-century AD Jewish historian, and to the

New Testament, the Pharisees believed that the bodies of the dead would be raised and reunited with their souls, while Jewish groups such as the Sadducees did not. Daniel 12:2–3 is the earliest text that unequivocally affirms the bodily resurrection of at least some of the dead, and the rewards and punishments that await them in the life to come, is. That passage was written in the context of one of the darkest events in early Jewish history, during the persecution and forced Hellenization by the infamous Antiochus IV Epiphanes in the mid-second century BC. It is ironic that this development was possible in part because of the influx of Hellenistic ideas, many of which had been so strenuously opposed by the Maccabees and other members of the Jewish resistance movement.

In discussing the events of the afterlife, the author of Wisdom is understandably vague. The book presumes separation of the just and the wicked at death. The just "are at peace" (3:3), for "their hope is full of immortality" (3:4); their portion is with the holy ones, the "sons of God" (5:5), who constitute the divine family. Dire things are said about the wicked, who go to a place of torment (4:19). Other texts speak of judgment (3:7, 13, 18; 4:6, 20), though we are not told when this occurs, whether immediately after death or at the end of time (see 5:17–23). Furthermore, we are not sure whether the author is speaking merely of physical death, of physical death followed by spiritual death, or of spiritual death alone. The author seems to pass over physical death, directing attention toward spiritual death. In the New Testament, Paul the ex-Pharisee faces the same question when dealing with the unexpected deaths of Christians in 1 Thessalonians 4:13–18. Unlike the answer of the author of Wisdom, his answer is specific.

Questions to Ponder

1. What, for you, is the theme or message of the Wisdom of Solomon?
2. What contribution does the book of Wisdom make to your understanding of wisdom?
3. In what significant ways does the book of Wisdom affirm traditional Jewish wisdom?
4. In your estimation, does the author of Wisdom of Solomon go too far in accommodating to Hellenistic and pagan views of God and the universe? Explain your answer.

5. In what ways do you find the Sage's methodology actually helpful in your struggle with faith, science, and reason?
6. Should the book of Wisdom be in the Jewish canon? Explain your answer.
7. Should the book of Wisdom be in the Christian canon? Explain your answer.
8. Can you detect ways whereby the book of Wisdom helped early Christians develop their Christology? Their doctrine of the Trinity?
9. In your estimation, does the Sage's introduction of the doctrine of the afterlife strengthen or weaken his overall thesis? What role does the afterlife play in your worldview?

PART IV

Liturgical Wisdom

CHAPTER 8

Wisdom Psalms

Overview: The Psalms functioned in a twofold manner in Jewish liturgical life, as hymns of praise and as prayers, both communal and private. Worship inevitably expresses a conviction about who God is and how humans relate to God and to one another. Israel's sages and liturgical leaders often expressed themselves in verse because poetry enhances worship by appealing to emotion and imagination. The hymns in the Psalter represent a wide variety of styles and moods, ranging from thanksgiving hymns, festival psalms, national and historical psalms, wedding psalms, royal psalms, laments, penitential psalms, and wisdom psalms. Of those considered wisdom psalms, we examine seven, each connected with topics central to the books of Proverbs (Ps. 1), Ecclesiastes (Ps. 49), Job (Pss. 8; 13; 139), Song of Songs (73:1–3), Sirach, and Wisdom of Solomon (Ps. 119).

Assigned Reading: Read Psalms 1; 49; 8; 13; 139; 73:1–3; 119.

Central Theme: God is to be praised in every season of life.

Contextual Analysis

The word "psalms" (meaning "praises") refers to a collection of 150 songs of supplication, thanksgiving, and praise found in the Bible. Throughout the biblical period, Israel's primary bond of unity was worship of God. According to the Bible, the enslaved Israelites were liberated from

Egyptian bondage so that they might worship God at Sinai (Exod. 3:12). During the period of the tribal confederacy, instituted by Joshua, the Israelites gathered at cultic centers such as Shechem and Shiloh to celebrate the great annual festivals and to renew the covenant tradition. During the time of David, Jerusalem became the cultic center of the nation, to which Solomon added the impressive Temple. During the period of the divided monarchy, when the northern kingdom became independent from Judea and Jerusalem, the kings of Israel gathered at pilgrimage shrines in their own territory, especially at Bethel. When the exiles returned from Babylon, their first thought was to rebuild the Jerusalem Temple. Throughout its history, Israel was a worshipping community, recalling God's actions in narrative and written traditions but also addressing God in bold, honest, and deeply personal ways. For this reason the book of Psalms represents the very heart and center of the Hebrew Bible, Israel's "conversation" with Yahweh.

About one third of the Hebrew Bible is poetry. Awareness of this feature of Israel's liturgical and literary expression is invaluable for reading and interpreting scripture. Poetry is a personal way of expressing faith, both individually and communally. Poetry appeals to our human nature, making us realize the importance of emotion and signifying that we are more than intellect. Worship, like other interpersonal communication, involves both head and heart.

The book of Psalms in its present form is the product of postexilic Judaism. Insofar as the Psalter reflects the liturgical practice of this period, one can speak of it as the Hymnbook of the Second Temple, though this material continues to be chanted in Jewish synagogues. The collected psalms were intended to be sung, generally as a kind of chant and often accompanied by instrumental music. Some psalms provide hints of the original musical setting in the titles, headings, and opening words, generally added later but still preserving ancient tradition. In addition to their use as hymns, the psalms also function as prayers, recited corporately and privately.

The book of Psalms is divided into five parts, probably in imitation of the Torah, the first five books of the Bible. This is also suggested by the content of Psalm 1, a wisdom psalm that introduces the entire collection by describing reward for those who observe Torah and punishment for those who fail to do so. The five collections are:

1. Book I (Pss. 1–41): characterized by the use of the word Yahweh ("Lord") for God, is thought to be relatively early;

2. Book II (Pss. 42–72): characterized by the use of the word Elohim ("God"), is a collection of "northern" psalms (from the northern kingdom of Israel during the period of the divided monarchy);

3. Book III (Pss. 73–89): characterized by instructions given for singers in the headings, was designed for use in the Temple;

4. Book IV (Pss. 90–106): taken from a royal collection, was often used in the celebration of Jewish festivals in the fall of the year: Sukkot ("Booths") and Rosh Hashanah ("New Year");

5. Book 5 (Pss. 107–150): appears to be a second collection of Davidic royal psalms. It includes Psalms of Ascent and Hallel Psalms, pilgrimage psalms describing the ascent of the people to the Temple in Jerusalem.

Each of the first four of these divisions ends with a blessing (Ps. 41:13; 72:18–19; 89:52; 106:48). The final psalm, Psalm 150, may be considered a conclusion to the fifth division as well as to the book of Psalms as a whole.

An important clue to the origin of the Psalter is found in the postscript following Book II: "The prayers of David son of Jesse are ended" (72:20). This passage indicates that at one stage in the formation of the Psalter the "Davidic" collection ended here. In this first division almost all of the psalms are prefixed with the words "of David." This does not mean that they were composed by David, however, but it does point to the antiquity of the collection. The psalms were composed by many individuals over a long period of time and collected under the patronage of David, in part because he was regarded as the ideal king with whom the people identified as they approached God in worship and as the prototype of the messiah (God's "anointed one"; Ps. 2), who would fulfill the hopes of Israel. The Psalms are quoted in the New Testament some seventy-five times; more than fifty represent Christ as the speaker or are directly applied to him.

In addition to David, the Psalms ascribe authorship or association with "the sons of Korah," one of the principal priestly families in Jerusalem; twelve are attributed to Asaph, a musician associated with David and one of the sons of Korah; ten are attributed to King Hezekiah. Within the book of Psalms there are other collections as well, including the Songs of Ascents (Pss. 120–134), so called because pilgrims used these psalms as they went up to Jerusalem to participate in the annual festivals; some psalms deal with divine kingship (Pss. 93–99), and another group, known as "Hallel" psalms, open or close with "hallelujah" ("praise Yahweh"; see Pss. 104–106; 111–113; 135; 146–150).

Additional evidence that the book of Psalms is an anthology is the repetition found therein. Thus, Psalms 14 and 53 are identical, except for the shift of the divine name from Yahweh to Elohim; Psalm 40:13–17 is the same as Psalm 70; and Psalm 108 is a combination of Psalms 57:7–11 and 60:5–12. The book of Psalms is therefore the result of a long process of compilation and editing. Perhaps the final editing was done by Ezra the scribe (c. 450–400 BC), the same person who is said to have edited the five books of Torah, putting them into their final form.

Modern scholars have attempted to classify the Psalms according to literary genre and sometimes by content. The main categories are individual and communal laments, songs of thanksgiving, royal psalms, hymns of praise, historical and national psalms, processional psalms (for festivals in Jerusalem), wedding psalms, and wisdom psalms. Some thirteen psalms are considered wisdom psalms (Pss. 1; 18; 19; 36; 37; 49; 73; 78; 112; 119; 127; 128; 139), though scholars disagree on the number of psalms classified under this topic.

Textual Analysis

In this segment we examine select psalms associated with topics from the Jewish wisdom literature, themes central to the books of Proverbs (Ps. 1), Ecclesiastes (Ps. 49), Job (Pss. 8; 13; 139), Song of Songs (73:1–3), Sirach, and Wisdom of Solomon (Ps. 119). Wisdom psalms, as a category, focus on the divine source of wisdom and on human need for wisdom.

A Psalm on Wisdom in General: Psalm 1 [associated with the book of Proverbs]

Psalm 1 serves as an introduction to the Psalter in general. This psalm presents a strong contrast between virtue and vice, much as the book of Proverbs personified the Two Ways as two women: Lady Wisdom and Lady Folly. Psalm 1 underscores the traditional law of retribution, connecting virtue with prosperity and vice with disaster. The first word in the psalm, translated "happy" or "blessed," prefigures the beatitudes in Jesus' Sermon on the Mount (Matt. 5:3–12), the first of Matthew's five collected sermons of Jesus. The Sermon on the Mount, described by scholars as "the new Torah," correlates well with Matthew's portrayal of Jesus as "The New Moses."[1] According to the psalmist, one acquires wisdom by meditating on Torah. Such a devotional life consists of pondering biblical texts, thinking and rethinking their meaning and application. This way of life, depicted as a tree "planted by streams of water" (1:3), is often associated with the Garden of Eden and the tree of life, its leaves and fruit ever green and always in season.

A Psalm for Uncertainty: Psalm 49 [associated with the book of Ecclesiastes]

Like the advice of Qoheleth, Psalm 49 provides instruction about life and death and insists that wealth cannot save one from death. In verses 1–4 the psalmist takes up his harp to apply wisdom to the problem he faces. As verses 10–14 indicate, this problem of the psalmist is similar to Qoheleth's: the inevitability of death. Numerous synonyms appear for death, including "the pit," "the grave," and "Sheol." The answer the psalmist receives in verse 15, that God will restore justice, is the answer Qoheleth pondered but was unable to accept.

Prayers (Psalms) in Times of Suffering [associated with the book of Job]

Prayer has been characterized as a "habit of the heart" because for many believers, prayer lies at the center of their devotional life. Despite prayer's paradoxical nature (believers are exhorted to pray to God despite being assured that God knows in advance their desires and needs), people of faith rarely consider the inconsistency, since for them prayer is a matter of obedience. In addition to its pious dimension, prayer also has therapeutic value, for prayer puts us in right relationship with God, others, and ourselves. Like regular physical exercise, prayer creates discipline and leads to greater health of body, mind, and spirit. The habit of prayer and meditation is not simply beneficial for the present, but it helps prepare people for the "lean years," for the calamities and disappointments of life. Like Job and his friends, suffering, disaster, and personal loss often result in a sense of desolation, creating anxiety and guilt that urge victims to

---

1. For additional information on Matthew's Christology, see chapter 10.

dwell on faults and mistakes. Such negative patterns can result in anger against God and in deep depression. The message of the book of Job is that God desires our honest response, for God is big enough to accept human anger. God would rather have our attention than be ignored.

In this segment we examine three psalms that provide wisdom in the face of suffering and uncertainty. Psalm 8 reminds us that God works providentially in our lives, not in small-minded, faultfinding ways or even in daily miraculous interventions, but rather as Creator and ruler over all things. Psalm 8 reminds believers that God is in control, enacting a loving and caring plan for their lives (cf. Rom. 8:28: "We know that all things work together for good for those who love God, who are called according to his purpose"). Human desolation, whether caused by suffering, guilt, or self-deprecation, results in distorted ways of thinking. All desolation bears some untruth, and the starting point for endurance is recognizing the distortion. Psalm 8 puts things into perspective. Humans have free will, and freedom produces consequences. Humans need wisdom to deal prudently with their awesome freedom.

Psalm 13 is a prayer for deliverance in the face of unspecified trouble. This psalm illustrates a three-stage process in the healing of body, mind, or spirit, progressing from a state of disintegration, followed by a transitional period, culminating in integration. As with Psalm 13, many psalms begin with complaint; verses 1–2 show that the psalmist has hit rock bottom. The first step to healing is honesty: sometimes the silence of God feels like abandonment, and the Psalmist's "how long?" (repeated four times) sounds hopeless. The psalmist has entered the transitional stage.

In their reading of the Psalms, readers need to discern moments of transition, progressive changes in the author's life or mood, propelling momentum from anger, sadness, or despair to faith, hope, and praise. Transitions in life, successfully negotiated, provide hope for renewal and can result in changed perspective. The key to navigating the crisis, as verses 4–5 indicate, is to keep hoping and praying, to keep the conversation going. Verses 5–6 represent a "sea-change" in attitude, a state of integration. The spiritual tenacity of the sufferer, believer, or worshipper results in a change of perspective, a new mindset. Such change requires time, and one can imagine that a period of time has transpired between verses 4 and 5. Reading the psalms holistically requires that we note the gaps in time, realizing that changes in perspective often take time. Finally, however, light comes with the dawn of a new day. The night is over;

suffering has ended. As verse 6 indicates, the psalmist has reached a state of integration, based upon two pillars: (a) his trust in God's unfailing love, and (b) his past experience of God's goodness. As we learned in Job 38–42, God's silence doesn't last forever. When God speaks, silence turns to song (13:6); the voice of God provides the power of positive thinking, increasing faith and trust.

Psalm 139, a prayer for God's help, further exemplifies trust in God's providential care. This psalm can be divided into five sections. Verses 1–6 speak about God's watchful care, both night and day. Verses 7–12 speak quite frankly about how the psalmist wishes to hide from God's presence. Verse 8 speaks of Sheol, the traditional place of the dead, including it under God's watch. The allusion here is neither to heaven nor hell, but merely to the poet's faith in God's cosmic rule. Verses 13–18 refer to God's personal care, not only through the years of our lives, but even in the nine months we spent in the womb (see verses 15–16). Verses 19–22 are a prayer for the defeat of personal enemies, including one's own inward thoughts and doubts. The psalm closes with the famous words: "Search me, O God, and know my heart; test me and know my thoughts" (verses 23–24), a passage in which the psalmist prays for honesty and integrity, even if they require change of attitude and lifestyle.

Like Job, the psalmist acknowledges living with insufficient knowledge. But he prays in trust even when the solution to his problem is not clear. He is not altogether sure things will work out the way he hopes, but like Jesus in the garden before his crucifixion, his attitude is one of relinquishment to God's will: "Father, if you are willing, remove this cup from me; yet, not my will but yours be done" (Luke 22:42).

A Wisdom Psalm for "Purity of Heart": Psalm 73:1–3 [associated with Song of Songs]

Biblical wisdom is essentially practical, a wisdom of the heart as much as of the head. One's inclinations, desires, and attractions, like one's schedule and affairs, can be badly as well as easily ordered. To give one's heart to God (see 73:25) as to a spouse or lover, as the Song of Songs suggests, requires a deep purity of heart (cf. "pure of heart," Matt. 5:8). When we consider the "heart" in the Bible, especially in the Hebrew scriptures, we must keep in mind the unified anthropology that informs such concepts. Like the Hebrew term *nephesh*, sometimes translated "soul" but meaning "life" or "living being," the Hebrew word *lev* ("heart") refers to the center or core of one's being, not to a specific organ.[2] This brief passage, like Psalm 1, presents a contrast between opposites, in this case between those who are "pure in heart" and those who are "arrogant." The issue of the wicked prospering (being healthy and pain free) is apparent here, as in the book of Job. Whereas the psalmist is tempted to abandon the disciplines of the Torah, that is, his traditional religious or Jewish upbringing ("my feet had almost stumbled," 73:2), "purity of heart" involves seeing things from God's perspective and persevering in that perspective. Purity of heart (love of God), like fear of God, are practically synonymous. In Jewish wisdom literature, faithfulness and loyalty—to God and Torah—are ways to show love for God. Again, the idea here cannot be limited to attitudes, but includes actions and all of one's being, for in the Hebrew Bible, heart, mind, soul, and body are a unity.[3]

Thematic Conclusion

Psalm 1:3, as Proverbs 3:18, connects wisdom with the "tree of life" in the Garden of Eden, its leaves and fruit ever green and always in season. This image reappears in the closing vision of the book of Revelation, the culminating vision of the Bible. There, in the New Jerusalem the tree of life produces twelve kinds of fruit, one kind each month of the year, and "the leaves of the tree are for the healing of the nations" (Rev. 22:2). Wisdom is the referent in these passages, inspired by the vision in Genesis 2:9 of the primordial paradise. Passages in the New Testament speak of the "fruit of the Spirit" (Gal. 5:22) and of the "gifts of the Spirit" (1 Cor. 12:8–10; Rom. 12:6–8; Eph. 4:11–12), and it is altogether certain, based on the connection between wisdom and the spirit of Yahweh in Wisdom of Solomon 7:24–27, that a strong biblical correlation exists between wisdom, the tree of life, the Spirit of the Lord, and the messiah. The sages who composed the latter books of the Jewish sapiential tradition joined in that effort, endowing wisdom with a cosmic role and thereby winning for wisdom a status almost equal to that of Torah and Prophecy.

---

2. In like manner the term *yamin* ("hands"), used liturgically, does not refer to a body part but to one's actions.

3. A Wisdom Psalm on Torah: Psalm 119 [associated with Sirach and the book of Wisdom], is covered in essay 8: "Wisdom and Torah."

When Isaiah described the ideal Davidic king who would govern in justice and wisdom, he states that the spirit of the Lord rests upon him, "the spirit of wisdom and understanding, the spirit of counsel and might, the spirit of knowledge and the fear of the Lord" (Isa. 11:2). To that list the Septuagint added "piety." Jerome followed the Septuagint in the Vulgate translation, resulting in the "seven gifts of the Spirit." For Christians, these are the qualities that Jesus Christ as messiah embodies and shares sacramentally with his adopted sisters and brothers. The first in the list, as of primary importance, is the "spirit of wisdom."

Essay 8: Wisdom and Torah

Our study of early Jewish wisdom literature reveals that in their interpretations of the major areas of human experience, the Jewish sages arrived at a more profound grasp of meaning than did any Near-Eastern neighbors. What produced this achievement? The Jewish answer is that they did not reach these insights entirely on their own. They are based on revelation, on divine disclosure about God's nature and God's will for nature and for humanity.

While there has been a tendency to approach revelation as though primarily verbal, the Bible indicates that God's revelation came foremost in actions—not words but deeds. This comes out clearly in Moses's instructions to his people: "When your children ask you in time to come, 'What is the meaning of the decrees and the statues and the ordinances that the Lord our God has commanded you?' then you shall say to your children, 'We were Pharaoh's slaves in Egypt, but the Lord brought us out of Egypt with a mighty hand'" (Deut. 6:21–22). From the goodness of God's nature it followed that God wanted people to be fair and honest, showing love and mercy to one another. Hence a covenant—a constitution for the grateful community—was established at Mount Sinai.

While the word Torah, in its narrowest sense, refers to the Ten Commandments, the term acquired the secondary meaning of the five books of Moses (the Pentateuch) and then of the twenty-four books that make up the Hebrew Bible. Eventually the term expanded to its most inclusive sense as reference to the totality of God's revelation to the people of Israel, including the oral interpretations that became incorporated in the Mishnah and Talmud.

As we learn from the Deuteronomic passage, Torah is both story and law. The story provides the reasons for keeping the laws. The basic plot of the Hebrew Bible is simple: it narrates the history of covenant. The central focus of the Torah is the record of liberation from bondage and the freedom that is possible for those who live under God's promise; the remainder is commentary.

Equating wisdom with Torah proved to be a significant development in Jewish thought. Reason and revelation became fused. Although, on the one hand, wisdom became locked to the written text of scripture, on the other hand, the written text was freed from the limitations of a literal reading. In late biblical Judaism, Torah became subjected to constant and ever-expanding interpretation, for wisdom became viewed as a process of thinking and reflection, as well as a received body of formulated truths.

As the latter books of biblical wisdom literature often emphasize the connections between wisdom and Torah (see Sir. 24:22–29 and the "Book of History" segment in Wis. 10–19), so too do many psalms. This essay examines Psalm 119, the longest of the psalms and also the most formal in its structure. This psalm consists of twenty-two stanzas, each corresponding to one letter of the Hebrew alphabet. In addition, each stanza contains eight verses, every line in the stanza beginning with the same letter of the alphabet. Psalm 119 is a celebration of love for God's gift of Torah. The chapter has been titled, "The Love of God's Law," based on the exclamation in verse 97: "Oh, how I love your law!" The reference to "love" in this psalm should not be taken as an emotional outburst of support or delight at specific commandments. The psalmist is not displaying a feeling but a commitment, a commitment to God and to Torah as God's greatest gift. In a larger sense, Psalm 119 is a prayer for wisdom.

The psalm opens by saying, "Happy are those whose way is blameless, who walk in the law of the Lord" (119:1). The wording and sentiment are similar to the opening of Psalm 1; in both cases, the focus is on the delight of pondering Torah day and night, much as does someone who enjoys chemistry, computer science, history, literature, mathematics, music, or some other academic discipline. As scholars love their subject, so people are exhorted to love and study Torah. There is a difference, however, for the psalmist is speaking of a cultivated devotion to God that results from committing oneself to study of Torah. The desired result is to be transformed by study and thereby inspired to live the life that the study of Torah requires.

In accord with one of the deep concerns of the sapiential tradition, the psalmist exhibits a holy fear of the Lord, not a servile fear, but a mature state of reverence. Psalm 119 represents a prayerful approach to living devoutly and to letting one's study inform the structure of a devout life. The psalmist expresses gratitude for the covenant God has made with devout followers, yet prays for protection from mere legalism. He acknowledges the cost involved in obeying God's law, which means letting go of certain attitudes and acquiring new ones. He is willing to pay the price, courting wisdom as Solomon or the sages are said to court Lady Wisdom. The entire psalm is about courtship: "With my whole heart I cry" (119:145). For the psalmist, a life of study and devotion form the structure for piety: "Your word is a lamp to my feet and a light to my path" (119:105). Knowing that he needs God's grace to persevere, he concludes: "Let your hand be ready to help me, for I have chosen your precepts" (119:173), and "I have gone astray like a lost sheep; seek out your servant, for I do not forget your commandments" (119:176).

Joseph Koterski likens the demeanor depicted in Psalm 119 to that of Socrates, the Greek philosopher. In the *Dialogues of Plato* Socrates tells how the Delphic oracle announced that no one was wiser than Socrates. Rather than being inflated by the remark, Socrates took it humbly, as a reference to knowing how much he didn't know. This led to a lifetime search for wisdom, characterized by perpetual listening, pondering, and inquiring.

Torah is a relational term, conveying from generation to generation the way of interaction between God and people. For the psalmist, courting wisdom means giving freely of oneself, living in covenant relation with God and others, and meditating on Torah, understood as God's guidance for living. In answer to the question, "How can I be wise?" Israel's latest sages reply: "Live Torah."

Questions to Ponder

1. In Psalm 1, what is the point of the "tree" imagery?
2. In Psalm 1, what does the psalmist mean by meditating on the law "day and night"? Is such a view unrealistic in today's demanding world?
3. In wisdom literature generally, do you agree or disagree with the concept of "two ways"? Is there a "third" way? Why or why not?

Part IV: Liturgical Wisdom

4. In Psalm 8, what verse or concept do you find most intriguing? Why?

5. In Psalm 13, what makes the psalmist hopeful at the end?

6. Describe the nature of the psalmist's hope in Psalm 49?

7. In Psalm 139, what verse or concept do you find most hopeful? Why?

8. In your estimation, what does it mean "to love the law of God"? How could one foster such devotion?

9. Psalm 119 speaks of God's justice and God's mercy. How do you understand these concepts? How are these reflected in how you relate to God, others, and yourself?

10. In the New Testament, what is meant by the "gifts of the Spirit"? How do they relate to wisdom motifs? What forms can they take in daily life?

PART V

New Testament Wisdom

CHAPTER 9

The Wisdom of Jesus

Overview: Like the Hebrew scriptures and other early Jewish writings, the New Testament contains important strands of wisdom thought. Paul refers to Christ as the wisdom of God (1 Cor. 1:24), and the hymn of Colossians 1:15–20 is also based on the figure of divine wisdom. Wisdom themes appear in the Epistle of James, an early Jewish Christian sapiential writing. A Wisdom Christology is evident in the Gospels, particularly in Matthew and John. Jesus appears in the Synoptic Gospels as a Jewish "prophetic sage" who communicates primarily in wisdom forms of utterance.

Assigned Reading: Luke 10:29–37; James 1–5

Central Theme: Through his teaching and way of life, Jesus models "counter-order" wisdom.

Outline:
    I. Wisdom Language and Imagery in the New Testament
        A. Early Christological Hymns
        B. The "Q" Document
        C. The Letter of James
        D. The Synoptic Gospels
        E. The Gospel of John

II. Jesus as a Jewish "Prophetic Sage"

III. Jesus as Counter-Order Sage

   A. Aphorisms

   B. Parables (narrative *meshalim*)

Contextual Analysis

Wisdom Language and Imagery in the New Testament

The study of Jewish wisdom literature as found in the Hebrew Bible (Old Testament) and in the Intertestamental wisdom literature provides readers of the New Testament with an entirely new and intriguing perspective on Jesus and early Christianity. Following the resurrection of Jesus, when early Christians were looking for language and concepts to express their experience and understanding of Jesus, one of the most helpful resources was the wisdom literature. Of course, other parts of the Hebrew Bible were valuable, such as the prophets, the psalms, and the historical traditions of Israel, but the authors of the New Testament and the leaders of the early Christian communities saw in the wisdom literature, particularly in the books of Sirach and Wisdom, important resources for understanding Jesus and their new life in Christ.

In *Jesus the Sage*, Ben Witherington divides early Jewish wisdom into two major traditions: conventional wisdom (as found in Proverbs and Sirach) and counter-order wisdom (as found in Ecclesiastes and Job). He maintains that through his teaching and way of life Jesus modeled the latter tradition, particularly in his parables and aphorisms of reversal (as exemplified by his care for weak and marginalized individuals).

The Jewish wisdom tradition profoundly influenced the New Testament community. Wisdom images and ideas appear in every layer of the New Testament, from the letter of James, an early document attributed to the brother of Jesus,[1] to the Gospels, which portray Jesus as a wisdom teacher, to the letters of Paul, where Christ is called the wisdom of God (1 Cor. 1:24). Early Christological hymns, embedded in the New Testament, utilize wisdom motifs to express Christian belief in the incarnation of Jesus (John 1:1–18) and in his cosmic rule (Col. 1:15–20; Heb. 1:1–4). Among the various influences on the New Testament was the identifica-

---

1. This topic is discussed further in essay 9.

tion of wisdom (Jesus) with divine spirit (2 Cor. 3:16–18), word (John 1:1), and law (Matt. 5:17–20; 7:24–29). Like wisdom in Sirach and in the book of Wisdom, Jesus is said to have preexisted his historical incarnation; having lived in intimate relation with God, Jesus is now exalted and enthroned in heaven (Phil. 2:6–11).

Wisdom traditions influenced the document called "Q," an early sayings source that circulated independently and was believed to have been used by the authors of the Gospels of Matthew and Luke. This source, whether oral or written, consisted mainly of Jesus' teachings. While drawing on diverse genres, the majority of the sayings are wisdom sayings, which portray Jesus as a sage or teacher of sapiential truth.

The first three Gospels in the New Testament are called "synoptic" because they draw from one another and look at Jesus with similar eyes. In all three, Jesus is portrayed as a wisdom teacher, displaying a style of instruction similar to that of the sages, teaching disciples through parables (often as narrative *meshalim*) and wisdom sayings (aphorisms) that tease the mind. The parable, as we learned earlier, is a proverbial form of wisdom, an implied comparison. The primary purpose of a parable is to instruct, but more importantly to move the listener/reader to decision or action. As a sage, Jesus teaches to persuade, but never to coerce. Like Lady Wisdom, Jesus invites hearers to decide, to choose for or against him, to seek the Kingdom of God or its opposite, folly and death. As in Proverbs 9 and Sirach 24, which feature the wisdom banquet, the Synoptic Jesus emphasizes table fellowship and festive banquets in his teaching and practice. Unlike John the Baptist, who came "neither eating nor drinking" (Matt. 11:18), Jesus speaks in his parables of meals and banquets and participates regularly in table fellowship. The underlying theme here is inclusiveness; all are invited to God's wisdom banquet, particularly outcasts and the poor.

Of all the Gospels, John is the most persistent in regarding Jesus as incarnate wisdom descended from on high to offer humans life and truth. Understanding what has been said about wisdom in the Jewish sapiential literature, particularly wisdom's origin, mission, benefits, and relation with God, is key to understanding Jesus' identity in John's Gospel: (a) as wisdom's origin is divine, so is Jesus' (John 1:1–2); (b) as wisdom existed before creation and was active in creation, so is Jesus (John 1:3); (c) as wisdom is God's agent on earth, so is Jesus (John 5:36); (d) like wisdom,

Jesus speaks in discourses using the first person pronoun. In the seven "I am" sayings Jesus is described as living bread (6:35, 51), light of the world (8:12), the gate (10:7, 9), the good shepherd (10:11, 14), the life (11:25), the way (14:6), and the vine (15:1, 5). All of these images are found in wisdom literature as proceeding from or characterizing wisdom. Thus, for instance, in Proverbs 8:36 wisdom says: "he who finds me finds life and obtains favor from the Lord." In Wisdom 7:26 wisdom is said to be a reflection of eternal light. In Sirach 24:17, 21, wisdom is compared to a vine: "Like the vine I bud forth delights, and my blossoms become glorious and abundant fruit. . . . Those who eat of me will hunger for more and those who drink of me will thirst for more." This passage also seems to inform Jesus' statement in John 4:13-14: "Everyone who drinks of this water will be thirsty again, but those who drink of the water that I will give them will never be thirsty." One may also compare Jesus' saying, "I am the bread of life. Whoever comes to me will never be hungry, and whoever believes in me will never be thirsty" (6:35) with Proverbs 9:5-6, where wisdom beckons: "Come eat of my bread, and drink of the wine I have mixed. Lay aside immaturity and live and walk in the way of insight"; (e) like wisdom, one's destiny hangs on whether one accepts or rejects Jesus (3:18; 14:6); (f) finally, like wisdom, Jesus is said to be the bearer of eternal life (3:16).

The Gospel of Matthew, more than any other book in the New Testament, represents Jesus as wisdom incarnate. Matthew's "Wisdom Christology" is evident throughout, but especially at critical junctures such as the Sermon on the Mount (Matt. 5–7), where Jesus is identified as the true Torah, much as Ben Sira characterizes wisdom as Torah incarnate in Sirach 24. In terms of the Jewish Christian debate on the nature and location of wisdom, Matthew's approach epitomized the Christian answer: wisdom is found in Jesus and his teaching.[2]

Jesus as a Jewish "Prophetic Sage"

It is possible to argue that the Jesus tradition (as found in the New Testament and espoused by the first Christians) is the next logical development of the Jewish wisdom tradition. The New Testament draws on the entirety of that tradition, particularly on Sirach and the book of Wisdom.

---

2. Matthew's Gospel and his Christology are the subject of chapter 10.

The Gospels introduce Jesus as a Jewish prophetic sage who communicates primarily in wisdom forms of utterance and who, like Ben Sira and the Sage before him, cross-fertilizes them with sapiential adaptation of prophetic and legal forms of utterance. What makes the category of "sage" most appropriate for describing Jesus is that he either casts his teaching in recognizable sapiential forms (aphorism, beatitude, or riddle) or else uses the prophetic adaptation of sapiential speech—the narrative *mashal*. In either case, he speaks figuratively, addressing his audience with indirect speech. It is in part this teaching style that makes Jesus so enigmatic, particularly for modern people, who value communication based on self-evident propositions and syllogistic logic.

Textual Analysis

The majority of authentic Jesus sayings are either aphorisms (*meshalim*) or parables (narrative *meshalim*), and it is these we will now examine. It is important to note that Jesus never uses the classic prophetic formula, "thus says the Lord." The closest approximation of this formula is in a Q saying found in Luke 11:49: "Therefore also the Wisdom of God said." As this passage indicates, Jesus' chosen way to communicate is the way of a sage, persuading by indirect and figurative speech. It has been estimated that at least 70 percent of the sayings of Jesus are some sort of wisdom utterance such as an aphorism, riddle, or parable. While the Gospels portray Jesus as speaking in parables (one scholar counted 247 *meshalim* in the Synoptic Gospels), they should not be seen as mere illustrations of Jesus' preaching; they were, in fact, his primary vehicle of proclamation. Their distinctive connection to Jesus' ministry is borne out by the fact that other than in the Gospels, the term "parable" appears nowhere else in the New Testament except in Hebrews 9:9 and 11:19.

We need to distinguish between proverbs, which are universally acceptable forms of communication, and aphorisms, which are enigmatic and innovative in nature. Whereas proverbs are associated with traditional wisdom, aphorisms are associated with counter-order wisdom. Jesus, like Qoheleth, represents the latter, for there is little in the Jesus tradition that is purely proverbial. Surprisingly, many major themes of proverbial wisdom are absent from the teachings of Jesus. For example, none of his proverbs urge the seeking of wisdom, nor does he declare that the fear of the Lord is the beginning of wisdom. Jesus utters no proverbs or sayings urging hard work, nor does he offer conventional patriarchal wisdom about women such as found in Proverbs, or much less in the misogynist evaluation in Sirach 25:24.

Jesus' aphorisms are said to represent "wisdom from below," for they regularly challenge prevailing assumptions, giving voice to the poor and marginalized rather than to the privileged classes. Numerous sayings illustrate the parameters of the possible implied in God's new social order. For example, we think of an aphorism like, "But many who are first will be last, and the last will be first" (Mark 10:31), or the riddle, "For those who want to save their life will lose it, and those who lose their life for my sake ... will save it" (Mark 8:35). And we notice the absurdity in the aphorism, "It is easier for a camel to go through the eye of a needle than for someone who is rich to enter the kingdom of God" (Mark 10:25). The saying, "The sabbath was made for humankind, and not humankind for the sabbath" (Mark 2:27), suggests that Jesus is appealing to creation theology, which is characteristic of Jewish wisdom thought. But his appeal is turned into an aphorism of counter order in that he stands on his own authority in making a pronouncement that challenges the Mosaic/levitical cultic tradition. In the statement about new wine and fresh wineskins ("no one puts new wine into old wineskins; otherwise, the wine will burst the skins, and the wine is lost, and so are the skins; but one puts new wine into fresh wineskins," Mark 2:22), Jesus is pointing to his own ministry and mission as representing the coming of a new order.[3] Some of Jesus' beatitudes exemplify "wisdom from below," such as the aphoristic "Blessed are you who are poor" (Luke 6:20) or "Blessed are you who are hungry now" (Luke 6:21).

The study of Jewish wisdom literature indicates that parables (narrative *meshalim*) were not characteristic of the canonical sages. Rather, parables seem to have been a prophetic phenomenon, or at least prophetic adaptations of a wisdom form of utterance (see, for example, the court prophet Nathan's parable of condemnation of King David in 2 Samuel 12:1-4 or the allegorical riddle in Ezekiel 17:3-10). In Sirach we note a new development or understanding of the sage's role, the claim to be inspired as were the prophets: "I will again pour our teaching like prophecy" (24:33).[4] Similarly, in Wisdom 7:27 the Sage informs his audience that when the spirit of wisdom passes into people's souls, she makes

---

3. Though these citations are from Mark, they appear in Matthew and Luke as well.

4. This statement is unexpected, given the common Jewish belief that prophecy had ceased during the Restoration Period, following the classical prophets.

them "friends of God and prophets." Here the sage is seen as the one who delivers the prophetic word. Like these predecessors, Jesus seems to have viewed himself as a Jewish prophetic sage, appropriating various traditions in his role as teacher.

When we think of Jesus' parables, we ordinarily think of the Prodigal Son or the Good Samaritan, classic stories about how God relates to humans and how they should relate to one another. However, many, if not most of the parables, are distinctly eschatological in nature. These parables have a prophetic element, in that they tend to reverse conventional values rather than reinforce them. Though many reflect "wisdom from below," the source is "from above," for the means of the expressed counter-order is the inbreaking eschatological Kingdom of God.

The parable of the yeast (leaven) in Matthew 13:33 (also Luke 13:20-21) is misleading as translated in the NRSV: "The kingdom of heaven is like yeast that a woman took and *mixed in with* three measures of flour until all of it was leavened," since the original Greek speaks of yeast that is "hidden in" the measures of flour. Could this story be about Jesus' mission, about how he is planting (hiding) the Kingdom message in his audience through his *meshalim*? If so, the parable suggests that Jesus is God's agent of change on earth, thereby performing the traditional role of wisdom. The woman kneading the dough may also be seen as an allusion to wisdom. In either case, the parable reflects an eschatological optimism about how things will finally turn out.

The parable of the Good Samaritan (Luke 10:29-37), one of Jesus' most beloved parables, has been called an "example story" rather than a comparative *mashal*, since it appears only in Luke, and only Luke contains example stories (10:30-37; 12:16-21; 16:19-31; 18:10-14). Furthermore, the parable exhibits clear marks of editorial activity (10:29, 36-37). Despite Luke's editorializing, this story likely goes back to Jesus, who intended it not as an example of "proper" behavior but as a counter-order *mashal*, a parabolic portrayal of how the inbreaking of the Kingdom of God transforms people and reorders their thinking. The focal point of the story cannot be the Samaritan's good deed of kindness or compassion, since the Samaritan exceeds all bounds, "not merely ethnic bounds, but even the suggested bounds in the Old Testament of what compassion would look like."[5] What we have here is an ethnic reversal, used to challenge current attitudes regarding ritual standards. The notion of a "good

---

5. Witherington, *Jesus the Sage*, 195.

Samaritan" was a contradiction in terms for a traditional Jew, but such reversal is typical of Jesus the sage, "who seems to specialize in oxymorons like good leaven, light burdens, and here a good Samaritan."[6] The underlying issue in this parable is ritual holiness. There is surely some degree of contrast in this parable between the Samaritan and the priest and levite, the latter paragons of holiness and virtue in Jewish society. Both Jesus and the Jewish religious leaders wished to spread holiness throughout the land, but they disagreed on procedure. The Pharisees wished to apply levitical laws to everyday life of ordinary Jews, but the net effect of their program was to further divide and separate Jews from Samaritans, Gentiles, and others. Jesus by contrast stressed an intensification only of the basic moral demands of the Old Testament such as fidelity in marriage, honoring parents, and loving neighbor, coupled with a benign neglect or outright dismissal of the more divisive of the ritual requirement. The net result was conflict over holiness between Jesus and the Pharisees.

Perhaps what the passage represents is an apologetic for the scandalous behavior of Jesus and his disciples, who broke levitical laws by associating with tax collectors and sinners. The Pharisees, together with "priests and levites," would have viewed Jesus and his followers as ritually unclean and therefore, like the Samaritan, outcasts (cf. John 8:48). Jesus seems to be asking, not "who is my neighbor?" (Luke's editorial question in 10:29) but "how is one a neighbor?" If that is Jesus' primary concern in this passage, then his answer to the question is not "show compassion," but "demonstrate lavish compassion." As we know, the Samaritan not only acts compassionately, he becomes personally involved in the restoration of the victim, seeing him through to full health and wellbeing.

The parable, then, is eschatological at its core, for it teaches that when God's Kingdom breaks into human lives and situations, it results in shocking patterns of behavior, where old prejudices die and new ways of life emerge. In this case Jesus is not relinquishing but rather intensifying the basic moral demands of Torah, exemplifying fully what it means to love one's neighbor. For Jesus, compassion trumps ritual holiness as a weightier matter of the law.

---

6. Ibid, 194.

Essay 9: The Letter of James

Wisdom language appears in every layer of the New Testament, dramatically so in the letter of James, a document of early Christianity best understood as Jewish Christian sapiential writing. This letter is traditionally attributed to James the Just, the brother of Jesus who became the leader of the church in Jerusalem (Acts 15:13; 21:18) and who was martyred prior to the outbreak of the Jewish War of AD 66–70. His loyalty to the Jewish law would explain the high importance attached to law in this letter (1:25; 2:8–12; 4:11–12). However, the memory of James was widely revered in the early church, and his name may have been used by another writer to give authority to his teaching. The general nature of the letter's contents makes it difficult to attach it positively to a specific time and place. The document opens with greetings, but has no comparable ending; it is a letter in literary form only, not an authentic letter. It has been described as Christian wisdom literature because, like Proverbs or Sirach, it is concerned with ethical teaching and often seems to string together unrelated admonitions.

The author writes in Greek with grammatical accuracy and some elegance. He has a wide vocabulary, including many words not found elsewhere in the New Testament. He makes allusions to the Septuagint, but some of his imagery is drawn from the nonbiblical Hellenistic world. The author presumes a real audience. His antagonism toward the rich (1:10–11; 2:6–7; 4:13–17; 5:1–6) suggests that most members of his community are poor or disadvantaged. His address to them as "the twelve tribes in the Dispersion" (1:1), his reference to their meeting in or as a "synagogue" (2:2), his appeals to the status of the law (2:8–11), and his affirmation of the one God (2:19) seem to indicate that they were Jewish Christians; however, there is no concern with characteristic features of Judaism like circumcision, the Sabbath, or food laws. His audience may have been drawn from the "God-fearers," non-Jews who were attracted to the monotheism and morality of Judaism without becoming full proselytes. He and his readers represent a form of Christianity emphasizing prayer and morality and loyalty to the teachings of Jesus, calling him Lord and awaiting his return (5:7–8).

The author of James is heavily indebted to the wisdom material in the Hebrew Bible, particularly Proverbs, but shows even greater dependence upon the wisdom of Sirach and the book of Wisdom. In addition, the author draws deeply from the wisdom sayings of Jesus. In this book there are more parallels to the sayings of Jesus, particularly to the material in the Sermon on the Mount, than there are in any other book of the New Testament. Often relying on sayings or proverbs, the author of this letter exhorts his readers through a series of instructions. Themes familiar to those in the book of Proverbs include the dangers of an unbridled tongue (3:1-12), of presumptuous planning (4:13-17), and of ill-gotten wealth (5:1-6). To these James adds his own warning, such as denunciations of the callous rich.

This author stands in the same stream of thought as Ben Sira. His is basically not counter-order wisdom, as was true with Jesus and Qoheleth, but rather the traditional and conventional form of wisdom found in Proverbs and Sirach; half of the book's 108 verses are imperatives (an impressive number appear in 4:7-10). The book of James is an example of a form of early Jewish Christianity heavily indebted to Jewish sapiential traditions, including the Jesus tradition, but the writer is also conversant with the larger world of Hellenistic discourse.

The author of James focuses on traditional topics, like guarding one's speech and passions, enduring suffering, and seeking wisdom, topics notably absent in the Gospels. Missing in James is any real sense of God's inbreaking reign in the present, a sense dominant in Paul and the Gospels, which makes possible a new social order. Instead, James's audience is exhorted only to be patient until the coming of the Lord (5:7). If James is early, written by one of the first Jewish Christians, this might explain his indebtedness to Hebrew sapiential thinking and literature. Being a wisdom teacher like Ben Sira, James may well have believed that the way forward is in large measure to return to conventional wisdom.

The parallels between James and the sayings of Jesus, particularly those found in the material now called the Sermon on the Mount, go back to Q, an early source underlying Matthew's Gospel. That the book of James is not just indebted to earlier Jewish wisdom material, but more specifically to the Jesus tradition, can be supported by the extensive parallels between James and the Q material. The parallels may be listed as follows:[7]

James 1:2 = Matthew 5:11-12/Luke 6:22-23
James 1:4 = Matthew 5:48
James 1:5 = Matthew 7:7

---

7. This list is taken from Witherington, *Jesus the Sage*, 240.

James 1:17 = Matthew 7:11
James 1:22 = Matthew 7:24/Luke 6:46-47
James 1:23 = Matthew 7:26/Luke 6:49
James 2:5 = Matthew 5:3, 5/Luke 6:20
James 2:10 = Matthew 5:18-19 (cf. Luke 3:9)
James 2:11 = Matthew 5:21-22
James 2:13 = Matthew 5:7/Luke 6:36
James 3:12 = Matthew 7:16-18/Luke 6:43-44
James 3:18 = Matthew 5:9
James 4:2-3 = Matthew 7:7-8
James 4:4 = Matthew 6:24/Luke 16:13
James 4:8 = Matthew 5:8
James 4:9 = Matthew 5:4/Luke 6:25
James 4:11 = Matthew 7:1-2/Luke 6:37-38
James 5:2-3 = Matthew 6:19-21/Luke 12:33
James 5:6 = Matthew 7:1/Luke 6:37
James 5:10 = Matthew 5:11-12/Luke 6:23
James 5:12 = Matthew 5:34-37

While some of these parallels, on close scrutiny, seem weak or nonexistent, taken as a whole they indicate that the author of James was familiar with some of Jesus' sayings in a pre-literary form or with a collection of Jesus' sayings. That the book of James is not simply indebted to earlier Jewish wisdom material, but more specifically to the Jesus tradition may also be suggested by the author's use of the narrative *mashal* form (cf. Jas. 1:23-24; 2:2; 2:15-17), which was not characteristic of wisdom books antedating the time of Jesus.

One immediately notices that the author of James does not cite the Jesus material directly, but rather gathers various ideas, themes, and phrases from that tradition to form his own argument. Unlike Q, the material in James is not presented as sayings of Jesus, but rather as the teaching of James that has been influenced by the Jesus tradition.

The general impression left from examining the letter of James is that the author espouses conventional wisdom for its practicality, which his readers should embrace in order to cope with the trials and temptations of life (1:2-6). James provides the sort of ethic one finds in Sirach and in the book of Wisdom, set forth to help readers survive in a hostile environment. James's aim is to have his audience control all three zones of human behavior, including those of impulses (1:14-16; 3:16-18), speech (3:1–12), and purposeful action (2:1–26).[8] This emphasis lacks the unconventionality and radicality of the Jesus tradition, which speaks of Jesus' free association with sinners and his reaching out to the least and the lost. The difference can be attributed to the absence in James of a sense of the inbreaking Kingdom of God and the way it reorders individuals and society. James's audience is not exhorted to seek first the Kingdom of God, or to learn the teachings of Jesus, but rather to pray to God for wisdom from above. Unlike sages who urge their audience to observe life or nature to gain wisdom, for James wisdom is obtained from one's teachers or directly from God. Hence, while the book reflects knowledge of the "hidden" quality of divine wisdom, James does not develop the idea of personified wisdom. Despite the pervasive sapiential content of the book, there is in James no reflection on the concept of Jesus as wisdom. James clearly handles the Jesus tradition as though it were traditional proverbial wisdom.

In many ways the letter of James comports with what other sources suggest to have been the attitude, lifestyle, and teachings of James the Just (Acts 15:12–21; 21:17–26; Gal. 1:18—2:10; 1 Cor. 9:5). Whether Jesus' brother James was actually responsible for this book, either as a source or as its author, this book represents early Jewish Christian sapiential material, suggesting that at least one dimension of early Christianity could be quite traditional, even though it drew also on the Jesus tradition in numerous ways.

Questions to Ponder

1. In your estimation, why did Jesus use aphorisms to communicate his message?
2. In your estimation, why did Jesus use parables to communicate his message?
3. Do you view Jesus primarily as conventional sage or as counter-order sage? Support your answer.
4. When scholars call Jesus a "prophetic sage," what do they mean?
5. What do scholars mean by "wisdom from below"? Provide an example from Jesus' teaching.

---

8. Ibid., 246.

6. Explain how the parable of the Good Samaritan might be about conflict between Jesus and the Pharisees over the issue of ritual holiness rather than an object lesson about performing deeds of kindness.

7. Explain the eschatological dimension of Jesus' parables and aphorisms.

8. Scholars disagree on the authorship and date of the letter of James. In your estimation, is James an example of primitive Christianity or the product of a second- or third-generation Christian mind? Support your answer.

CHAPTER 10

Jesus as Wisdom of God: Matthew's Wisdom Christology

Overview: This chapter explores Wisdom Christology in Matthew's Gospel and in early Christological fragments embedded in New Testament passages such as John 1:1–18 and Colossians 1:15–20. Matthew was written around 80 AD, probably from Antioch, Syria, where there was a large Jewish community. The Gospel is addressed to Jewish Christians who organized an academy that operated as a training school for Christian scribes and teachers. Their task was the ongoing study, transmission, and interpretation of the Jesus tradition. In this setting, sapiential thinking and Jewish wisdom literature were important influences. Matthew's Christology revolves around an understanding of Jesus as "Wisdom of God," one to whom God had given all authority in heaven and on earth.

Assigned Reading: Read Matthew 1–28; Philippians 2:6–11; Colossians 1:15–20; Hebrews 1:1–4; and John 1:1–18

Central Theme: Jesus can best be personified as "Wisdom of God."

Outline:
  I. Jesus as the "Wisdom of God"
  II. The Setting of Matthew's Gospel
  III. General Characteristics of Matthew's Gospel
  IV. Matthew's Christology

A. Jesus' Role as Master Teacher
   B. The Disciples' Role as Pupils
   C. Jesus as Wisdom of God
V. Points of Connection between Jewish Wisdom and the Gospels

Contextual Analysis

Jesus as the "Wisdom of God"

At various points in the development of the Jewish wisdom tradition stress was placed on the hiddenness of wisdom, and therefore on the need for it to be revealed. It may be that in early Judaism the personification of wisdom arose, at least in part, to cope with and make clear not only that wisdom is hidden, but also that God intends to reveal it. During the biblical era, no human, either before or after Jesus, identified himself or herself with personified wisdom. Early Jewish followers of Jesus, having viewed him as both sage and revealer of God's will for humanity, pondered the possibility of going one step further, identifying him as the embodiment of wisdom on earth. Bearing in mind Jesus as prophetic sage, there were times in the prophetic literature when prophets presented themselves as living symbols of God's message for God's people. In this regard, Jesus may be understood not merely as a teacher of wisdom *meshalim* but as a *mashal* himself, as wisdom in person. With respect to the Kingdom of God, the dominant aspect of his teaching, Jesus was not content with merely announcing its coming, for in a profound way he believed he embodied it. Personified wisdom is after all the highest form of *mashal*, and thus the development from being a *mashal* to embodying wisdom is not unnatural. The portrayal of the role of Jesus in the earliest authentic Gospel material is much like the role of wisdom as described by one of Jesus' near contemporaries: "Wisdom rescues from troubles those who served her . . . she guided him on straight paths; she showed him the kingdom of God, and gave him knowledge of holy things" (Wis. 10:9–10).

This brings us to Matthew 11:28–30, a text crucial to our discussion, with both a precedent and a close parallel in Sirach 6:23–31. In Sirach it is clearly wisdom's yoke the disciple is to put on, whereas in Matthew it is Jesus' yoke. The authenticity of the Matthean saying must be seriously considered, in view of the fact that the idea of Jesus as wisdom can be found in most strata of the Synoptic sources (Matthew 12:42 and Luke 11:31 are taken from "Q"; Luke 21:15 from "L"; and Matthew 11:19 from "M"). If Jesus saw himself as a sage, these passages suggest that he did not see himself as just another sage, or even as the final Jewish sage, but rather that he maintained a transcendent self-understanding. Matthew's exalted portrayal of Jesus is substantiated by how people relate to Jesus. In this Gospel, insiders (disciples) regularly address Jesus as Lord (8:21, 25; 14:28; 16:22), a term for Yahweh in the Old Testament, whereas when Jewish leaders or strangers address Jesus, it is generally as rabbi or teacher (8:19; 12:38; 19:16; 22:16, 24, 36). Even more revealing is the fact that only Judas among the disciples calls Jesus rabbi (26:25, 49), and only after he is prepared to betray Jesus. What this indicates is that for Matthew it is inadequate simply to call Jesus a rabbi or teacher. Others may call him teacher, which he is, but Jesus alone is the master teacher, as 23:8–10 makes plain: "for you have one teacher, and you are all students. . . . Nor are you to be called instructors, for you have one instructor, the Messiah." This passage exhibits Matthew's Christology most distinctly, for it is uniquely Matthean; the Markan and Lukan parallels have nothing similar (cf. Mark 12:38–40; Luke 20:45–47).

The Setting of Matthew's Gospel

Matthew's Gospel is said to have been written during the eighth decade of the first century, some ten years after the cataclysmic destruction of Jerusalem and the Temple by the Romans in AD 70. This Gospel was written by a Jewish Christian for a predominantly Jewish Christian audience. It was probably written from Antioch, a Syrian port city, where many Jews relocated after the Jewish War with Rome and where the followers of Jesus were first called Christians (Acts 11:26). In early Christianity there was urgency to legitimate itself as offering the true interpretation of Jesus, Judaism, Torah, and related matters. To this end early Jewish Christians set up schools or academic settings where teachings of and about Jesus as well as new interpretations of Torah were introduced and passed on to a generation of Christians who had neither been in contact with the historical Jesus nor involved with his earthly ministry. Schools in early Judaism had been established to conserve religious heritage and it is likely that this conservation was the primary purpose of early Christian schools as well. Matthew's community is believed to have been organized as such a "school" or academy, and it is quite likely that the author of Matthew was a scribe writing for a particular element within that community, a select group trained as scribes and teachers tasked with the ongoing study, transmission, and interpretation of the Jesus tradition.

Numerous characteristics of Matthew's Gospel support this contention: (a) Matthew displays an interest in arranging material in numerical groupings or divisions of threes and sevens, probably for pedagogical purposes, as an aid in teaching and as a device for learning and remembering; (b) it is also clear that Matthew was written to an audience for whom the Hebrew scriptures had great significance. This Gospel contains more quotations from the Old Testament than does any other Gospel, more than all the other Gospels together. In his account of the birth of Jesus, Matthew describes everything as happening according to a divine plan and in fulfillment of scripture. Not only in his birth narrative but also throughout the entire book, Matthew emphasizes Jesus' fulfillment of scripture by using the formula quotation "in order to fulfill," a phrase not found in the other Gospels, thereby indicating the unity between the Hebrew Bible and Christianity; (c) Matthew shapes the opening stories to show that Jesus' life fulfills the stories of Moses. The parallels are hard to ignore: Herod is like the Egyptian Pharaoh; Jesus' baptism is like the crossing of the Red Sea; the forty days of testing are like the forty years the Israelites wandered in the wilderness; and the Sermon on the Mount is like the Torah Moses delivered on Mount Sinai.

These parallels tell us something significant about Matthew's portrayal of Jesus: he is the new Moses, come to set his people free from bondage and give them his teachings, the new Torah. Matthew, alone among the Gospels, organized the teachings of Jesus into five principal discourses, each ending with a similar statement:

1. Discourse on ethics (Sermon on the Mount): Matthew 5–7, ending with 7:28;

2. Discourse on mission: Matthew 10, ending with 11:1;

3. Discourse on the Kingdom of God (a collection of parables): Matthew 13, ending with 13:53;

4. Discourse on the church (and church discipline): Matthew 18, ending with 19:1;

5. Discourse on eschatology: Matthew 24–25, ending with 26:1.

Textual Analysis

In Matthew, numerous passages depict Jesus as master teacher and provide textual support for a training school for Jewish Christian scribes. Indeed, throughout this Gospel one finds an emphasis on pedagogy not found in the other Gospels. For example, the end of the Sermon on the Mount makes clear that the First Evangelist (the author of Matthew) wishes to distinguish between Jesus the sage, who teaches as one who has independent authority, and "their scribes" (7:29), that is, Jewish teachers. In summary passages of Jesus' ministry, Matthew cites "teaching" ahead of preaching and healing as the chief task of Jesus (4:23; 9:35; and 11:1). This is significant when one notes that in Matthew's Markan source (Mark 1:39) there is no mention of teaching and no parallel to Matthew 9:35. In the Lukan parallel to Matthew 11:1, instead of "teach," one reads "after Jesus had finished all his sayings." When one examines the style of Jesus' teaching in Matthew, wisdom language predominates. Jesus offers beatitudes, aphorisms, parables, and wisdom discourses. In short, Jesus is portrayed as a Jewish sage. In 26:18 Jesus refers to himself as "The Teacher"; the assumption is that the reading audience knows who "the Teacher" is, and that those who hear are disciples.

Many scholars suggest that the statement in 13:52 provides a clue to how the Evangelist saw himself: "Therefore every scribe who has been trained for the kingdom of heaven is like the master of a household who brings out of his treasure what is new and what is old." This uniquely Matthean saying indicates as much about the audience for whom this Gospel was intended as it does about the author. The Evangelist is one scribe showing other scribes the proper content and form of their teaching before they are sent out to make further disciples chiefly by teaching (cf. 28:19–20). Whereas Mark views the disciples as hardheaded and obtuse, not understanding the parables of Jesus, Matthew's inner circle of disciples understands even the more enigmatic wisdom teachings of Jesus (13:51).

Several additional passages reveal Matthew's purposes and aims in producing this Gospel. In 16:17–19, Peter is given the keys of the Kingdom, explained as binding and loosing (in 18:18 the entire church is given this authority). One way to interpret this imagery is as referring to the teaching authority of the church, in this case, the commissioning of scribes with authority to teach, transmit, and interpret the Jesus tradition. Matthew 10:24–25a, the first commissioning scene in Matthew's

Gospel, states that a disciple is not to be above "*the* teacher," but rather is called to be *like* his teacher. This passage, unique to Matthew, prepares readers for the culminating scene in 28:18–20, where the Evangelist summarizes various wisdom and pedagogical themes, particularly obeying commandments and teaching others, two tasks of disciples.

Thus at crucial junctures in Matthew's Gospel—at the end of the first discourse (7:28–29); at the first commissioning of the disciples (10:24); at Caesarea Philippi, when Peter is granted the keys (16:19); at the close of the chapter on parables (13:52); and at the Great Commission that ends the book (28:19–20)—Jesus is portrayed as Teacher and the disciples as teacher-scribes.

Matthew's Wisdom Christology

Among the various attempts to highlight what is distinctive about Matthew's portrayal of Jesus, one of the most popular is to view Jesus as the new Moses, delivering five discourses, the first from a mount. While the depiction has some merit, Matthew nowhere specifically likens Jesus to Moses, and in the series of comparisons in 12:6, 41, and 42, where the Evangelist speaks of one present who is greater than the Temple, or Jonah, or Solomon, there is no reference to Moses. It seems clear that the author is more interested in how Jesus is unlike Moses as in ways he is like him. Perhaps Matthew's most distinctive Christological contribution is to depict Jesus as "Wisdom of God," the messianic Son of David (1:1) like unto but greater than Solomon (12:42), whose intimacy with the Father is modelled in part on the way wisdom and God are described in earlier sapiential literature.[1]

The starting point for Matthew's Christological understanding is the statement, "something greater than Solomon is here" in 12:42, a Q passage (see Luke 11:31). Whereas Luke ends the pericope with the Jonah analogy, "something greater than Jonah is here" (11:32), Matthew closes the segment with the Solomon analogy, depicting Jesus as superior to Solomon, the biblical figure most representative of divine wisdom. In the following chapter (13:1–58), Matthew inserts a collection of narrative *meshalim*, using traditional wisdom genre to underscore that Jesus is God's sage, speaking God's wisdom. At the climactic point in the chapter, just before the saying about the scribe, Jesus asks his disciples if they

---

1. Witherington, *Jesus the Sage*, 350.

have understood all he has said, and like wise learners, their response is an unequivocal "Yes" (13:51). In light of the Gospel's conclusion, where the disciples desert Jesus and even after the resurrection some continue to doubt (28:16), it seems clear that Matthew wants to stress that for all disciples, whether of Jesus or of Matthew, the process of growing in faith and understanding continues, even after Easter.

If Jesus is greater than Solomon, a royal person who personifies divine wisdom, then one would expect an extraordinary birth, with signs in the heavens announcing his coming, a visit by royal counselors or seers, and involvement in power struggles with other so-called kings; and that is precisely what one finds in Matthew 2: a great star, visits by magi, royal presents fit for a king, and conflict with Herod.

The genealogy in chapter 1 is equally revealing, for there we learn that Jesus is the "Son of David" (1:1; Joseph is said to be the son of David in 1:20). Matthew also organizes his genealogy according to a pattern of three sets of fourteen generations, as he states in 1:17. In order to create this symmetry, he takes some liberties, relying on Jewish gematria, whereby Hebrew letters equal numbers (the letters for the name "David" add up to the number fourteen). In Judaism the name of David was connected with messianic titles and promises, thus enabling Matthew to construct a genealogy for Jesus that supports his contention that the royal birth of Jesus signified the coming of Emmanuel, which means "God with us" (1:23), thereby fulfilling Isaiah's prophecy (Isa. 7:14).

The sapiential character of the Sermon on the Mount (Matt. 5–7), which might be better called the Teaching on the Mount, is well known. Suffice it to say that this material consists primarily of wisdom material, including beatitudes (5:3–12); metaphors to promote virtuous deeds (5:16); instructions to uphold Torah and its commandments (5:17–20); practical teaching on self-control (5:21–30); prohibition of oaths and revenge (5:33–42); exhortation to love of enemies (5:43–48); exhortation to almsgiving, prayer, and fasting (6:1–18); advice on wealth, health, and loyalties (6:19–23); nature wisdom meant to produce a less anxious lifestyle (6:24–34); prohibitions of judging others and of profanations (7:1–6); and exhortations to seek the will of God, obey the Golden Rule, follow the narrow path, avoid false teachers, and to maintain integrity in word and deed (7:7–23). The discourse ends with the parable of two foundations, which, like the two ways in the book of Proverbs, is fairly typical wisdom imagery. While these topics represent conventional wisdom, Matthew's Jesus is not a conventional teacher, a fact he stresses in the six antithetical sayings in 5:21–48, where the Greek introductory formula adds the emphatic personal pronoun (*egō*) to *de legō* ("I say"), meaning, "But I, I say unto you," thereby accentuating the authority of Jesus, and at the conclusion of the discourse, where Jesus' authority is distinguished from that of the early Jewish scribes (7:29). The contrast is between Jesus, who has independent authority (the Teacher), and all other teachers and authorities. For Matthew, Jesus is no mere scribe: he is teacher par excellence, greater and wiser than Solomon.

Matthew 11 is crucial for evaluating the intent of the Evangelist. There we are told that "wisdom (i.e. Jesus) is vindicated by her deeds" (11:19). Using parallels and allusions with Israel's wisdom tradition, this passage sums up the first ten chapters of the Gospel. People are offended by Jesus (cf. 11:6), for he associates with tax collectors, sinners, and other undesirable elements of society (11:19), and even John the Baptist wonders about Jesus' identity (11:2–3). Their concerns are answered in 11:19: Jesus is Wisdom, God's agent who reveals God's ways but is often rejected. The book of Proverbs speaks of wisdom in similar ways: as being refused (1:24–25), as associating with an unlikely audience (1:22–23), and as inviting scandalous guests to her feast (9:4–6). Another wisdom motif appears in Matthew 11:28–30, using words about Jesus found in Sirach 6:23–31 and 51:26. In chapter 12, people again ponder Jesus' identity. Matthew's answer is found in 12:42; there, the ultimate witness is the Queen of Sheba, who heard the wisdom of Solomon and was amazed. The metaphor in 13:52 indicates that Jesus, as the Wisdom of God, embodies the entire wisdom tradition, uniting conventional and unconventional wisdom, traditional with new.

Chapter 22:41–46 is a pivotal passage in Matthew's Christology. Here one learns that it is not enough to say merely that the messiah is Son of David, for proclaiming Jesus to be the Son of David falls short of the truth. As the quotation from Psalm 110:1 indicates, Jesus is understood to be David's Lord. If Jesus is by implication claiming to be David's Lord (22:45), then surely he must be seen in more transcendent categories than sage, teacher, or even Son of David. According to Matthew, two ascriptions fit such a claim: Son of God and Wisdom. Like Solomon, Jesus is son of David, only greater. Like Solomon, Jesus is the embodiment of wisdom; indeed, he is greater than Solomon, for he is God's Wisdom. It is in this light that we can understand Matthew's intention in 28:18: "All authority in heaven and on earth has been given to me." It is hard to imagine a higher Christology than one that begins with a person called Emmanuel (1:23) and ends with a proclamation that to this one has been given all authority in heaven and on earth. Matthew, like the church and its Evangelists, was deeply influenced by wisdom literature; he simply would not have been able to develop his Christology apart from the teaching, speculation, and imagery revealed through the Jewish sapiential tradition.

Thematic Analysis

The New Testament cannot be understood in a historical or theological vacuum. There is profound continuity between early Christian belief and late Jewish hope. Particularly when combined with sapiential adaptations of Jewish prophetic and apocalyptic teaching, Jewish wisdom literature provides a logical bridge between the history and hopes of Israel and Christian interpretations of Jesus. The following list is illustrative of the many points of connection between the Jewish wisdom literature, the Gospel of Matthew, and the New Testament Christology:

1. In Jewish wisdom literature, Solomon is the exemplar of wisdom; for Matthew ("Q"), Jesus is greater than Solomon (Matt. 12:42).

2. The book of Proverbs contains many parallels with Matthew's Sermon on the Mount:

    a. The narrow path (Prov. 2:8–15 with Matt. 7:13–14);

    b. Exhortation to keep the commandments (Prov. 3:1 with Matt. 5:17–20);

    c. Honoring God in one's dealings with material goods (Prov. 3:19 with Matt. 6:19–21);

    d. Beatitudes (Prov. 1:13 with Matt. 5:3–12);

    e. Acknowledging God's wisdom in nature (Prov. 3:19–20 with Matt. 6:25–33);

    f. Warnings against sexual impurity (Prov. 5:1–23 with Matt. 5:27–32);

    g. Exhortations to guard one's speech (Prov. 6:1–2 with Matt. 5:33–37);

    h. Exhortations to perform industrious deeds (Prov. 6:4–14 with Matt. 5:16).

3. Qoheleth, like Matthew, uses counter-order aphorisms and narrative *meshalim*.

4. The book of Job addresses the topic of innocent suffering; Matthew and the other Gospels focus on the passion of Jesus, who suffers vicariously, the just for the unjust. In the New Testament, suffering can be redemptive, but only in connection with the resurrection. Job's prose tale concludes with reward for faithfulness, the Gospels with resurrection.

5. Job and Qoheleth struggle with the inequities in the law of retribution; Matthew 5:45 provides context to those inequities.

6. The Song of Songs depicts Solomon as bridegroom; Matthew 9:14–17, together with the other Synoptic Gospels, depicts Jesus as bridegroom.

7. The book of Sirach includes parallels with Matthew and John:
   a. Wisdom is connected with the prophets (Sir. 24:33 with Jesus as "prophetic sage");
   b. List of beatitudes (Sir. 25:7–10 with Matt. 5:3–12);
   c. Wisdom extends an invitation to her disciples (Sir. 24:19–22; 51:26 with Matt. 11:28–30);
   d. Wisdom is associated with Torah (Sir. 24 with Matthew's antithetical sayings, which portray Jesus' teachings as the new Torah);
   e. Wisdom is God's word (Sir. 24:3a and John 1:1).

8. The book of Daniel and Jesus' use of the apocalyptic genre (see Matt. 24; Mark 13; Luke 21), especially references to "desolating sacrilege" (Dan. 9:27 with Matt. 24:15); also use of "Son of Man" in Dan. 7:13 and Matt. 16:27.

9. Many Psalms, royal and wisdom in nature, are viewed in the New Testament as references to Jesus.

10. The book of Wisdom is essential for understanding New Testament Christology:
    a. Wisdom grants eternal life (Wis. 5:15), as does Jesus;
    b. Wisdom is related to the divine Spirit (Wis. 9:17); in John, Jesus gives the divine Spirit (John 16:5–6; 15:26; 20:22);

c. Solomon's prayer in Wisdom 9 and the Lord's Prayer in Matthew 6:5–15;

d. Wisdom as creator and savior (Wis. 9:18—10:1); the same roles are given to Jesus in the New Testament Christological hymns, particularly in John's prologue.

Essay 10: Christological Hymns and the Jewish Wisdom Tradition

Once wisdom became identified with Jesus of Nazareth, and Jesus became an object of worship for early Jewish Christians, some of these same people, steeped in Jewish wisdom traditions, appropriated the hymn-like praise of personified wisdom in order to express their devotion to Jesus Christ. The Christological hymn fragments found in the Pauline corpus (Phil. 2:6–11; Col. 1:15–20; 1 Tim. 3:16), the Gospel of John (1:1–5, 9–14), and Hebrews (1:2–4) are fundamentally expressions of a wisdom Christology that goes back to early Jewish Christianity and demonstrate that the earliest thinking about Jesus grew out of worship practices that were modelled after the synagogue service, a pattern that consisted of readings from scripture, singing, and prayer. Such Christology, influenced by Hellenized Jewish traditions, ultimately led to the doctrine of the preexistence of Jesus and in due course to a doctrine of the incarnation.

The earliest use of Christological hymn fragments is found in the Pauline corpus, and Paul likely heard such hymns in contexts where Greek was the primary language of worship, since hymns such as the one in Philippians 2 and particularly in Colossians 1 so clearly draw on the Greek text of the Wisdom of Solomon and were surely first composed in Greek. To judge from the fact that one finds hymn fragments in places as varied as Hebrews, the Fourth Gospel, and the Pauline corpus, such hymns and their composition must have been widespread. These hymns suggest a widely held common form of wisdom Christology in early Christianity.

Three primary sources seemingly were influential in the composition of Christological hymns: (1) Jewish discussions about personified wisdom; (2) early Christian preaching about Jesus, particularly about his death and resurrection; and (3) the Christological use of the Psalms, particularly Psalm 110 but also Psalm 8.[2]

---

2. Ibid., 253. The material in this essay is adapted from *Jesus the Sage*, 249–94.

Wisdom thinking, to the extent that it is theology, is essentially a form of creation theology, and one should not be surprised to find in Christian wisdom hymns a considerable emphasis on what was true of the Son before and during the event of creation, including the doctrine of his preexistence and in due course a doctrine of the incarnation. In these hymns, Christ's career is envisioned as having both heavenly and earthly scope, and the attempt to express adequately the theological significance of this career led early Jewish Christians to draw on the most exalted language they could find—Jewish wisdom speculation, coupled with messianic interpretation of the Psalms and soteriological reflections on Christ's death.

In view of the degree of development of the personification of wisdom in early Judaism long before these hymns were composed, there is no reason in principle why this material could not have been used by early Jewish Christians when these hymns were first composed. Indeed, the use of both sapiential material and the Christological use of the Psalms to compose these hymns points to Jewish Christians still closely connected with Judaism and its ways of contemporizing scripture as composers. If any elements were added later by Paul and others, it was to make explicit that the rejection of wisdom in the person of Christ entailed death on a cross.

There are some who are skeptical that the Christological fragments in the New Testament were originally parts of hymns. One notable trait most skeptics share is failure to evaluate these hymns in light of the Jewish sapiential tradition, especially the personified wisdom material that in some cases appears to have been liturgical. When one thinks of liturgical appropriation, one should not assume that the New Testament writers were simply "quoting" hymn fragments. Rather they took the tradition, modifying it to suit their intended purposes and literary contexts.

The Servant (Kenotic) Hymn: Philippians 2:6–11

This hymn, inserted by Paul in his letter to the Philippians, exhorts believers to unity by means of humble service, for which the example of Christ serves as a model. In 2:8 the phrase translated "he humbled himself" is important, for ancient secular writers did not view humility as virtuous. The word had a negative connotation, something like shabby or base-minded, in its adjectival form meaning the mentality of a slave.

But this is Paul's meaning, that Jesus, the exemplar of what humility truly means, took the form of a servant (*doulos*, 2:7).

In the Hebrew scriptures one occasionally finds humility and lowliness exalted. Some scholars ask whether the servant language, which is unique to this hymn, draws primarily on material from the Servant Songs of Isaiah or on Jewish wisdom material. If there is correspondence with Isaiah, particularly 52:13—53:12, such correspondence is indirect. It is more likely that the wisdom ideas here predicated of Christ, including the concept of servanthood, are drawn from material in Sirach and the Wisdom of Solomon. For example, after talking about the wisdom that formed humans, "Solomon" in Wisdom 9:4-5 prays: "give me the wisdom that sits by your throne, and do not reject me from among your servants, for I am your servant (*doulos*), the son of your servant girl" (i.e. "wisdom").

Paul's Servant Hymn is divided into two parts, namely, what Christ chooses to do (he is the actor in 2:6-8) and what God does for him (2:9-11). Both halves are illumined by the material in Wisdom 5-7. For example, in Wisdom 5:16 one hears of the righteous ones (called "servants of [God's] kingdom" in 6:4) who will receive "a glorious crown," or again in 6:3, "for your dominion was given you from the Lord, and your sovereignty from the Most High," for being obedient servants while on earth. These comments culminate in the discussion of hypostasized wisdom in 7:22-23. Seen in this light, Philippians 2 becomes a hymn about a royal figure who, like Solomon, humbles himself by becoming God's servant, obeys God, and is rewarded in royal fashion in the end. Similar is material in Sirach such as "The wisdom of the humble lifts their heads high, and seats them among the great" (11:1) or "The greater you are, the more you must humble yourself. . . . For great is the might of the Lord; and by the humble he is glorified" (3:17-18).

Like these passages, Philippians 2 tells about the exaltation of the obedient servant, who humbled himself willingly. The juxtaposition of preexistence language, servant language, humility and exaltation language, and the bestowal of kingship and kingdom in Philippians 2 are also found in Sirach and Wisdom of Solomon. Indeed, the whole of Philippians 2:6-11, except such Pauline additions as "even death on a cross" (2:8c), probably derived from early Jewish Christian attempts to paint an adequate portrait of Christ reflecting on and utilizing Jewish wisdom material.[3] With regard to this hymn, one can say with confidence that as

---

3. Ibid., 261-62.

early as the mid-50s, when Paul adopted and modified it, a new view of monotheism was emerging in Jewish Christian circles, which involved viewing Christ as God's wisdom in person—as someone who once had and continues to have equal attributes with God, and in the end is given the same throne name ("Lord," 2:9–11). N. T. Wright views the reference to "the name of Jesus" in Philippians 2:10 as an example of "Christological monotheism," which, while affirming the divinity of Christ, at the same time "never intends to assert that Christ is divine in a sense apart from or over against the one true God."[4] Confessing "Jesus is Lord" (likely the earliest Christian confession) does not detract from but in fact enhances God's glory (2:11).

The Wisdom Hymn: Colossians 1:15–20

Due to the numerous parallels between this hymn and the Wisdom of Solomon, we can be fairly certain that barring editorial additions by the author of Colossians (such as "the head of the body" and "the church" in verse 18 and much of verses 18–20), the rest of the hymn is dependent on the book of Wisdom.[5] While the authorship of Colossians is disputed, the majority of scholars are likely right in seeing the Wisdom Hymn as pre-Pauline. First, there is the sapiential influence, coupled with distinctive non-Pauline vocabulary and context (e.g. Paul calls Christ the "first fruits" from the dead in 1 Corinthians 15:20, not the "firstborn" as in Colossians 1:15). Secondly, this hymn manifests the distinctive V pattern so characteristic of early wisdom hymns, in this case chronicling the Christological drama in its three stages, viewing Christ as creator, sustainer, and redeemer.

As in Philippians 2, the hymn in Colossians 1 boldly attributes to Jesus divine names as well as ascribing to him deeds only deity can perform. In regard to the meaning of the hymn, two terms used in 1:15 of Jesus need clarification: (a) when Jesus is said to be the "image" of the invisible God, the term used is "icon," meaning Christ makes visible what is invisible. If God could be seen, then this is what God would look like (cf. Col. 2:9); (b) when Jesus is called the "firstborn of all creation," this

---

4. Wright, *Climax of the Covenant*, 116.

5. Witherington identifies points of correspondence between the following passages: Col. 1:15a and Wis. 7:26; Col. 1:15b and Wis. 6:22; Col. 1:16a and Wis. 1:14; Col. 1:16d and Wis. 5:23d; 6:21; 7:8; Col. 1:16–17, 19 and Wis. 7:24b; Col 1:17b and Wis. 1:7–8; and Col. 1:17a, 18d and Wis. 7:29c; see *Jesus the Sage*, 267.

does not mean that he is himself created, for the hymn declares Jesus to be the agent of all creation. "Firstborn," used legally, declares Christ to be the sole heir of the Father, meaning that he stands on the side of the Creator in the creator-creature distinction. "Firstborn" emphasizes Christ's relationship to the creation, just as "image" emphasizes the relationship to the Creator. "Firstborn" possibly reflects the idea in Psalm 89:27 where God promises to make the king the firstborn, meaning "supreme in rank." In 1:18, where "firstborn" is used in conjunction with "beginning" and resurrection, the meaning is priority and supremacy; the notion of being created is not present. In the writings of Philo, the first-century Alexandrian Jewish author, "image" and "beginning" are used interchangeably and are predicated of heavenly wisdom. Similar statements are made about wisdom in Wisdom 1:7 and Sirach 43:26.

The concept of incarnation, present in every Christological hymn, is most likely a development of the idea found in Sirach 24:23, which suggests that wisdom expressed herself in concrete historical form in the Torah, the law of Moses. While this association is not equivalent to the idea of personal incarnation, such development is not totally unexpected, particularly by early Christians who began transferring what had previously been said about wisdom, in particular wisdom as manifested in Torah, to Jesus. The notion of incarnation, not so much stated as implied, is present in Colossians 1:19–20. While it is unique to talk about the preexistence and incarnation of a personal being who took on flesh and became Jesus Christ, the Jewish wisdom tradition prepare the way for such an idea. It is not accidental that the most clearly incarnational hymn, the Johannine prologue, is also the most clearly sapiential.

The Character Hymn: Hebrews 1:2b–4

The influence of wisdom on the hymn fragment in Hebrews 1 is clear and may be summed up in the following points: (1) verse 2, with its idea of an agent through whom God created all worlds, is found in the Wisdom of Solomon, where wisdom is called "the fashioner of all things" (7:22), an "associate in [God's] works," and the "active cause of all things" (8:4–5), but it may already be present in Proverbs 8, where wisdom is seen to be at God's side during the creation, "like a master worker" (8:30); (2) verse 3, which speaks of Christ as the "reflection of God's glory," seems to be a direct use of Wisdom 7:25; (3) Hebrews 1:3b ("and he sustains all things by his powerful word") is related to Wisdom 1:7 (cf. Sir. 24:3), which describes wisdom as holding all things together; (4) Hebrews 1:3d ("he sat down at the right hand of the Majesty on high") is related to Wisdom 9:4, which speaks of wisdom sitting beside God's throne (see 9:10), and Psalm 110:1; (5) the reference to angels and superiority over them in Hebrews 1:4 ("having become as much superior to angels as the name he has inherited is more excellent than theirs") may in part reflect 1 Enoch 43, where wisdom is said to take her place among the angels, yet as being superior to them.[6]

The Logos Hymn: John 1:1–18

This passage has impacted belief in the divinity and preexistence of Christ more than any other New Testament passage. Here the early church derived its Logos Christology (i.e. the Son of God as the "Word") and its basic understanding of the incarnation.

Four beautifully crafted poetic stanzas make up the Logos Hymn in John's prologue: first strophe (1:1–2); second strophe (1:3–5); third strophe (1:10–12b); and fourth strophe (1:14). Some include 1:16–18, though probably they should not. The following themes appear to be central in this hymn: (1) the preexistent Logos (1:1–2); (2) the Logos and creation (1:3–5); (3) the rejection of those created (1:10–12b); (4) the incarnation and revelation (1:14a); and (5) the response of the faithful community (1:14b).[7]

There is in this hymn an obvious dependence on Genesis 1. Both documents begin with the words, "In the beginning," and in both God creates by means of the spoken word. The use of the Genesis material in the hymnic material about wisdom both in the Hebrew scriptures (see Prov. 3; 8:1—9:6) and in the later Jewish wisdom tradition inspires the ideas in this hymn. In that tradition one learns that personified wisdom was present at creation, and that she calls God's people back to ethical living and offers them life and divine favor. These are the same things said of the Word in John's prologue. By the time of Ben Sira, this sort of wisdom speculation includes Torah, seen as the consummate expression of wisdom (cf. Sir. 24). At the end of the Logos Hymn it is said that the

---

6. Ibid., 281–82.
7. Ibid., 282–83.

Son eclipses this Torah, for through Torah came the law, but through the Logos come grace and truth (1:17).

One need not reiterate all the parallels between this hymn and the Jewish wisdom literature, although central to that correspondence is that wisdom provides life and light (see John 1:4 and Wis. 7:26, where wisdom is said to be the reflection of eternal light, and 7:25a, where she is the very life breath of God). Some question why *logos* ("word," a masculine term) and not *sophia* ("wisdom," a feminine term) is used of Jesus in John 1. Although the answer cannot be known with certainty, it seems doubtful that the reason is because Jesus was male, for other Evangelists certainly used *sophia* of Jesus (cf. Matt. 1:19; Luke 11:49). In Wisdom 9:1–2 "word" (*en logo*) and "wisdom" are used in synonymous parallelism, an idea that Philo explores fully. The Wisdom of Solomon personifies *logos* in 18:15, when it declares that God's "all-powerful word leaped from heaven, from the royal throne" (18:15). Since 9:10 had already said that wisdom was present and sent forth from the throne, one can see how interchangeable the terms "wisdom" and "word" are in Wisdom of Solomon. This is also the case in Sirach 24:3, where wisdom is said to come forth from the mouth of God. As Witherington explains, "It may be that [John] simply used the term *logos* to better prepare for the replacement motif—Jesus superseding Torah as God's *logos* [1:17]."[8] Another idea unique to John's prologue, the tabernacling of the *logos* with God's people (1:14), is also manifest in Sirach 24:8, where the Creator is said to choose a place for wisdom to tent, namely in the earthly tabernacle in Zion (24:10).

Conclusion

When the early Jewish Christian composed Christological hymns, they were looking for exalted language from their heritage that gave adequate expression to their newfound faith in Jesus Christ. No language seemed better suited for their task than the poems about personified or hypostasized wisdom found in Proverbs 8, Job 28, Sirach 24, and Wisdom 7 and 9. In particular, it was the latest of these sapiential writings, the Wisdom of Solomon, that had the greatest impact. It seems unlikely that one Christological wisdom hymn spawned the others, or that some sort of borrowing occurred, whereby the Colossians hymn grew out of the Philippians hymn or the Johannine hymn grew out of earlier hymns.

8. Ibid., 285.

Each hymn is distinctive enough to make such an argument implausible. Rather, it seems that sapiential themes were widely shared and expressed in a variety of ways by early Jewish Christians.

When the sapiential liturgical material was applied to the historical Jesus, the result is a very high Christology, not abstract speculation or mere mythical cross-fertilization. The result was the predication of preexistence, incarnation, and even divinity to a historical person. The existence of these hymns in so many different sorts of sources—Pauline, Johannine, and in Hebrews—strongly suggests that wisdom Christology was "both widespread and popular with a variety of Christian writers and their audiences. The fact that one finds such Christology already in nearly full flower used by Paul in Philippians 2, suggests that this Christology had already developed within the first two or three decades of early Christianity. That is, this Christology had developed *before* the writing of any of the canonical Gospels. To be sure, John 1 may be a further amplification especially of the ideas of incarnation and divinity, but such ideas are already present, though not as fully expressed, in the earlier hymns."[9]

Questions to Ponder

1. In your estimation, was early Christianity primarily a Jewish phenomenon or a radically new one? Support your answer.
2. In your estimation, what is the function of the beatitudes in the Sermon on the Mount?
3. In your estimation, what is the central teaching of the Sermon on the Mount? Support your answer.
4. What does it mean to call Jesus a *mashal*, rather than simply a wisdom teacher?
5. In Matthew 11:29–30, what does Jesus mean by "taking up his yoke"? How can Jesus' yoke be "easy" and his burden "light"?
6. How is the setting of Matthew's Gospel important for understanding Matthew's Christology?
7. What passage in Matthew do you consider pivotal for understanding Matthew's Christology? Support your answer.
8. What does it mean to characterize Jesus as "Wisdom of God"?

9. Ibid., 290.

9. How can Christology be said to have developed from early Jewish Christian worship?

Appendix

Chronological Timeline

Biblical (Hebraic Period)	c. 2000–605 BC
Patriarchal Period	1850–1700
Egyptian Period	1700–1250
The Exodus from Egypt	c. 1250
Period of the Judges	1200–1025
United Monarchy	1025–926
Northern Kingdom (Israel)	926–722
Southern Kingdom (Judah)	926–586
Neo-Babylonian Period	605–539
Babylonian Exile	587–539
Persian Period	539–332
Hellenistic Period	532–63
Alexander the Great's Conquests	336–323
Ptolemaic Period	323–198
Seleucid Period	198–142
Maccabean Revolt	167–142
Hasmonean Period (Home Rule)	142–63
Roman Period	63 BC–AD 324
Herod the Great	40–4 BC
Birth of Jesus	c. 6 BC
Ministry of Jesus	AD 27–30
Apostolic Period	30–100
Paul's Missionary Journeys	46–58
Jerusalem Council	49

Destruction of Jerusalem	70
Patristic Period	100–451
Council of Nicaea	325
Council of Chalcedon	451
Byzantine Period	324–640
Early Islamic Period	630–1174
Crusader Period	1099–1291
Late Islamic Period	1174–1918
Modern Period	1918–present

Bibliography

Anderson, Bernard W. *Understanding the Old Testament*. 5th ed. Upper Saddle River, NJ: Pearson, 2007.
Bergant, Dianne. "Reading Guide: The Wisdom Books." In *The Catholic Study Bible*, edited by Donald Senior and John J. Collins. The New American Bible. 2nd. ed., 235-279. New York: Oxford University Press, 2006.
Berlin, Adele, and Marc Zvi Brettler. *The Jewish Study Bible*. New York, Oxford University Press, 2004.
Brown, Raymond E. *The New Jerome Biblical Commentary*. Upper Saddle River, NJ: Prentice Hall, 1990.
Clifford, Richard J. "Introduction to Wisdom Literature." In *The New Interpreter's Bible Commentary* 5:1-16. Nashville: Abingdon, 1997.
———. *The Wisdom Literature*. Nashville: Abingdon, 1998.
Coogan, Michael D. *A Brief Introduction to the Old Testament*. New York: Oxford University Press, 2009.
Crenshaw, James L. *Ecclesiastes*. Old Testament Library. Philadelphia: Westminster, 1988.
———. *Old Testament Wisdom: An Introduction*. Atlanta: John Knox, 1981.
———. "Sirach." In *The New Interpreter's Bible Commentary* 5:601-867. Nashville: Abingdon, 1997.
Fox, Michael V. *A Time to Tear Down and a Time to Build Up: A Rereading of Ecclesiastes*. Grand Rapids: Eerdmans, 1999.
Good, Edwin M. "Job." In *Harper's Bible Commentary*, edited by James L. Mays, 407-32. New York: HarperSanFrancisco, 1988.
Gordis, Robert. *The Book of God and Man: A Study of Job*. Chicago: The University of Chicago Press, 1965.
———. *Koheleth—The Man and His World: A Study of Ecclesiastes*. 3rd. ed. New York: Schocken, 1968.
———. *The Song of Songs and Lamentations*. Rev. ed. New York: KTAV, 1974.
Gruber, Mayer. "Job." *The Jewish Study Bible*. New York: Oxford University Press, 2004.
Habel, Norman C. *The Book of Job: A Commentary*. Old Testament Library. Philadelphia: Westminster, 1985.
John Paul II. *On the Christian Meaning of Human Suffering*. Boston: Pauline Books, 2005.
Kolarcik, Michael. "Book of Wisdom." In *The New Interpreter's Bible Commentary* 5:435-600. Nashville: Abingdon, 1997.

Koterski, Joseph W. *Biblical Wisdom Literature*. Lecture Transcript of Thirty-Six Lectures. Chantilly, VA: The Great Courses. 2009.
Kreeft, Peter. *Three Philosophies of Life*. San Francisco: Ignatius, 1990.
Kushner, Harold S. *When All You've Ever Wanted Isn't Enough*. Boston: G. K. Hall, 1987.
———. *When Bad Things Happen to Good People*. New York: Avon, 1983.
L'Engle, Madeleine. *The Irrational Season*. New York: Seabury, 1977.
Lewis, C. S. *A Grief Observed*. New York: Bantam, 1976.
———. *The Problem of Pain*. New York: HarperCollins, 2001.
Machinist, Peter. "Ecclesiastes: Introduction." In *The Jewish Study Bible*. New York: Oxford University Press, 2004.
Matter, E. Ann. *The Voice of My Beloved: The Song of Songs in Western Medieval Christianity*. Philadelphia: University of Pennsylvania Press, 1990.
Meeks, Wayne A. *HarperCollins Study Bible*. New Revised Standard Version. New York: HarperCollins, 1993.
Murphy, Roland E. *The Song of Songs*. Hermeneia. Philadelphia: Fortress, 1990.
———. *The Tree of Life: An Exploration of Biblical Wisdom Literature*. 3rd ed. Grand Rapids, MI: Eerdmans, 2002.
Newsom, Carol A. *Book of Job: A Contest of Moral Imaginations*. New York: Oxford University Press, 2003.
———. "Job." In *The New Interpreter's Bible Commentary* 4:317–637. Nashville: Abingdon, 1996.
O'Connor, Kathleen M. *The Wisdom Literature*. Collegeville, MN: Liturgical, 1990.
Rowley, H. H. *The Book of Job*. The New Century Bible Commentary. Grand Rapids, MI: Eerdmans, 1980.
Sanders, J. T. *The New Testament Christological Hymns*. New York: Cambridge University Press, 1971.
Seltzer, Robert M. *Jewish People, Jewish Thought: The Jewish Experience in History*. Upper Saddle River, NJ: Prentice Hall, 1980.
Senior, Donald, and John J. Collins. *The Catholic Study Bible*. The New American Bible. 2nd. ed. New York: Oxford University Press, 2006.
Smith, Huston. *The World's Religions*. Rev. ed. New York: HarperSanFrancisco, 1991.
Towner, W. Sibley. "Ecclesiastes." In *The New Interpreter's Bible Commentary* 5:265–360. Nashville: Abingdon, 1997.
Van Leeuwen, Raymond C. "Proverbs." In *The New Interpreter's Bible Commentary* 5:17–264. Nashville: Abingdon, 1997.
Von Rad, Gerhard. *Wisdom in Israel*. Nashville: Abingdon, 1972.
Weems, Renita J. "Song of Songs." In *The New Interpreter's Bible Commentary* 5:361–434. Nashville: Abingdon, 1997.
Witherington III, Ben. *Jesus the Sage: The Pilgrimage of Wisdom*. Minneapolis: Fortress, 1994.
Whybray, R. N. *Ecclesiastes*. The New Century Bible Commentary. Grand Rapids: Eerdmans, 1989.
———. *Proverbs*. The New Century Bible Commentary. Grand Rapids: Eerdmans, 1994.
Wright, N. T. *The Climax of the Covenant: Christ and the Law in Pauline Theology*. Edinburgh: T & T Clark, 1991.
Yancey, Philip. *Disappointment with God*. Grand Rapids, MI: Zondervan, 1988.
———. *Where Is God When It Hurts*. Grand Rapids, MI: Zondervan, 1977.

Subject/Name Index

acrostic poem, 13, 27, 29, 31, 42, 78, 121, 122, 123, 125, 127, 180
afterlife, belief in, 15, 27, 49, 50, 59, 94, 118, 122, 140, 145–47, 154, 163, 164–66
  See also immortality; Sheol
Akiva (rabbi), 107
Alexander the Great, 142, 143, 147–48, 153
allegory, allegorical, 12, 17, 63–64, 107, 109–11
Ambrose, 109
Amos (prophet), 21
Anderson, Bernhard, 77
Antiochus IV, Epiphanes (Seleucid ruler), 121, 135, 137, 138, 141, 142, 143, 144, 145, 149, 166
apocalypse, apocalyptic(ism), 4, 135, 139–40, 144, 146
  and wisdom, 21, 206
aphorisms, 37, 187, 189–90, 202
Apocrypha, 132, 152
Aquinas, Thomas, 104
Aramaic, 5, 55, 138, 141
Aristotle, 154
Augustine, 109

Babylonian Exile, 2, 4, 5, 13, 14, 77
Beard, Charles A., 5
Ben Sira, 11, 117, 119, 120, 121, 122, 127, 129, 130, 132, 148, 163, 189, 194, 213
  theology of, 118
Bernard of Clairvaux, 104, 110

Blake, William, 75
Booths. *See* Sukkot

Carlyle, Thomas, 74
Cassian, John, 109
chiasmus, chiastic, 57, 60, 89, 106, 156, 157, 160, 162
Christianity, origins of, 3, 4, 140, 147, 186
Christology, ix, 38, 42, 185, 198, 200, 205, 206, 207
  Christological hymns, 163, 186, 208–15
  Wisdom, 185, 188, 198, 203–6
  See also Logos, Christology; Suffering Servant
Clement of Alexandria, 152
Clifford, Richard J., xiii, 96, 163
covenant, 49–50, 180, 181
creation theology, 37, 41, 47, 91–92, 97, 107, 160, 164, 187, 190, 209, 211–12, 213
Crenshaw, James L., xiii, 121
Cyrus the Great, 2, 143

Daniel, book of, ix, 135–47
  and apocalyptic, 139, 207
  authorship, 137, 138–39
  contextual analysis, 136–39
  date of, 137, 138–39
  literary analysis, 139–40
  overview, 135
  textual analysis, 140–44
  thematic analysis, 144–47

David (ruler of Israel), 7–8, 49, 172, 173, 190, 204
   Son of, 204, 205
Dead Sea Scrolls, 133, 140
death, 13, 15, 18, 21, 30, 36, 39, 47, 57, 58, 62, 67, 86, 98, 145–46, 155, 157, 158, 164–66
   images of, 64
dialogue (literary genre), 12, 78, 81, 84, 106
Diaspora. *See* Judaism, Diaspora
diatribe (literary genre), 79, 156
dualistic thought, 140, 154, 158–59, 164, 165

Ecclesiastes, book of, ix, 1, 5, 8, 17–18, 20, 47–71, 111, 175
   and afterlife, 15
   and God, 69–71
   and Greek philosophy, 53, 54, 55, 58, 61, 66
   and injustice, 53–54, 59
   and Torah, 53
   and truth, 54, 66
   authorship, 51–55
   contextual analysis, 48–50
   date of, 5, 55
   literary analysis, 56–57
   overview, 47
   place in Jewish canon, 55
   textual analysis, 57–65
   thematic analysis, 55, 60, 61, 62, 63, 65–71
   See also Qoheleth
encomium (literary genre), 120, 122
Epicurean(ism), 54, 66, 120, 154–55
   view of death, 155
   view of God, 155
Essenes, 4, 133, 148
Eucharist, 110, 126
eulogy (literary genre), 156
evil (cosmic), 67, 90, 92, 101, 117, 139, 140, 143
   human suffering as, 92, 101
   See also pain; suffering
   human wickedness as, 50, 59, 62, 67, 68, 140, 165–66
Exile. *See* Babylonian Exile

Ezekiel, 2, 14, 132, 145
   book of, 136, 190
Ezra, 3, 8, 174
   book of, 137

fate. *See miqreh*
fear of the Lord, 7, 13, 38, 55, 62, 66, 111, 124–25, 128, 128–29, 130, 178, 181, 189
Festival of Booths (Sukkot). *See* Sukkot
Five Scrolls (Megillot), 55, 106
free will, 71, 176
friendship, 129–30

gematria, 57, 204
God
   and suffering, 94, 98, 158, 175–77
   humans and, 89–91, 98–100, 101
   justice of, 90
   mystery of, 94, 101
   providential role in history, 144–45
Gordis, Robert, xiii, 87
Gregory the Great (pope), 104
grief, grieving
   stages of, 84, 86

Hasidim, 137, 142, 143, 146, 149
Hasmonean(s), 3
heart. *See* purity of heart
hebel (vanity), 56, 57, 66
Hebrew poetry, 27–28, 106, 156, 172
Hebrew scriptures (Tanakh), 5, 65, 96, 131, 132, 133, 152, 153, 154, 172, 177, 179, 185, 186, 201, 210, 214
   and wisdom, 20–22, 186
Hellenism, 119–21, 124, 129, 130, 135, 147–50, 153–55, 156, 165, 193
   See also Sirach (Ecclesiasticus), book of, and Hellenism
Holocaust, 77
Holy Spirit. *See* Spirit of God
Honoris Augustodunensis, 109–10

immortality, 133, 146, 154, 156, 158–59, 160, 163, 164, 165
incarnation, 110, 186–87, 208, 209, 212, 213, 215
inclusiveness. *See* table fellowship

Intertestamental Literature, 131
Isaiah, book of, 6, 8, 20, 76, 132, 133, 179, 204
  Second (Deutero), 5, 14, 165
  Servant Songs, 210
Isis (goddess), 154, 160, 161

James, Epistle of, 119, 133, 163, 185, 186, 193–96
  and book of Wisdom, 193, 195
  and Proverbs, 193
  and Q material, 194–95
  and Sirach, 193, 195
  audience, 193
  authorship, 193, 196
  date of, 193
Jeremiah (prophet), 2, 49, 132, 143
Jerome, 109, 118, 179
Jesus Christ
  as Jewish prophetic sage, 189, 199
    See also sage(s), Jesus as
  as Torah, 188
  as wisdom of God, 185, 186, 198–206
  as wisdom teacher, 185–92, 199–200, 202–3, 204–5
  See also Christology; incarnation
Job, book of, ix, 1, 5, 6, 17, 18, 20, 73–101, 111, 146, 175–76, 177, 207
  and afterlife, 15
  and design in nature, 90
  and divine justice, 90
  and retribution, 91–92
  and suffering, 77, 91, 93, 97–102
  authorship, 76
  contextual analysis, 74–77
  date of, 5, 76–77
  literary analysis, 78–82
  overview, 73
  soliloquy of, 88
  textual analysis, 82–91
  thematic analysis, 71, 91–102
  theme of, 14
John, Gospel of. *See* wisdom, and Gospel of John
John of the Cross, 104
John Paul II (pope), 75
Josephus, 165

Judaism, 3, 111, 124, 149, 209
  and Hellenism, 147–50, 163
  Diaspora, 6, 98, 148, 153, 161, 193
  Jewish identity, 18, 155
  Palestinian, 6
  Pharisaic, 4, 15, 118, 133, 146, 149, 164, 166, 192
  Rabbinic, 3, 133–34, 147

Kingdom of God, 127, 145, 187, 190, 191, 192, 196, 199, 201, 202
Koterski, Joseph W., xiii, 181
Kreeft, Peter, xiii, 67–69, 71, 112–13
Kübler-Ross, Elisabeth, 84
Kushner, Harold, 69–71

Lady Folly, 19, 37–40, 43, 61, 174
Lady Wisdom, 19, 27, 37–43, 61, 111, 123, 124, 125, 127–28, 159, 160, 174, 181
lament (literary genre), 13, 78, 83–84, 87, 88
L'Engle, Madeleine, 95
life, 16–18, 21, 30, 31, 37, 38, 47, 57, 62, 66, 68–69, 95, 111, 112, 158, 177, 214, 215
logos, 161, 214
Logos, 154
  Christology, 213–15
  doctrine of, 6, 133
  Hymn, 6, 213–15
love, 71, 104, 108, 109, 111–13, 129, 177–78, 179, 180, 192
Lucretius, 155
Luther, Martin, 74

Maccabees, 11, 143, 145, 149, 166
  Maccabean War, 3, 119, 137, 149
MacLeish, Archibald, 75
Maimonides, 75
mashal, meshalim, 20, 27–29, 65, 70, 82, 187, 189, 190, 191, 195, 199, 203, 207
Masoretes, 64–65
Matthew, Gospel of, 198–208
  and book of Sirach, 199
  audience, 200–201, 202
  authorship, 200–201, 202

Matthew, Gospel of, *(continued)*
  date of, 200
  setting, 200–201
  textual analysis, 202–3
  thematic analysis, 206–8
  Wisdom Christology, 198, 200, 203–6
  See also wisdom, and Gospel of Matthew
medieval quadriga, 108–11
merism(s), 59, 125
messiah, messianic, 4, 109, 143, 173, 178, 203, 204, 205
midrash, midrashic, 156, 162
miqreh (fate), 58, 71
Mishnah, 6, 133, 179
misogyny. *See* Sirach (Ecclesiasticus), book of, and misogyny
Moses, 8, 49, 133, 162, 179, 201, 203
  new, 175, 201, 203
Murphy, Roland E., xiii, 19, 56, 66, 69, 121

Newsom, Carol, 81, 100–101

O'Connor, Kathleen, xiii, 18, 34
Old Testament. *See* Hebrew scriptures
Origen (of Alexandria), 109

parable(s), 2, 12, 17, 187, 189–92, 202, 204
  Good Samaritan, 191–92
pain, 89, 101–2
  See also suffering
Passover, 106
Paul (apostle), 79, 134, 146, 158, 163, 166, 185, 186, 194, 208, 209, 210, 211, 215
  and Wisdom of Solomon, 208, 210, 211
Persian empire, 3, 5, 138, 142, 143
  Jews and, 3, 5, 13–14
Pharisees. *See* Judaism, Pharisaic
Philo, 6, 148, 150, 153, 156, 212, 214
Plato, 74, 154, 157, 160, 164
Platonism, 154
Pompey (Roman general), 3
prayer(s), 129, 171, 172, 175, 193, 196

  for wisdom, 160, 161, 180
priest(s), priesthood, 3, 4, 5
prophet(s), prophecy, 4, 5, 14, 128, 136, 139, 190–91, 199
Prophets (Nebiim), 2, 4, 6, 131, 132, 135, 156, 178
  themes of, 16
proverb(s), 2, 7, 12, 16, 27–29, 61, 189–90, 194, 202
  definition of, 27–29
  See also *mashal, meshalim*
Proverbs, book of, ix, 1, 5, 7, 17, 18, 20, 25–43, 48–49, 111, 174, 188, 193, 204, 205, 212
  and Sermon on the Mount, 206
  and Sirach, 117
  contextual analysis, 26–29
  date of, 5, 8, 26–27
  Egyptian source of, 9
  genres of, 12, 13
  king sayings, 10
  literary analysis, 29–31
  overview, 25
  purpose of, 27
  social justice and, 27
  Solomon and, 9
  thematic analysis, 31–37
Psalms. *See* Torah, Psalms and; Wisdom Psalms
pseudepigrapha, pseudepigraphic, 8, 133
Ptolemaic empire, 3, 55, 118, 144, 148, 153
purity of heart, 177–78

Qoheleth, 1, 11, 13, 51–55, 146, 175, 189
  as philosopher, 69
  as scribe, 11
  disciples of, 51, 64

Restoration, the (Second Temple period), 3, 5, 11, 13–14
resurrection of the dead, 95, 96n13, 118, 139, 140, 144, 145–47, 164–66
  See also afterlife

retribution, doctrine of (rewards and punishments), 15, 21, 25, 47, 49–50, 51, 59, 62, 64, 66, 80, 91–92, 93, 94, 104, 139, 146, 147, 158, 164, 165, 174, 207
revelation, 5–6, 40, 67, 69, 85, 108, 126, 129, 130, 141, 150, 154, 179, 213
Revelation, book of, 139, 178
riddle(s), 7, 9, 12, 17, 28, 189, 190
Roman empire, 3

sage(s), ix, 4, 5–6, 7, 10–11, 15, 136, 139, 171, 179, 181, 190–91, 200
   activities of, 11, 190
   goal of, 16–18
   Jesus as, 189, 199–200, 202, 203, 205
Sage, the, 153, 155, 156, 157, 160, 162, 165, 189
satan, ha (the Adversary), 76, 79, 83, 90, 99
scribe(s), 2, 3, 4, 10, 128, 201, 202, 205
scripture, canonical and deuterocanonical, 130–34, 160, 165
Seleucid empire, 3, 55, 119, 137, 139, 141, 143, 144, 148, 149, 153, 154
Septuagint, 2, 59, 76, 95, 131–32, 148, 150, 153, 179, 193
Sermon on the Mount, 174–75, 188, 194, 201, 204, 206
   and Proverbs, 206
   and Torah, 201, 204
   and wisdom, 204
Sheol, 59, 62, 64, 145, 164, 175, 177
sickness (illness), 89
simhah (enjoyment), 55, 58, 70
Sirach (Ecclesiasticus), book of, ix, 1, 6, 18, 21, 49, 118–30, 132, 133, 148, 205, 214
   activities of sages, 11, 190
   and Ecclesiastes, 133
   and Hellenism, 120, 127, 129, 148
   and incarnation, 212
   and misogyny, 39, 190
   and New Testament, 133, 186, 199, 207, 210, 212, 213
   and Proverbs, 117

   and Torah. *See* Torah (Law), Sirach and
   authorship, 117, 119
   contextual analysis, 118–21
   date of, 119
   description of wisdom, 7, 40–41, 123–28, 188, 212
   literary analysis, 121–23
   overview, 117
   textual analysis, 123–28
   thematic analysis, 128–30
Socrates, 181
soliloquy (literary genre), 13, 84, 88
Solomon, 5, 8, 9, 10, 16, 109, 172, 181, 203, 210
   and Jesus, 203–4, 205, 206
   Proverbs and, 26
   Song of Songs and, 104
   Wisdom of Solomon and, 153, 157, 159
Song of Songs (Song of Solomon), ix, 8, 9, 20, 103–13, 177
   and Solomon, 10
   authorship, 104–5
   canonical status, 106–7
   contextual analysis, 104–6
   genre, 106
   literary analysis, 107–8
   overview, 103
   thematic analysis, 71, 111–13
sophia, 214
sorites, 159
soul, 177–78
   See also life
Spirit of God, 6, 42, 178
   wisdom and, 161, 164, 178–79, 187
spirituality. *See* wisdom, and spirituality
Stoic, Stoicism, 66, 120, 154, 160–61
suffering, 14–15, 16, 18, 38, 53–54, 59, 77, 83, 85, 87, 89, 91, 92, 93, 94, 97–102, 104, 112, 122, 158, 175–77, 194, 207
   meaninglessness and, 86
   vicarious, 98
   See also evil; pain

Suffering Servant, 98
  See also Isaiah, book of, Servant Songs
Sukkot (Booths), 55, 70, 173
summum bonum, 17, 58, 67, 68, 71, 130, 154
symposium (literary genre), 78, 120
Synoptic Gospels, 185, 187, 207

table fellowship, 187
  See also wisdom, banquet
Talmud, 133, 179
Tanakh. *See* Hebrew scriptures (Tanakh)
Temple, 118, 120, 121, 125, 126, 142, 144, 149, 172, 173
  destruction of, 2, 149
  ritual, 3
Tennyson, Alfred Lord, 74
theodicy, 78, 89–91, 92, 146
theophany, 178
Torah (Law), 2, 3, 4, 14, 42, 49, 53, 55, 120, 121, 129, 131, 132, 148, 154, 156, 174, 175, 178, 179, 180, 181, 201, 204, 212, 213, 214
  and early Christianity, 200
  and Jesus, 175, 189, 192, 212, 214
  definition of, 179
  new, 175, 201, 207
  Psalms and, 172, 175, 178, 180
  Sirach and, 42, 49, 117, 120, 121, 125–27, 128, 129, 132, 188, 212, 213
  themes of, 16
  Torah-centric, 120, 121
  Wisdom of Solomon and, 156, 207
  See also wisdom, and Torah
Tournier, Paul, 84n6
Toynbee, Arnold, 67
tradition, 93, 130
Trinity, 38
truth, 100–101

Vaughan Williams, Ralph, 75
Virgin Mary, 39, 109
visions, 89, 135, 136–37, 140–43, 144
Vulgate, 109, 118, 153, 179

wisdom, 5–6, 18, 26, 28–29, 42, 48, 87, 123–28, 128, 158, 178–79, 180
  and Epistle of James, 193–96
  and freedom, 176
  and God, 41–42, 43n4, 161
  and Gospel of John, 187–88, 213–14
  and Gospel of Matthew, 188, 198–208
  and Hebrew scriptures, 20–22
  and New Testament, 186–96, 198–215
  and prophecy, 136–37
  and Sermon on the Mount, 204–5
  and spirituality, 18–20
  and Torah, 42, 117, 121, 126, 127, 164, 179–81, 188, 213, 214
  and worship, 123–24
  as Creator, 41, 208
  as way of life, 158
  as Holy Spirit, 161, 162, 164, 178–79, 187, 207
  as Savior, 160, 161, 208
  banquet, 17, 30, 125, 126, 127, 128, 187
    See also table fellowship
  conventional, 15, 48–50, 62, 85, 186, 189, 194, 195, 204, 205
  counter-order (unconventional), 15–16, 49–50, 186, 189, 190, 191, 205
  gender stereotypes, 39, 61
  genres of, 7, 12–13
  historical emergence of, 1
  images of, 188
  literary profile, 163–64
  literature, 2, 15–16, 19–22, 37, 77, 104, 111, 133, 136, 178, 179, 180, 186, 190, 206, 214
  mediatorial role, 41
  movement, 4–5
  origins of, 6, 7, 40, 41, 125, 163
  personification of, 6–7, 37–43, 121, 126–27, 128, 196, 199, 208, 209, 213, 214
    See also Lady Folly; Lady Wisdom
  pragmatic value of, ix–x, 7
  qualities of, 40–41, 125, 160

sources of, x, 4–5, 6, 10–11, 65, 124, 163
task of, 65
themes of, 13–16
See also Christology, Wisdom
Wisdom of Solomon, book of, ix, 1, 6, 7, 21, 42, 49, 133, 151–63, 178, 210
and afterlife, 15, 164–66
and Hellenism, 133, 153, 154–55, 156, 159–61
and New Testament, 133, 186, 207–8, 210, 211, 212, 213, 214
authorship, 154
See also Sage, the
contextual analysis, 152–55
date of, 153
description of wisdom in, 7, 158, 160–61, 188, 190–91, 212, 214, 215
literary analysis, 156, 157, 159
overview, 151
Paul and, 208, 210, 211
textual analysis, 156–63
thematic analysis, 163–64
Wisdom psalms, 171–79, 207
contextual analysis, 171–74
date of, 172, 173
overview, 171
textual analysis, 171–74
Witherington, Ben, xiii, 186, 214
worship, 172
Wright, N. T., 211
Writings (Ketubim), 2, 55, 75, 107, 131, 135, 136, 156

Zealot(s), 148, 149
Zionism, 111

www.ingramcontent.com/pod-product-compliance
Lightning Source LLC
Chambersburg PA
CBHW062019220426
43662CB00010B/1390